ROADMAP™ B2+

STUDENTS' BOOK
with digital resources and mobile app

Jonathan Bygrave, Hugh Dellar and Andrew Walkley

Contents

EXTENDED ROUTE

Contents

1A ▶ Give it a go

▶ **Goal:** persuade people to try different activities

▶ **Grammar:** cleft sentences

▶ **Vocabulary:** free-time activities

Vocabulary

1 a Work in pairs. Look at free-time activities 1–8 and check you understand the words in bold. Which activities can you see in photos A–E?

1 do **crosswords** or other puzzles
2 do gardening, dressmaking or another **creative pastime**
3 do a **martial art** like judo or karate
4 do **keep-fit** activities like yoga or running
5 go camping and hiking or do another **outdoor pursuit**
6 do **online gaming** or play other computer games
7 see the latest **blockbuster**
8 sing in a choir or do some other kind of **performing**

b Look at 1–8 again in Exercise 1a and discuss:
- which are easy or difficult to learn.
- what the positive or negative aspects of doing each one might be.
- if people you know do any of them.

2 a Complete the sentences with the phrases in the box.

fancied taking up	grow on me	hopeless at
the hype	let off steam	nothing beats	switch off
take to it	very encouraging	

1 I tried it, but I didn't really _____ . It was a bit too slow for me. I prefer something more energetic.
2 I didn't like it to begin with, but then it started to _____ and I'm completely addicted now.
3 I'm a bit put off by all _____ around it. I just know it can't be that good and I'll be disappointed by it.
4 I gave it a go, but the teacher wasn't _____ , so I felt a bit useless and, since everyone else took it rather seriously, I stopped going.
5 I'm _____ that kind of thing. I don't have the patience, the imagination or the skill!
6 I love it – _____ the feeling when you do it well and you get a great reaction from the audience.
7 I've always _____ some kind of martial art. I've just never got around to doing it.
8 It's a great way to _____ and get rid of all the frustrations from the day. I've also made friends from all over the world doing it.
9 It keeps you fit. You're surrounded by nature and I find I can just _____ and forget all the stresses of life.

b Work in pairs. Which activities from Exercise 1a <u>might</u> each person in Exercise 2a be talking about?

3 Discuss the questions.

1 Have you ever started an activity and found you either really took to it or were hopeless at it? What? Why?
2 What activities have had a lot of hype around them recently? Do you think the hype is justified?
3 Is there an activity you've always fancied taking up? Why haven't you done it yet?
4 What do you find are the best ways to let off steam or switch off from work?

 Go to your app for more practice.

Listening

4 ◁)) **1.1** Listen to four conversations. Find out:
1 what free-time activities the people talk about.
2 if both speakers enjoy doing each activity.

5 In which conversation (1, 2, 3 or 4) is a speaker:
a concerned about comfort?
b concerned about what others might think?
c not into a particular kind of TV programme?
d persuaded to change their mind?
e addicted to something?
f talking about letting off steam?

6 Have you ever persuaded anyone or been persuaded to do something you weren't sure about? How did it turn out?

Grammar

7 a **1.2 Read the pairs of sentences. Then listen and complete the second sentences.**

    1   a I've found it's just a great way to get rid of all those frustrations from work.

        b _____ I've found _____ it's just a great way to get rid of all those frustrations from work.

    2   a The pain put me off!

        b _____ put me off _____ the pain!

    3   a The way they make it relevant to now is great.

        b _____ the way they make it relevant to now.

    4   a I love how friendly people are.

        b _____ I love _____ how friendly people are.

    5   a No one in this class takes it too seriously, which is great.

        b _____ this class _____ no one takes it too seriously.

b **Work in pairs. Look again at the pairs of sentences in Exercise 7a. Why might a speaker use the structure in the second sentence rather than the first?**

c **Complete the examples in the grammar box with one word in each gap.**

Cleft sentences

Speakers often use the following sentence patterns to draw attention to something they feel strongly about:

¹_____ I've found ²_____ it's a great way to let off steam.

The ³_____ that is great (about it) is the way they make it relevant to now.

The other thing (that) I love (about it) is how friendly people are.

One thing (that) I don't understand (about it) is how anyone gets enjoyment from it.

We can use the same patterns to talk about feelings we had in the past.

⁴_____ put me off ⁵_____ the pain.

What I found interesting was the variety of people who work there.

What I loved was the ⁶_____ that no one took it too seriously.

8 a **1.3 Listen to the sentences and notice the emphasis on the underlined sounds. When said at normal speed, the other words around them may be less clear.**

    1 What I <u>like</u> about it is the fact I can just com<u>plete</u>ly switch <u>off</u>.

    2 The thing I <u>love</u> about it is the way the teacher <u>or</u>ganises the class.

    3 What's <u>bad</u> about it is the amount of time you spend <u>wait</u>ing around.

    4 The <u>only</u> thing I <u>didn't</u> like so much was the <u>venue</u>.

    5 What I find <u>fun</u> is learning something <u>new</u> every time.

b **Listen again and repeat.**

9 **Rewrite the sentences using *What* or *The thing* and the words in brackets.**

    1 I go to a choir. It's great. I especially like meeting new people. (most).
        The thing (that) I like most about going to the choir is meeting new people.

    2 Making a cake without eggs just doesn't make any sense to me. (don't understand)

    3 Everyone was much better than me, which made the class difficult. (found difficult)

    4 I love hiking because you're out in the countryside all day. (being)

    5 I wasn't really progressing, which was frustrating. (the fact that)

    6 I'd really like to learn how to fly, but the cost is a bit off-putting. (puts me off)

10 a **Write true sentences about your free time using these sentence starters.**

    1 What I most love to do at the weekend …

    2 The thing I love most about …

    3 What I find difficult …

    4 What was great about …

    5 The only thing I didn't like about …

    6 What I'd like to do …

    7 What puts me off … -ing is …

b **Work in pairs. Compare your sentences and explain your ideas.**

Go to page 136 or your app for more information and practice.

Speaking

PREPARE

11 **Work in pairs. Choose two activities in Exercise 1a or think of other things you do. Think of ways you might persuade someone to take up these activities.**

SPEAK

12 **Work with a new partner. Take turns to be Student A or B. Use the Useful phrases to help you.**

Student A: You want Student B to do one of the activities you thought of in Exercise 11. Ask them if they fancy doing the activity and persuade them why they should.

Student B: You aren't sure you want to try the activity suggested by Student A. Give reasons.

Useful phrases

Do you fancy … -ing tonight?
Have you ever thought of taking up …?
You should give it a go.
What's great about it is …
What puts me off is …

Develop your writing
page 116

1B Kind acts

> **Goal:** narrate a short story in detail
> **Grammar:** narrative tenses
> **Vocabulary:** helping people

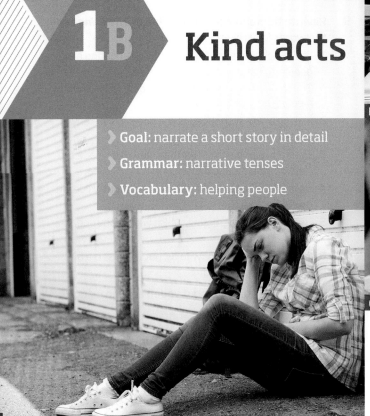

Vocabulary

1 **Look at the photos and discuss the questions.**

1 What do you think the people in the photos need?
2 When was the last time you helped someone you know? What did you do?
3 Do you ever help people you don't know? How?

2 **Complete the sentences with words in the box.**

> babysit/let down   comfort/mourning
> desperate/an apprenticeship   down/the bill
> mentor/expertise   rough/grab
> stranded/pulled over   welcoming/rave

1 She acted as a _____ to me when I first started. She was always happy to share her _____ .
2 She was a real _____ to me when I was _____ the loss of my grandfather.
3 He was sleeping _____ and so I decided to _____ some food for him from the local store.
4 I offered to _____ for them because they'd been _____ by the person they usually use.
5 They'd been incredibly _____ while we stayed there, so we gave them a _____ review.
6 I was _____ on the side of the road and he _____ and offered me a lift.
7 We went out the other night. I was feeling a bit _____ because I'd lost my job, so when we asked for _____ at the end of the evening, she paid for everything.
8 I'd been unemployed for ages and was getting _____ . Then they offered me _____ .

3 **Work in pairs. What do you think the relationship is between each of the pairs of people in the sentences in Exercise 2?**

Go to page 156 or your app for more vocabulary and practice.

Reading

4 **Look at the title of the article. What do you think the bystander effect might be? Read and check.**

5 **Read the article again. Are the sentences true (T) or false (F)?**

1 People can usually tell whether someone needs help.
2 If you don't react in an emergency, others are more likely to react.
3 We're more likely to help someone when there aren't many people around us.
4 Bystanders may not want to risk getting involved.
5 The author sometimes offers help to people when they don't need it.

The bystander effect

A few years ago, I was on a bus. It was quite crowded at the front so I pushed my way to the back, where I found a man lying on the floor, apparently asleep. Passengers were standing around him, occasionally glancing down. When the back door opened at the next stop, some people saw him and didn't get on, others just stepped over the man and took a seat. I had no idea how long he'd been lying there but, finally, a couple got on. They were shocked and started asking what had happened. Had anybody told the bus driver? No one knew. They got the bus driver to stop and an ambulance was called.

Some days later I saw a piece on the news about the man. Apparently, he'd passed out because of his diabetes, but, thanks to the couple, he'd made a complete recovery. The news didn't mention how many other people, including me, had let him down. Why had that crowd stood by and not helped? I have since learnt we were in the grip of what's known as the 'bystander effect'.

Psychologists have identified several causes of this phenomenon. Firstly, we may not realise it's an emergency, and if others show little reaction it confirms to us there's no need to help. Secondly, crowds reduce our feelings of personal responsibility. The more people there are watching, the more likely we are to think someone else will help. And finally, we may be scared that our help will lead to greater problems.

Understanding this now, if I have any doubt in similar situations, I always help. In the end, the worst thing that happens is that there really is no problem and I feel slightly embarrassed – but that's a much better feeling than the guilt of having done nothing.

6 Work in pairs and discuss the questions.

1 Have you seen or heard of any other examples of the bystander effect? If so, what happened?

2 Do you think you'd be more likely to help strangers having read the article? Why/Why not?

Grammar

7 a Look at four incorrect sentences from the story in the text. Cover the box below and correct the tense in each.

1 I pushed my way to the back, where I was finding a man lying on the floor apparently asleep.

2 Passengers have been standing around him, occasionally glancing down.

3 I had no idea how long he was lying there.

4 I saw a piece on the news about the man. He passed out because of his diabetes.

b Work in pairs. Compare your ideas then read the grammar box and check.

Narrative tenses

Past simple

Use the past simple to talk about past habits or to list single completed actions in chronological order.

*I **pushed** my way to the back, where I **found** a man lying on the floor.*

Past continuous

Use the past continuous for actions that were in progress around the time another action happened.

*Passengers **were standing** around him, occasionally glancing down.*

Past perfect simple

Use the past perfect simple to talk about single, complete actions that happened before another action or event in the past.

*I saw a piece on the news about the man. He**'d passed out** because of his diabetes.*

Past perfect continuous

Use the past perfect continuous to talk about actions that were in progress before, or that continued up to, another action or event in the past. The emphasis is on the duration.

*I had no idea how long he**'d been lying** there but, finally, a couple got on.*

The past perfect isn't necessary when we use words like *after* and *before,* as the order of events is already clear.

8 a 🔊 1.4 When we speak at normal speed, the auxiliary verb *had* is sometimes impossible to hear. Listen and notice the way it is reduced or is said as /d/ before a vowel.

1 I'd acted as a mentor to her.

2 We'd grabbed some food beforehand.

3 She'd let me down before.

4 We'd been thinking about it for a while.

5 They'd offered me a job.

6 We'd been saving up.

b Listen again and repeat.

9 Complete the story by putting the verbs in brackets into the correct tense. Use continuous forms wherever possible.

One holiday I ¹_____ (work) in a toy store. A woman ²_____ (come) in one day wearing a lovely cap. I ³_____ (compliment) her on it, and ⁴_____ (ask) her where she ⁵_____ (buy) it because I ⁶_____ (look for) something similar for years, but ⁷_____ never _____ (see) that style before. She ⁸_____ (tell) me and then she ⁹_____ (leave). When I ¹⁰_____ (come) back after lunch, she ¹¹_____ (wait) there. She ¹²_____ (buy) me the cap!

10 Work in pairs. Think of two different ways you could complete sentences 1–6, one with the past perfect simple and one with the past perfect continuous.

1 We ended up stranded at the airport because …
the flight had been cancelled.
it had been snowing hard and we couldn't take off.

2 It was a huge relief when I was finally offered an apprenticeship as …

3 He was sleeping rough. He told me that …

4 … and so I wrote a rave review.

5 … so I was feeling a bit down.

6 … so I picked up the bill for the meal.

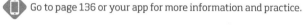 Go to page 136 or your app for more information and practice.

Speaking

PREPARE

11 🔊 1.5 Listen to a short story about a time when a stranger was kind. Answer the questions.

1 Where did the story take place?

2 What was the problem?

3 How and why did the stranger help?

12 You're going to tell a story. Choose one of the topics in the box below and plan what to say.

a time you helped a stranger	a surprise
a time a stranger helped you	a stupid mistake
an example of the bystander effect	
something amazing you saw in the street	

SPEAK

13 Work in groups. Tell each other your stories and respond to them. Use the Useful phrases to help you.

Useful phrases

I can imagine.
You must've been (terrified).
That must've been (a relief).
I think I would've … in that situation.
What a (great) story!

Develop your listening
page 86

1c  How annoying!

A
B

> **Goal:** talk about annoying incidents
> **Language focus:** exaggeration
> **Vocabulary:** at work

Reading and vocabulary

1 a Look at the pictures. What's happening in each one? Why are the people irritated?

b Work in groups. Discuss how annoying you find each thing in the list below. Put them in order from most annoying (1) to least annoying (6).
- having to sit in long, unnecessary meetings
- people eating food noisily
- people complaining about work, school or university
- a colleague or fellow student making you look bad
- your computer crashing
- poor wifi

2 Read the article about a survey into things people find annoying at work.
1 In what order did the survey put the list in Exercise 1b?
2 Find three other annoying things mentioned in the text.

Have you ever thought, I'd really love my job, if only …
• my boss wouldn't **have a go at me** for the tiniest mistakes?
• my colleagues wouldn't spend all day gossiping?
• they'd just buy a photocopier that didn't **jam** every ten seconds?

A recent survey has revealed that you are not alone. The report lists fifty things that drive us mad and found over a quarter of us want to work from home because of work **irritations**, while another 25% have considered quitting their job and working for themselves.

Unfortunately, it's often our colleagues who are **at fault**. For example, ranked number 5 in the report are colleagues who **go on and on about** what's wrong with everything without **coming up with** any solutions themselves. And at number 8, there's the colleague who makes us look bad. They **undermine us** by **pointing the finger of blame** for mistakes while taking all the credit for success.

Then at 7, there are those **pointless** meetings that are called to decide that nothing has been decided! Though apparently, this isn't as bad as colleagues who snack at their desk, **distracting** you with their loud chewing (number 6).

But while our **fellow workers** can be annoying, it's the machines that really make us lose our temper. The survey showed that the biggest irritation is computers crashing – no doubt taking your last three hours' work with it – followed by the hours spent looking at the slow spin of the wheel as a webpage loads. They're enough to make you want to pick up your device and **smash it into little pieces**!

And now you *can* (kind of)! First appearing in Australia, so-called 'rage rooms' are starting to spread around the world. They provide a special space with a variety of **gadgets** – from keyboards to printers – for you to destroy to the sound of your favourite music. Fans claim that it's fantastically satisfying and, as a way to get rid of your frustrations, it is certainly easier than finding a new job!

3 Work in pairs and discuss the questions.
1 Can you think of other annoying things about work or study that weren't mentioned in the article?
2 What do you think of the idea of rage rooms?
3 Can you think of better ways to get rid of irritations?

4 Complete the sentences using some of the words in bold from the article. Use one word in each gap.
1 I think we need a new printer. It's incredibly slow and the paper always seems to _____ . I'm so sick of it.
2 A customer had a real _____ at me today because his credit card didn't work. It was hardly my fault!
3 What I find annoying is that when things go wrong, politicians are very quick to point the _____ of blame at other people, but they never seem to consider that they could be at _____ themselves.
4 I get sent about 150 emails a day and even though most of them are fairly _____ , I still have to check them all before deleting. It's one of my biggest _____ at work.
5 The guy I sit next to is constantly _____ me. Most of the time, he's just going _____ about the latest football news or celebrity gossip.
6 I came _____ with the idea originally and helped develop it, but then in the meeting, in front of all my _____ workers, my boss took all the credit and hardly mentioned me at all.
7 I keep suggesting things but my colleagues always _____ me and it's beginning to affect my confidence.
8 I get so annoyed by other students playing with their _____ in class that sometimes I just want to grab the things and _____ them into little pieces.

5 Work in pairs and discuss the questions.
1 Why might a customer have a go at a shop assistant? Why might a teacher have a go at a student?
2 What different gadgets and equipment do you have in an office? What might go wrong with them?
3 What things might happen to undermine your confidence? What might undermine a team working together?
4 In what ways might you get distracted from working or studying?
5 What things might get smashed? How?

 Go to page 156 or your app for more vocabulary practice.

Listening

6 **1.7 Listen to two conversations about work. Which of the irritations a–d do they talk about?**

a uncomfortable room conditions

b a boss having a go at them

c students behaving badly

d a colleague making them look bad

7 Work in pairs. Try to complete the sentences from the conversations. Then listen again and check your ideas.

1 They've been going _____ about how hot and stuffy the room is.

2 It is _____ in that room. Seriously, we're _____ in there. It must be 35 degrees.

3 They have this supposedly _____ air filtering system.

4 I bet they _____ it, too.

5 I waited _____ for the bus to come.

6 I was rushing around _____ to get everything done.

7 Seriously, I _____ !

Language focus

8 a Work in pairs. Read the language focus box, then match the sentences from Exercise 7 with categories A–D. Some sentences go in more than one category.

Exaggeration

We sometimes exaggerate when telling a story or reporting something that happened to us, to get an extra reaction from the listener. We may exaggerate in one of the following ways.

A Exaggerated time, distance, amount, etc.

*If they'd just buy a photocopier that didn't jam **every ten seconds**!*

*The photocopier is **miles** away from my desk.*

B Repetition (with *and*)

*I had to walk for **miles and miles**.*

*I told him **over and over** again.*

C Comparisons

*It's **like** the Arctic in there.*

*I looked **as if** I'd been dragged through a hedge backwards.*

D Death metaphors

*I was absolutely **dying of** hunger.*

*I could **murder** a curry.*

b Discuss whether you exaggerate in the same way in your language. Give an example.

9 a 🔊 **1.8 Listen and notice how the speaker introduces an exaggerated statement by placing the stress on *Honestly* and *Seriously*.**

1 Honestly, I almost died of boredom.

2 Honestly, I could've killed him.

3 Seriously, the room was like a fridge.

4 Honestly, we were waiting for hours and hours.

5 Seriously, I must've mentioned it about a thousand times.

b Listen again and repeat.

10 a Use exaggeration to write one or more examples of each of the following complaints.

1 He's constantly distracting me.
   Honestly, he asks me something every ten seconds.
   He's constantly chewing or eating something.
   Seriously, he's like a cow or something.

2 It was a pretty boring, pointless meeting.

3 I wish they would do something about the air con at work.

4 They should get a new photocopier.

5 My colleague lost all the work I had done.

6 My boss is incredibly demanding.

b Work in pairs. Compare your examples. Which do you like best? Why?

📱 Go to page 136 or your app for more information and practice.

Speaking

PREPARE

11 Think of two things that you find annoying. Make notes about incidents that have happened which illustrate each of these irritations and why these things particularly annoy you.

SPEAK

12 a Work in groups. Tell each other about what irritates you and give some examples. Use the Useful phrases to help you.

b Who had the most interesting experience? Did anyone share the same irritation as you?

Useful phrases

There's this ... at work/school/uni that drives me mad!
I find that really annoying too.
I know exactly what you mean!
I have to say, things like that don't bother me.
Something similar happened to me the other day.

Develop your reading
page 96

> **Goal:** negotiate solutions to disputes
>
> **Vocabulary:** fights and disputes

Vocabulary

1 Work in pairs. Look at the photos. What disputes or arguments do you think could happen in the following places?
- an airport or on a flight
- a car rental place
- a restaurant
- an apartment block

2 Match the situations in the box with comments 1–6 below.

> a dispute between neighbours   a pay dispute
> a row between friends   a domestic dispute
> mediating in a dispute   a workplace dispute

1 The **tension** had been building up a bit in the office so we had a meeting to try and **clear the air**.

2 They were hardly **on speaking terms** for a while, which was a bit awkward if our usual group went out or had a party, but thankfully they've **made up** now!

3 We're not here to **side with** anyone. We're here to resolve this before it **escalates**.

4 They've had **an ongoing dispute** about a parking space and they even nearly **come to blows** a couple of times when they confronted each other!

5 They've always **quarrelled** a lot, but it seems she's actually **kicked** him **out** this time.

6 Hopefully it won't end up in a strike, but at the moment they've not **been willing** to **compromise**, so what can we do?

3 Replace the words in italics with the correct form of some of the words and phrases in bold from Exercise 2.

1 Are you someone who *is prepared to give up some of what you want* in an argument?

2 Have you heard of a dispute that *quickly got out of control* and where people then *physically fought*?

3 When friends or family members argue, do you ever *support* one person more than the other?

4 Do you know anyone who behaved so badly in a class or a team that they were *forced to leave*?

5 Do you know any people who often *argue and shout at each other*?

6 Have you heard of *an argument between two sides that has continued a long time*?

4 Work in pairs and discuss three of the questions in Exercise 3. Give some details.

Listening 1

5 🔊 1.9 Listen to a conversation between three people who are trying to resolve a dispute. Answer these questions.

1 Where are they?

2 What's the problem?

3 What has caused the problem?

4 How is the dispute resolved in the end?

6 Listen again. Complete the sentences with two or three words.

1 With all _____ , that's your problem. Not ours.

2 I'm awfully sorry about all of this and obviously if _____ to me …

3 So can we talk to whoever's _____ here?

4 I understand that this may not be down to you, but this is _____ .

5 Could you please not _____ at me? I'm just doing my job.

6 If you could just try and _____ a bit …

7 I mean, there must be some way we can _____ here, surely.

7 Work in pairs. Add the sentences from Exercise 6 to the correct section in the Useful phrases box.

> **Useful phrases**
>
> **Seeking compromise**
> Is there really nothing you can do?
> Well, would it be possible to …?
> a _____
> b _____
>
> **Expressing annoyance**
> There must be some mistake.
> You've got to be kidding me!
> c _____
> d _____
>
> **Apologising**
> I'm awfully sorry about all of this.
> I'm afraid the manager is not around at the moment.
> e _____
>
> **Dealing with anger**
> You're really not making this any easier.
> I do understand that you might be upset, but …
> I am going to have to ask you to …
> f _____
> g _____

8 a 🔊 **1.10** Read the information box below. Then listen to these two sentences and notice how an auxiliary verb is stressed or added.

1 I do understand that you might be upset.

2 I am only doing my job.

> **Sounding firm**
> When we have a dispute with someone, we often stress the auxiliary verb in statements. This makes our message sound more forceful. Where there is no other auxiliary verb, we can also use *do/did* in these kinds of statements.
> I asked you not to enter. → I <u>did</u> <u>ask</u> you not to enter.

b Listen again and repeat.

9 a Work in pairs. Practise saying these sentences more forcefully by stressing an auxiliary verb or adding *do/did*.

1 I'm afraid I'm going to need to see some ID.

2 I talked to someone about this last week on the phone.

3 I'm going to have to ask you to leave, I'm afraid.

4 You're going to need to come back tomorrow, I'm afraid.

5 I want to sort this out, but you're not making it easy.

6 I've warned you about this twice now.

7 You really have to return the keys today.

8 We're going to pay, but only once everything's sorted.

b 🔊 **1.11** Listen and check your answers.

Listening 2

10 🔊 **1.12** Listen to another conversation in which people try to resolve a dispute. Are the statements true (T) or false (F)?

1 The couple are buying a second-hand car.

2 They're planning to split the driving on their journey equally.

3 The man they're talking to needs to see some documents.

4 There's no record of their booking.

5 Adding an extra driver will cost them 100 euros a day.

6 They're not staying nearby.

7 They pay cash to cover the extra charge.

8 They manage to reach a compromise.

11 Listen again. Find the difference in sentences 1–5 with what the speakers actually said.

1 There must be a mistake. I'm absolutely positive I put both names down.

2 You've got to be kidding!

3 I really am awfully sorry about this.

4 I understand you might be upset, but could you please not raise your voice, sir?

5 I am going to have to ask you for an extra 100 euros.

12 Work in groups. Discuss the questions.

1 How do you think the people in Listening 1 and Listening 2 handled the situations? Would you have done anything differently?

2 Do you think the compromises they reached in each case were fair?

3 Have you ever had a dispute when travelling or buying something? What happened?

Speaking

13 a You are going to roleplay conversations to resolve disputes. Work in pairs. Student A: Turn to page 166. Student B: Turn to page 168.

b Roleplay the conversations.

 For more practice go to your Workbook or app.

Go online for the Roadmap video.

On the mend

> **Goal:** talk about recovery
> **Grammar:** the future in the past
> **Vocabulary:** injuries and illnesses

Vocabulary

1 **Look at the photos. What physical injuries and illnesses might people face doing these activities? How could they prevent or overcome them?**

2 **Match the problems in 1–8 with the results in a–h.**
   1 The cream they gave me really **irritated** my skin
   2 **I bumped** my head hard on the side of the cupboard
   3 **I came down with** a **stomach bug** on the last day of my holiday
   4 He **strained** a muscle in his leg during the game
   5 He suffered a serious **spinal** injury
   6 She suffered **kidney failure**
   7 I fell off my bike and **bashed** my arm
   8 As she got older, she **developed arthritis**

   a and was **out cold** for a few minutes.
   b and had to **limp** off. He'll be **out of action** for a while.
   c and she'd get sharp pains in her **swollen joints**.
   d and needs a **transplant** when they can find **an organ donor**.
   e and spent half the night **vomiting**.
   f and it was **black and blue** by the morning.
   g and made it very **itchy**.
   h and was left with **severely restricted mobility**.

3 **Work in pairs. What's the best way to deal with some of the problems in Exercise 2?**

4 **Complete the short story about an amazing recovery with one to three words in bold from Exercise 2.**

For any professional athlete, injuries are part and parcel of the job. Footballers are used to getting kicked and waking up black ¹_____ , while runners who have ²_____ muscles in their legs can end up ³_____ for weeks. You also often see tennis players with ⁴_____ ankles who have to ⁵_____ off court in the middle of a match and concede defeat. However, few have been through what Aries Merritt has and come back to perform at the highest levels. Having won gold in the 110 metre hurdles at the 2012 Olympics, Merritt learnt he had liver disease. He would find himself ⁶_____ after meals and eventually needed a ⁷_____ . Remarkably, within a matter of months, he was back in training and performing near his best!

 Go to your app for more practice.

Listening

5 a 🔊 2.1 **Listen to five people talking about recoveries. Take notes about the injuries and illnesses they had.**

   b **Work in pairs. Compare your notes and discuss how serious each injury or illness was. Put them in order from the most serious (1) to the least serious (5).**

6 a **Listen again. What do the speakers say about each of these things?**
   1 shoot - scan - training
   2 a meeting - operations - a friend
   3 make it - donor - chemicals
   4 cows - physical pain - pin codes
   5 the office - Barbados - Sunday

   b **Work in pairs and compare your ideas.**

Grammar

7 **Work in pairs. Look at sentences a–e below from the listening. Discuss questions 1–5.**
   1 What do they all have in common in terms of time?
   2 Which sentences refer to plans or intentions?
   3 Which structure refers to an action you intend to do immediately?
   4 Which sentences refer to predictions?
   5 Which words or structures show uncertainty?

   a She was just about to shoot when her foot got caught.
   b I honestly believed I was never going to walk again.
   c To be honest, we weren't sure she would make it.
   d The doctors thought she might never get her memory back.
   e I came down with it the day before I was due to go to Barbados for a holiday.

8 Read the grammar box to check your answers to Exercise 7. Then complete the examples with one word from sentences a–e in Exercise 7.

The future in the past

When we talk about the past, sometimes we want to refer to an action or event that was in the future at that time. We often do this when what we planned or predicted didn't actually happen. We can use the past of some future forms for this.

Past plans or intentions

I was going to spend some time in Australia in the summer.

I was just ¹_____ to leave, when I realised I had forgotten something important.

I was ²_____ to see the dentist the following week.

Was (just) about to refers to an action someone was intending to do immediately.

Past predictions

I thought I was ³_____ to die.

I knew it ⁴_____ work.

Use *might, wasn't sure, possibly,* etc. to show uncertainty.

I had a feeling it might be difficult.

9 Complete the sentences using the verbs in the box and the prompts in brackets.

affect develop get have leave park play want

1 I _____ my car when a motorbike bumped into the back of me. (just about)

2 I was worried that the accident _____ her mobility, but in the end she was fine. (going to)

3 It wasn't easy, but I kept telling myself that things _____ better over time. (would)

4 I saw him a few weeks ago and he _____ another operation the following day. (due to)

5 She _____ hospital when they decided they needed to do some more tests. (just about)

6 My son had a horrible stomach bug, so I knew he _____ to eat anything. (wouldn't)

7 The doctors were worried that he _____ heart disease in the future. (might)

8 The doctors said he _____ professionally again, but he refused to accept it. (never going to)

10 a 🔊 2.2 When we speak at normal speed, *to* often blends with the words around it. Listen and notice how the phrases with *to* sound in the sentences.

1 I felt like I was going to vomit.

2 I was due to start a new job the next day.

3 The train was just about to leave.

4 I knew it wasn't going to be easy.

5 I realised I was going to be out of action for ages.

b Listen again and repeat.

11 Work in groups. Use the structures in the grammar box to tell each other about two of the following:

* a time you changed your plans
* a time someone broke a promise
* a time you were very disappointed by something
* a silly accident
* an excuse you needed to make

📱 Go to page 138 or your app for more information and practice.

Speaking

PREPARE

12 Choose one of the options below to talk about. Decide what the original problem was, what effect it had and what the recovery involved.

* a time you recovered from an illness or injury
* someone you know who has made a recovery
* someone famous who made a good recovery

SPEAK

13 Work in pairs. Tell your stories and respond. Use the Useful phrases to help you.

Useful phrases

Seriously? How awful!

That must've been difficult for ... to deal with.

Wow! That's a really inspiring story.

That's brought a tear to my eye, that story.

I'm glad everything worked out OK.

14 Change partners and tell each other about the stories you heard. Which was the most remarkable recovery?

Develop your reading
page 98

> **Goal:** present a case
> **Grammar:** double comparatives
> **Vocabulary:** charities

Reading and vocabulary

1 **Work in pairs and discuss the questions.**

1 Can you think of any organisations that could help in the situations in the photos?

2 What could the organisations do exactly?

3 Why might organisations dedicated to helping not want to make a profit?

2 **Read the newspaper column quickly. Where might you see a feature like this? What is its purpose?**

3 **Match organisations 1–3 with statements a–c.**

a You can share your experiences and get help from others with the same problem.

b They mainly work with people living in war zones or in poverty.

c By working with politicians and local residents, they can improve the environment.

Non-profit spotlight

New non-profit organisations are formed each year to tackle different problems. But the more there are, the more difficult it becomes to decide which to support. Our new monthly column can help by giving charities a space to offer us a brief description of what they do.

1 Clowns without Frontiers organises free comic performances by professional clowns to children and families who are suffering the consequences of armed conflict, natural disasters and deprivation. Its aim is to provide emotional support through creating moments of laughter and joy in what can seem hopeless situations.

2 Sustrans campaigns for sustainable transport. It also lobbies governments nationally and internationally to change policy and city design in favour of pedestrians and cyclists. It works with communities to empower people to reclaim their streets by providing expertise and advice on how to change their neighbourhood into a greener, safer space. It also runs a national network of car-free routes connecting people.

3 BackCare raises money in aid of people suffering from chronic back pain, a problem that millions have to live with and that costs the economy billions each year. This organisation funds research into the causes and treatment of back pain and runs support groups for sufferers. It also distributes information packs to increase awareness of the condition.

4 **Look at the words in the box from the column in Exercise 3. Complete the questions with the correct form of the words.**

| aware | campaign | deprive | empower | expert |
| lobby | reclaim | sustain | tackle | worth |

1 What's the most important problem that needs to be _____ in your community?

2 What issues do we need to raise _____ of? Why?

3 Apart from charities, who else might _____ a government? What for?

4 What's the best way of encouraging _____ development in developing countries?

5 What more could be done to _____ women in society?

6 Do some parts of your country suffer worse social and economic _____ than others?

7 Why might people feel the need to _____ the streets?

8 What areas do you have some degree of _____ in? How could you use this to help charities?

9 Can you think of two things people sometimes _____ for? And two _____ you would support?

10 Which of the organisations mentioned in the feature do you think are most _____ of donations? Why?

5 **Work in pairs. Ask and answer five of the questions in Exercise 4.**

Go to page 157 or your app for more vocabulary and practice.

Listening

6 a 🔊 2.3 **You're going to listen to a radio show where two people each make a case for donating to a particular charity. Listen and complete the notes.**

Charity name 1: [1]_____

In aid of: *people with housing problems*

Action: *provide legal advice to people* [2]_____ *and lobby government to* [3]_____

Consequence: *government spends less on effects of homelessness*

Charity name 2 : [4]_____

In aid of: *people living in poverty*

Action: *they give donations to people, without* [5]_____

Consequence: *helps reduce stress and people make* [6]_____

---

b **Work in pairs and compare your notes. Then listen again and check.**

7 Think of two things you would want to know about each charity. Compare with a partner.

Grammar

8 a Try to complete the sentences from the radio show with two or three words in each gap.

1 _____ we do to tackle the causes of homelessness, _____ the government will have to spend on dealing with its effects.

2 _____ people have to decide on how to spend their money, _____ the donation will be.

3 _____ people are, _____ they are to make good decisions.

b 🔊 2.4 Listen and check your answers.

9 a Work in pairs and discuss the questions.

1 What do the gaps in Exercise 8a have in common?
2 What's the relationship between the two halves of each sentence?
3 Do all the comparatives use an adjective?
4 In these kinds of sentences, why might you need to use the word *fewer* instead of *less*?

b Read the grammar box and check your answers.

Double comparatives

We can use two comparatives in a sentence to show how one action/situation (e.g. an increase) can have an effect on another action/situation (e.g. to improve) as a consequence.
The less stressed people are, the better able they are to make decisions.
There can be more than one consequence.
The less stressed people are, the better able they are to make decisions, and the more successful those decisions will be.
Countable nouns
The more there are, the better it is.
The fewer there are, the harder it is.
The more people that take part, the quicker it will get done.
Uncountable nouns
The more you do it, the easier it becomes.
The less we do to help, the worse the situation gets.
The less money we have, the less we can do.
Adjectives
The smaller the problem, the less help people need.
The more difficult it is, the bigger the reward.

10 a 🔊 2.5 Listen to some of the sentences from the grammar box. Notice the way the first half of the comparative rises and the second half falls.

b Listen again and repeat.

11 Read the sentences about a charity that helps children in poor areas. Complete the examples using the correct comparative form of the words in brackets.

1 _____ (meals) they provide at school, _____ (likely) it is that kids will attend.
2 _____ (long) kids stay in education, _____ (great/opportunities) they have in life and the more they will be able to support their families.
3 They also want to provide kids with a place to play – _____ (big/space), _____ (good).
4 _____ (money) they raise, _____ (kids) they can help, so please donate generously.

12 Work in pairs. Say at least two beginnings or endings for each of the following:

1 _____ , the better.
2 _____ , the easier it is.
3 The sooner we get started, _____ .
4 The longer they have to wait, _____ .
5 The less free time people have, _____ .

📱 Go to page 138 or your app for more information and practice.

Speaking

PREPARE

13 Work in pairs. Imagine you work for a charity, either one from Exercise 2 or one of your choice. You want to apply for money from a large fund. Think about the following:
- what your charity is and how you will explain its work
- how much money you want/what you will do with it
- what effect this money will have now and in the future

SPEAK

14 a Present your case to the class. Use the Useful phrases to help you. Other students can ask questions to find out more.

Useful phrases
Thanks for your time.
I'm speaking in support of …
The more you can give, the better.
The money will go towards …
All the evidence suggests it's an effective way of …

b Vote for the charity that you think most deserve donations.

 **Develop your writing** page 118

Regeneration

> **Goal:** make suggestions about new uses for old buildings

> **Language focus:** negative questions

> **Vocabulary:** urban change

Reading

1   **Look at the photos and discuss the questions.**

1   What do you think these buildings and spaces are used for now?

2   What do you think they were used for in the past?

3   Why do you think they stopped being used like that?

4   What problems might arise when trying to change the way buildings are used?

2   **Read a review of a book on abandoned buildings. Decide which statements are true.**

1   The author gives a positive review of a book.

2   The author explains why the hotel was abandoned.

3   The hotel wasn't in as bad a condition as might have been expected.

4   The author found out someone was living in the hotel.

5   The author sees opportunities in the buildings photographed in the book.

3   **Work in pairs. Using the words below, retell the author's experience at the abandoned hotel.**

- rumours
- crawl under the fence
- thick with weeds
- neglected
- footsteps
- raced out
- eventually restored
- turned into

Vocabulary

4   **Complete the descriptions with the words in the box.**

abandoned	bankrupt	declined	demolished
neglected	outdated	restored	shrank
took over	turned into		

1   Part of Kelenföld Power Station near Budapest was shut down in 2005 because its machines had become _____ . However, because of its special architecture, the building is protected by law and cannot be _____ or altered.

2   Family School Fureai was a school in Yubari, Japan. Yubari was once a big coal-mining town, but then the industry _____ and families started leaving to look for work elsewhere. The population _____ dramatically and in 2007 the city went _____ and the school was left _____ .

3   In 1914, the beautiful gardens of Heligan house became _____ after the gardeners who looked after them went to fight in World War One and never returned. Weeds completely _____ . In the 1970s, the house was eventually _____ flats. However, in 1990, the story of the gardens was uncovered and over the next 20 years, the grounds were _____ to their former glory. Since their restoration, they've become a major tourist attraction.

When I was growing up, there was an abandoned hotel near my home. A high fence surrounded it, with signs saying 'Danger – Keep Out', and 'Security cameras in operation'. There were rumours (false, as it turns out) that a murderer had lived there and that a strange atmosphere could still be felt in some of the rooms. But all these warnings were like a challenge to us kids and one day a friend of mine and I managed to crawl under the fence. The grounds of the hotel were thick with weeds and we fought our way through them to the building. The lock and chain on the front door had been broken. We stepped inside.

Although it was badly neglected, the hotel lobby seemed almost to be waiting for guests to return: a bell remained on the reception desk; room keys still hung on a board behind it; there was a dusty red leather sofa and a coffee table with a single cup on it. We were about to go up a wide staircase when suddenly we heard footsteps above. We were so terrified we raced out, not waiting to find out who or what they belonged to.

The image of that hotel lobby, frozen in time, has stayed with me and I was reminded of it again by Martin ten Bouwhuijs' fascinating book, *The World of Urban Decay 2*. The Dutch photographer has explored abandoned buildings ranging from churches to schools to power plants, and his photos reveal the sad beauty behind those 'keep out' signs. The book also tells the stories that led to these buildings' decline and closure. While there is a certain sadness in the photos, there's also a feeling of excitement about what these places could one day become. Our abandoned hotel was eventually restored and turned into an amazing old people's home that includes a nursery for local kids. Who knows what a power plant could be in the future?

The World of Urban Decay 2 is published by Schiffer Publishing Ltd.

D

5 **Work in pairs and discuss the questions.**

1 Can you think of three machines that have become outdated? What replaced them?

2 Do you know any buildings where you live that cannot be demolished or altered?

3 What industries are declining where you live? Why?

4 Are there any neglected areas or abandoned buildings where you live that have been restored?

Go to page 157 or your app for more vocabulary and practice.

Listening

6 a 2.6 **Listen to a conversation about an abandoned glove factory. What is going to happen to the factory? What do the speakers suggest could happen to it?**

b **Work in pairs. Which suggestion or alternative solution would you choose for the factory? Why?**

Language focus

7 a 2.7 **Work in pairs. Try to complete the questions from the conversation with the correct words. Then listen and check.**

1 _____ they do something better with it than create luxury flats?

2 _____ they done that elsewhere?

3 _____ they just be better demolishing the whole thing and creating some nice park land?

b **Work in pairs. Answer the questions. Then read the language focus box and complete it with the examples in Exercise 7a.**

1 What do the questions in Exercise 7a have in common?

2 Why do you think they are they asked in this way?

Negative questions

We often ask negative questions with *isn't, don't, didn't, can't,* etc. We do this to get an answer, but also to show we have a particular attitude.

1 I think this is true, but want to check.

Isn't he already 18?

a _____

2 I'm surprised about this or have an opinion/ suggestion about this.

Can't you swim?

Don't you think it's a waste of time?

b _____

c _____

8 a 2.8 **Listen and notice the rising tones at the end of the questions.**

1 Weren't you scared?

2 Can't they do anything about it?

3 Didn't you think it was dangerous?

4 Wasn't it closed because it went bankrupt?

5 Wouldn't it be better to turn it into a school or something?

b **Listen again and repeat.**

9 a **Think of how you could respond to each statement using a negative question.**

1 She's not married.

Really? Didn't she say she was?

2 I don't have a car.

3 I never go to that part of town.

4 The building was previously owned by the government.

5 I don't really like this building.

6 They should just demolish it and start again.

b **Take turns to say one of the statements. Your partner asks a negative question. Try to continue the conversations.**

Go to page 138 or your app for more information and practice.

Speaking

PREPARE

10 **Work in pairs. Choose one of the photos on page 166. Discuss the questions.**

1 Where do you think it is?

2 What might it have been used for in the past?

3 Why do you think it has been abandoned?

4 What should or could they do with it now?

5 How could the different parts/areas of it be adapted?

SPEAK

11 a **Change partners. Take turns to introduce the place you chose and explain what you think should be done with it. Use the Useful phrases box to help you.**

- If you have chosen the same picture, you can 'correct' any 'facts' your partner tells you.
- You can also suggest alternative ideas.
- When you have discussed one place and come to an agreement, discuss the next.

Useful phrases

It's about time they did something about it.

I reckon they should …

It would (increase tourism in the area).

Wasn't it a … before?

Wouldn't it be better to …?

b **Tell the rest of the class about your decisions.**

Develop your listening page 87

Check and reflect: Units 1 and 2

1 a Match the sentence halves.

1 I didn't like this song to begin with, but it's growing
2 I love outdoor swimming. Nothing
3 I do judo. It helps me let
4 I've always been hopeless
5 I don't want to see it. There's been too much hype
6 I tried doing yoga, but I didn't really take
7 I grew up in a city, so I'm not really into outdoor
8 I've always fancied doing a martial

a to it.
b at crosswords.
c off steam.
d around it.
e pursuits.
f on me.
g art.
h beats it.

b Work in pairs. Tell your partner about two of the following:
- something that's really grown on you
- something you've always fancied doing or trying
- something you tried, but didn't really take to
- the best way of letting off steam
- something you've always been hopeless at

2 Complete the sentences with one word.

1 One thing _____ really helps me switch off is cooking.
2 _____ I like most about her is how encouraging she always is.
3 One thing I love about the game is the _____ that anyone can play it!
4 What I enjoyed most about the experience _____ how relaxing it was.
5 What I've never understood _____ why it's not more popular.
6 The _____ I love about it is that sometimes a beginner can beat an expert!

3 Complete the sentences with the best word. The first two letters are given.

1 I'm OK, I guess. I've just been feeling a bit do_____ recently.
2 I'd missed the last bus and so was st_____ at the airport overnight.
3 My family have been a real co_____ to me during this difficult time.
4 Everyone was very we_____ . They made us feel at home.
5 That new film has had ra_____ reviews. It sounds great.
6 What I found shocking was the number of people sleeping ro_____ on the streets.
7 My son's been offered an ap_____ with a local building firm.
8 I've been asked to act as a me_____ to one of the new members of staff.

4 Complete each pair of sentences with one of the verbs in the box. Use the past perfect simple in one sentence and the past perfect continuous in the other.

drive	make	offer	stay	try

1 a I _____ there before and liked it, so this time was a real disappointment.
  b He _____ with friends for weeks and was desperate to get his own place.
2 a It was weird. I _____ to remember his name when he messaged me unexpectedly.
  b She _____ loads of different keep-fit activities, but didn't really take to any.
3 a After I _____ the decision to move to Spain, I started to take Spanish classes.
  b They _____ noise for hours so eventually their neighbours called the police.
4 a We _____ all day so I decided to pull over and take a break.
  b It was the first time I _____ on the left!
5 a We _____ to meet and discuss it three times, but they always refused.
  b He _____ to babysit for us for ages so in the end, we decided to give him a try.

5 Complete the questions with the correct form of the verbs in the box. Then ask a partner three of the questions (1–6).

come up with	distract	go on	have
point	smash		

1 Have you ever _____ the finger of blame at someone and later found out they weren't at fault?
2 When was the last time someone _____ a go at you?
3 What kinds of things usually _____ you when you're trying to concentrate?
4 Do you think you're good at _____ solutions to problems?
5 Do you know anyone who always _____ about their problems – or about how great they are?
6 Have you ever lost your temper and _____ something? When? Why?

6 Complete the sentences with repetitive phrases based on the words in the box.

ages	cried	days	laughed	miles	over

1 The advert said the hotel was quite central, but it was actually *miles and miles* from the centre.
2 I just _____ when I turned forty. I felt like my life was already over!
3 Sorry I'm late. I waited _____ for the bus!
4 Honestly, I _____ when I first saw that video of the dog dancing!
5 I love that film. Seriously, I could just sit and watch it _____ again.
6 The airline lost my luggage and it took _____ for them to get it back to me.

7 Complete the sentences with the pairs of words in the box. You will need to decide which order to use the words in.

> action/strained   black and blue/bashed
> bumped/cold   transplant/donor   itchy/irritates
> swollen/arthritis

1 I _____ my leg on the car door. It was _____ when I woke up.
2 I can't use that cream. It _____ my skin and makes it all _____ .
3 As she got older, she developed _____ and had _____ joints.
4 I _____ my head when I stood up and was out _____ for a couple of minutes.
5 He's _____ a muscle, so he's going to be out of _____ for at least a month.
6 She's waiting for a kidney_____ , but they haven't found a _____ yet.

8 a Complete the sentences with one word.

1 It was awful! I thought I was _____ to faint.
2 I was _____ about to go out when it started raining.
3 We were _____ to land at six, but we got delayed.
4 I _____ going to call you, but couldn't find my phone.
5 I wasn't sure, but I had a feeling that this _____ happen.
6 We _____ about to give up and get a cab when the bus arrived.

b Work in pairs. Tell your partner about two situations you've been in that were similar to the ones in Exercise 8a.

9 a Complete each sentence with a preposition in the correct place.

1 In recent years, many organisations have lobbied a change in environmental policy.
2 We need to do more to raise awareness issues, such as pollution.
3 Most charities just aren't worthy donations.
4 I have a degree of expertise computing.
5 It's great that people are campaigning action on climate change.

b Work in pairs. How many sentences do you agree with? Why?

10 Match the sentence halves.

1 The lower wages are,
2 The fewer motorists there are on the roads,
3 According to new research, the more you lie,
4 The more we empower women educationally,
5 The more the government tackles corruption,

a the less likely accidents become.
b the more easily they can get out of poverty.
c the more money will be paid in taxes.
d the worse it is for the economy.
e the easier it gets.

11 a Complete the sentences with the best word. The first part of the word is given.

1 That shop was left ab_____ when its owner died.
2 Some gadgets very quickly become ou_____ .
3 A lot of old historic buildings have been tu_____ i_____ luxury apartments.
4 The building's protected by law, so it can't be de_____ or altered.
5 The amount of green space is sh_____ every year.
6 The company went ba_____ because of $18 billion in long-term debt.

b Work in pairs. What might be good or bad about four of the situations in Exercise 11a?

12 Complete the negative questions using the words in the box.

> Aren't you   Didn't you   Haven't we   Can't you
> Don't you   Won't you

1 _____ once tell me you wanted to be an actor?
2 _____ find it worrying when it's this hot in February?
3 What's the rush? _____ wait until I'm ready?
4 _____ met before? You look familiar.
5 _____ bored of it all? It's been going on so long.
6 _____ miss your train if you don't leave soon?

13 Put the words in the correct order to make sentences/questions.

1 have / going / leave / you / ask / to / am / to / I / to
2 be / you / have / got / kidding / to
3 do / really / is / you / can / nothing / there / ?
4 be / must / there / mistake / some
5 awfully / this / I / all / sorry / am / about / of
6 talk / can / whoever / in / is / I / to / charge / ?

Reflect

How confident do you feel about the statements below? Write 1–5 (1 = not very confident, 5 = very confident).

- I can persuade people to try different activities.
- I can narrate a short story in detail.
- I can talk about annoying incidents.
- I can negotiate solutions to disputes.
- I can talk about recovery.
- I can present a case for a donation.
- I can make suggestions about new uses for old buildings.

 For more practice go to your Workbook or app.

 Go online for the Roadmap video.

3A It'll brighten up

> **Goal:** talk about the weather and plan activities
> **Grammar:** ways of expressing the future
> **Vocabulary:** the weather

Vocabulary

1 Read the sentences and match the words in bold with the correct weather category in the box.

cold hot sunny wet windy

1 It was **blowing a gale** when we got to the top, so I didn't go too close to the edge.
2 I couldn't sleep at night because it was so **sticky** and **humid**.
3 It **brightened up** in the morning and then the rest of the weekend it was absolutely **glorious**.
4 Apart from one brief sunny spell, it was pretty **miserable** most of the time.
5 Oh, it was really **bitter**! I almost froze to death while we were watching the game.
6 It started **spitting**, so we decided to pack everything up, but then it started **pouring down** before we could get inside. We all got **soaked**.
7 It was a bit **chilly** at night. We definitely needed the extra blanket.
8 There was a **frost** on the ground in the morning and it was a lovely, clear **crisp** day.
9 It was so still. There wasn't even the slightest **breeze**.
10 There was a huge **thunderstorm** that **flooded** the pitch, so the game was called off.

2 Answer the questions about the words in bold in Exercise 1.

1 Which word describes a small amount of wind and which a small amount of rain?
2 What might happen if it's blowing a gale outside?
3 If it's spitting and it then gets worse, how do you describe the weather? And what about if it then gets better?
4 Why might a warning about the weather be issued?
5 Which three words can also describe a person or their mood?

3 Work in pairs. Tell your partner about three of the following topics:
• the weather you've had in your country this year
• the weather you had the last time you went on holiday
• any weather stories you have heard about in the news
• a great weather experience you've had
• a terrible weather experience you've had

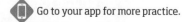 Go to your app for more practice.

Listening

4 🔊 3.1 Listen to four conversations about the weather. In which conversation (1–4) is each type of weather (A–H) mentioned?

5 Listen again. Match each sentence with one or more of the conversations 1–4.
a The weather is unexpected for the time of year.
b The weather is going to change.
c People may be in danger.
d Someone is busy.
e Someone is persuaded to change their mind.
f Someone is not dressed for the weather.

6 Have you experienced any similar situations to those described? When? What happened?

Grammar

7 a **3.2 Listen and underline which sentence in each pair the speakers say.**

1 It's going to warm up. / It's supposed to be warming up.
2 The hot weather is set to continue. / The hot weather is continuing.
3 So beware if you're considering travelling there. / So beware if you consider travelling there.
4 Temperatures should drop. / Temperatures are going to drop.
5 They'll serve us if we go now. / They'll still be serving if we go now.
6 I'm supposed to be visiting a friend. / I'm visiting a friend.

b Look at the examples in Exercise 7a. Complete the grammar box with the words in the box.

> formal   in progress   plans   pleasant   predictions
> reporting   unpleasant

Ways of expressing the future

be supposed to
Use *be supposed to* to talk about predictions we are ¹_____ or about plans that may change because of new circumstances.
It's supposed to be warming up.
I'm supposed to be visiting a friend.

be set to, be expected to
We usually use *be set to* and *be expected to* to make ²_____ in more ³_____ speech and writing.
It's set to continue.
It's expected to improve.

Present continuous
We use the present continuous form of verbs such as *consider, hope, think of,* and *plan* to talk about ⁴_____ that are in our minds now.
I'm considering travelling there.
I'm hoping to go away this weekend.

should
Use *should* for something ⁵_____ we expect to happen, and *shouldn't* for something ⁶_____ we expect won't happen.
Temperatures should drop.
The visit to the dentist shouldn't take long.

Future continuous (*will be + -ing*)
Use the future continuous to talk about a situation that will be ⁷_____ at a time in the future.
They'll still be serving.
You can use *may* instead of *will* to show a lack of certainty.
It may be pouring down by the time we get there.

8 a **3.3 Listen to five sentences. Notice the intonation of the future forms. Write what you hear. Each sentence is said twice.**

b **3.4 Work in pairs and compare what you wrote. Then listen and repeat.**

9 Choose the correct alternatives.

1 Moving on to the forecast for Wednesday, things *are set to/ are supposed to* improve with many sunny spells and only the odd shower. Thursday *should see/ is seeing* temperatures rise and, heading in to the weekend, we can expect fine, dry weather.
2 I'm not sure we'll do much when we get there because *it'll probably be raining/it should rain.*
3 *We think/ We're thinking* of going camping. *It's supposed to be/ It's set to be* gorgeous this weekend.
4 *I'm supposed to be going/ I'll be going* out tonight, but it's so hot I might just stay in with the air con on.
5 I'll see if we can change the tickets. *It's not set to be/ It shouldn't be* a problem, but I'll let you know if it is.

10 Work in pairs. Use different ways of expressing the future to talk about the following:
- the weather next weekend
- plans you have for the next holiday period
- the situation you'll find in your house or apartment when you get home
- how you expect the country to change over the next few years

 Go to page 140 or your app for more information and practice.

Speaking

PREPARE

11 a Write down four different forecasts for the weather.
> *It's supposed to be a cold, sunny day – nice and crisp!*

b Think about four or five different things you plan to do over the next week.

12 **3.5 Listen to a conversation about making plans. Answer the questions.**
1 What is the weather forecast?
2 Do the speakers arrange to do anything together?

SPEAK

13 Work in pairs. Have similar conversations to the one in Exercise 12. Use the Useful phrases to help you and follow this pattern.

Student A: Choose one of your weather forecasts. Start the conversation: *What are you up to [time]?*
Student B: Say your plan and invite Student A.
Student A: Continue the conversation and come to an arrangement. Mention the weather forecast.

Useful phrases

What are you up to (later)?
Weather permitting, (I'm going out).
Apparently, there's going to be (a frost).
It's supposed to be (miserable).
We might as well (stay at home).

> **Develop your writing**
> page 120

3B Law and order

> **Goal:** discuss legal cases and consequences
>
> **Grammar:** verb patterns and reporting
>
> **Vocabulary:** the law and courts

Vocabulary

1 a **Look at the pictures. What are these crimes? How serious are they? Put them in order (1 = least serious, 6 = most serious).**

  b **Work in pairs. Compare your answers, giving reasons.**

2 **Complete the sentences with a word or phrase in the box to make alternative collocations with the words in bold.**

access to information	of corruption	the patent
damages of $3 million	the defence	in favour of
~~not guilty~~	a nuisance	online fraud	the verdict

1 In court, the defendant **pleaded** *guilty* / *not guilty* .

2 The judge **awarded** *custody of the children to the mother* / _____ .

3 The government has **cracked down on** *petty crime* / _____ .

4 The judge **ruled** *against* / _____ the claimants.

5 The judge ruled the company was unfairly **restricting** *people's rights* / _____ .

6 He said he would fight on and is going to **appeal against** *the ruling* / _____ .

7 She denies all **the charges** *against her* / _____ .

8 In the trial, he **testified for** *the prosecution* / _____ .

9 They were **accused of causing** *the fatal crash* / _____ .

10 The judge found the terms of *the agreement* / _____ **had been broken**.

3 **Work in pairs. Choose five of the sentences in Exercise 2 and decide what the whole situation or story could be.**

> *The defendant faced charges of corruption and there was a lot of evidence against him, so he **pleaded guilty** to get a shorter sentence.*

 Go to page 158 or your app for more vocabulary and practice.

Reading

4 **Read about three legal cases that had ongoing consequences. For each case, answer the questions.**

  a Who were the defendants?

  b Who took them to court? Why?

  c What was the final verdict?

5 **Read the cases again. Are the statements true (T), false (F) or not mentioned (NM)?**

  1 Apple were awarded significant damages.

  2 Samsung are going to appeal against the decision.

  3 Before Bosman's case, clubs still owned players even after their contracts had ended.

  4 Bosman ended up getting the move to Dunkerque that he wanted.

  5 The Millers tried to sort out the dispute with the cricket club before going to court.

1 Tech giants Apple and Samsung **announced** that they have finally settled a long-running legal battle, with the South Korean firm agreeing to pay their US rivals over £400 million in damages. The dispute started back in 2011, when Apple **accused** Samsung of copying the iPhone's design and key software features. It dragged on for seven years. In the end, a jury decided that some of Apple's patents had been broken and Samsung **accepted** the ruling.

2 Footballer Jean-Marc Bosman became famous as perhaps the only player to have a landmark legal ruling named after him. When his contract with Standard Liège expired in 1990, he wanted to move to a French club called Dunkerque. However, his club **refused** to release him unless a transfer fee was paid. Bosman took his case to the European Court of Justice, where he **persuaded** judges that his freedom of movement was being restricted. The Bosman Ruling came into being, leaving out-of-contract players free to move wherever they wanted.

3 At the time Mr and Mrs Miller bought their recently-built house in the village of Lintz, the nearby cricket pitch had already been in use for over 70 years. As a few balls every year ended up in the garden or hitting their house, they went to court in a bid to **force** the local club to stop playing there. The club **denied** causing a nuisance and stressed that they'd offered to pay for any damage they caused. The judge hearing the case, Lord Denning, agreed and ruled against the Millers, who moved house soon afterwards.

6 **Work in groups. Discuss the verdicts in the three cases.**

  1 Do you think they were correct?

  2 What similar things might the verdicts prevent?

  3 What other consequences might there be?

E

F

Grammar

7 Look at the patterns described in the box. Then match the verbs in bold in the texts in Exercise 5 with the patterns, according to how they are used.

Verb patterns and reporting

We use different verbs to report what someone said, and these can be followed by a range of different patterns. Many reporting verbs can take more than one pattern.

1 verb + object
For example: *blame, criticise, discuss, reject*
Activists have **criticised the judge's decision**.

2 verb + infinitive
For example: *agree, demand, promise, threaten*
The government has **promised to crack down** *on tax avoidance.*

3 verb + object + infinitive
For example: *advise, ask, encourage, remind, warn*
The prosecution **asked the judge to refuse** *bail.*

4 verb + -ing
For example: *admit, deny, discuss*
The driver **admitted breaking** *the law.*

5 verb + (that) clause
For example: *admit, agree, argue, boast, confess, demand, suggest*
She **confessed that she knew who had done it**.

6 verb + object + (that) clause
For example: *advise, warn*
They **warned him that it was against the law**.

7 verb (+ object) + preposition
For example: *blame, criticise*
The airline **blamed the delay on** *technical problems.*

Note that when we use reporting verbs, we generally summarise the general content of what was said rather than report the exact words.

8 a Which of the past forms in the box end with:

    a a /t/ sound?   **b** a /d/ sound?   **c** an /ɪd/ sound?

| admitted | argued | asked | blamed | criticised |
| promised | warned | | | |

b 🔊 3.6 Listen to the sentences and write what you hear. Notice how the *-ed* endings are reduced or disappear.

c 🔊 3.7 Work in pairs and compare what you wrote. Then listen and repeat.

9 a Choose the correct alternatives. Sometimes both options are correct.

  1 I *warned/threatened* to report them to the police if it happened again.

  2 People were quick to *criticise/blame* the police for the rising crime rate.

  3 They've *promised/discussed* to do more to enforce parking rules in the area.

  4 All three defendants *admitted/denied* causing a public nuisance.

  5 The Prime Minister has *rejected/agreed* demands for his resignation.

  6 Police are *demanding/encouraging* anyone with any information to come forward.

  7 My dad *advised/suggested* me to take out a patent on my invention.

  8 He *boasted/confessed* that he'd stolen over a hundred thousand pounds from the company.

b Work in pairs and compare your answers. Change the sentence to use that verb that you couldn't use.

10 a Choose one of the topics and prepare to talk about it.
* something someone promised to do, but then didn't
* something someone you know was once accused of
* a time you did something you were warned not to
* a time someone was unfairly criticised for something

b Work in groups and share your stories.

📱 Go to page 140 or your app for more information and practice.

Speaking

PREPARE

11 🔊 3.8 Listen to two friends discuss one of the three cases you read about in Exercise 5.

  1 Which case do they discuss?

  2 How do they feel about the verdict? Why?

  3 What do they say about the implications of the verdict?

12 Work in pairs. Student A: Choose one of the two cases on page 166. Student B: choose one of the two cases on page 168. Prepare to talk about it.

SPEAK

13 Tell your partner about your case. Discuss what should happen. Use the Useful phrases to help you.

Useful phrases

Did you see/read that thing in the paper about …?
If you ask me, what should happen in cases like this is …
It's just plain wrong.
I think that's fair enough.

Develop
your
listening
page 88

25

3c Fair play

A Serena Williams

B Saina Nehwal

C Kim Yuna

D Fu Yuanhui

> **Goal:** talk about sports events and news stories
> **Language focus:** *even* and *hardly*
> **Vocabulary:** sports events, actions and news

Reading

1 Look at the photos and discuss the questions.
  1 What are the people doing in the photos?
  2 What do the people all have in common?
  3 Who are the most famous sportswomen in your country? Why are they well known?

2 Work in pairs. Discuss how far you agree with the statements. Explain why.
  1 Women in sport aren't as well-known as men in sport.
  2 Men are far more into sport than women are.
  3 It's only right that male athletes earn a lot more than female athletes do.
  4 More women used to do sport in the past.
  5 Women in sport aren't given enough opportunities.
  6 Women would be healthier if more women's sport was shown on TV.

3 Read the opinion piece. Would the author agree or disagree with the statements in Exercise 2?

Melody Phillips gets to the heart of sexism in sport

If you were to judge popularity only in terms of income and visibility, you'd be forgiven for assuming that women were far less interested in sport than men. Across sport as a whole, the top ten women earned just under a hundred million pounds between them last year, while the top ten men made more than nine times that amount. At the same time, around 80% of all sponsorship deals were for male-only sports, while TV companies devoted only 3.2% of airtime to women's sports on news broadcasts. Surely this must just be a reflection of relative levels of enthusiasm, right?

Wrong! The reality is that, round the world, women's participation in sport has soared, and more women are watching traditional male sports such as football as well. Indeed, in a survey carried out during the last World Cup, more than half the women interviewed said they were watching the tournament on a daily basis, while almost one in five even claimed they were more excited about it than their male partners were.

On one level, there are obvious financial opportunities being missed here. The more exposure that women's sport is given, the more it will be able to generate extra income, attract increased advertising revenue and make professional careers more possible for more women. In addition, it hardly needs saying that more women in positions of power in the world of sport would ensure a greater diversity of opinions and perspectives. However, perhaps the main cause for concern here is something far more fundamental: our health. Researchers at Birmingham University have claimed that the lack of focus on women's sport is directly linked to the fact that, despite rising participation levels, far fewer women and girls exercise to keep fit than men do. Put like that, it seems that the inequality is quite literally killing us. A game-changing moment is long overdue.

4 Which of the sentences best summarises the main purpose of the article?
  1 She wants to raise awareness of the many great sportswomen currently being ignored.
  2 She wants to see serious moves made towards greater equality in sport and the media.
  3 She wants fewer companies to sponsor men's sports.

Language focus

5 a Work in pairs. Look at extracts 1 and 2 from the article. Then answer questions a–c below.
  1 … women's participation in sport has soared, and more women are *even* watching traditional male sports such as football as well.
  2 … it *hardly* needs saying that more women in positions of power in the world of sport would ensure a greater diversity of opinions …
  a Which of the two adverbs in italics means 'almost not'?
  b Which is used to show surprise?
  c What do you notice about the position of these adverbs? What type of words do they come before or after?

b Read the language focus box. Choose the correct alternatives.

even and hardly

Even is often used to emphasise that something is surprising, unusual, unexpected or extreme.
Even usually comes **¹**before/after the thing that we want to emphasise.
We can also add emphasis by using **even** before a comparative:
Wow! That run was even faster than his last one.

Hardly is often used to say something is almost not true or **²**almost doesn't happen/never happens at all. It is a negative word and is often used with words like *any* and *ever*. Note that it **³**should/should not be used with other negative words.
Hardly comes before the main verb in a sentence. When there is a modal or an auxiliary verb, **hardly** usually comes **⁴**before/after it.

E | Ada Hegerberg   F | Danica Patrick

6 a  3.12 **Listen to six sentences and write what you hear. Notice that** *even* **and** *hardly* **are stressed.**

   b 3.13 **Work in pairs and compare what you wrote. Then listen and repeat.**

7 a **Rewrite the parts of the sentences in italics, using the word** *hardly.*

   1 He was rolling around on the floor, screaming, but I *hadn't even touched* him.

   2 We had terrible seats. We *couldn't even see* from where we were.

   3 By about halfway round, I was exhausted, but my running partner *wasn't even sweating.*

   4 It was a really bad injury. She *didn't even play* last year.

   b **Work in pairs. Discuss the difference in meaning between the sentences with** *even* **and those with** *hardly.*

8 **Complete the sentences by adding** *even* **in the most appropriate place.**

   1 She won the competition, but she didn't get a trophy.

   2 He played terribly. He didn't win a game in the last set.

   3 She actually seems to be playing better than she was before she got injured.

   4 I'm usually optimistic, but I thought they'd lose.

9 **Work in pairs. Take turns to complete the sentence starters. One of you use** *hardly,* **the other** *even.*

   1 The next day I was aching all over and I ...

   2 I was so out of shape I ...

   3 When the tickets came though, I was so excited ...

   4 After the race, I was so exhausted I ...

   5 The rain was so heavy that we ...

📱 Go to page 140 or your app for more information and practice.

Vocabulary

10 **Work in pairs. Discuss the meaning of the words in bold.**
- be accused of accepting **bribes**
- be **disqualified** after failing a drug test
- be **neck and neck** going into the final **lap**
- **burn off** a few calories
- **dive** to win a free kick
- dream of **turning pro**
- **foul** someone to stop them scoring
- have 70% **possession** in the game
- play some lovely **strokes**
- sign a major new **sponsorship** deal
- **talk back** to the referee

11 **Complete the sentences with the correct form of words in bold from Exercise 10.**

   1 The players' wages have increased thanks to the _____ they get from the national airline.

   2 She _____ after she won the amateur world championships. She's now a top-earning athlete.

   3 The referee gave a penalty first, but when they reviewed it, he realised the striker had _____ .

   4 We had most of the _____ , but they managed to score from their only shot on target!

   5 From the first _____ it was _____ , but the Kenyan athlete had a slightly quicker finish.

   6 He got kicked out of the team for constantly _____ to the coach.

   7 It was an amazing match. Both players played some incredible _____ .

   8 They tried to stop him by constantly _____ him, but eventually he scored a great goal.

   9 I've been trying to exercise most days to _____ all the extra calories I had on holiday.

   10 The club were _____ from the tournament after paying _____ to officials.

12 **Work in pairs. Discuss two different:**

   1 sports that feature a final lap.

   2 reasons you might be disqualified from a tournament.

   3 ways you could burn off a few calories.

📱 Go to page 158 or your app for more vocabulary and practice.

Speaking

▶ PREPARE

13 **Choose two of the topics to talk about. Decide what you want to say.**
- a game/tournament you enjoyed watching
- the way athletes behave while they're competing
- a personal sporting achievement/failure

14 3.14 **Listen to a conversation about one of the topics in Exercise 13. Answer the questions.**

   1 Which topic do the people discuss?

   2 What was good about it?

   3 What was bad?

▶ SPEAK

15 **Work in groups. Tell each other about the topics you chose. Use the Useful phrases to help you.**

> **Useful phrases**
>
> It caused a huge scandal when it happened.
> I'll remember it for the rest of my life.
> I bet that was ...
> That must've been ...

> Develop
> your
> reading
> page 100

> **Goal:** give a short, clearly structured presentation
> **Vocabulary:** gender stereotypes

A

Vocabulary and listening 1

1 a Work in pairs. Look at the photos and discuss the questions.

　1 What's happening in the photos?

　2 How do you feel about these images?

　3 How might they be connected to ideas about gender equality?

　4 How might kids' games influence their adult lives?

b Do you generally associate any of the words and phrases in the box with either men or women? Why?

> engineering   talking about your feelings
> the caring professions   expressing anger   strength
> cars and robots   self-esteem   inequality

2 　🔊 **3.15** You're going to hear the start of a presentation. Listen and find out:

　1 the key question the speaker begins with.

　2 the main topic of the presentation.

　3 how the presentation is going to be structured.

3 Look at the Useful phrases 1 box. Can you remember which of the phrases the speaker uses? Listen again and check.

> ### Useful phrases 1
>
> In the introduction to a presentation, we generally refer to *why* we are talking about the subject (or why the subject is important). Then we often explain the structure of the talk and what we will do in each part.
>
> **Explaining the structure**
> I'm going to talk to you about …
> What I'll do first is …
> After that, I'll …
> I'll then go on to …
> To conclude, I'll …
> … before finally … -ing
>
> **Outlining what will happen**
> … give you a brief outline/overview of …
> … provide some background/context
> … explain the reasons for this problem
> … put forward some solutions/suggestions
> … give some of my own thoughts (on) …
> … examine the pros and cons of …
> … summarise what I have covered.
> … open up the floor for discussion.

B

4 a Work in pairs. Choose one of the topics for a presentation. Decide the structure of the presentation, then write the introduction using phrases from the Useful phrases 1 box.

- an annoying issue at work or college
- a remarkable recovery
- a non-profit organisation
- what to do with an abandoned building in your area
- a court case
- women and sport
- your own idea

b Read out your introduction to other students.

Listening 2

5 Work in pairs. Before you listen to the rest of the presentation discuss these questions.

　1 Do you think there are differences in behaviour or likes and dislikes between seven-year-old boys and girls? What? Why?

　2 What about between older boys and girls or adult men and women?

　3 Do you think differences are natural or more cultural?

6 a 🔊 **3.16** Now listen to the rest of the presentation and take notes about the questions in Exercise 5.

b Work in pairs and compare your notes.

7   Read the Useful phrases 2 box. Which of the different kinds of signposting did the speaker in Exercise 6a use? Listen again and check.

8 a Think about the presentation you heard in Exercise 5 and write:
- a comment describing how you feel about the arguments discussed.
- ways the speaker kept the listeners' attention.
- two questions you would like to ask the presenter about the topic.

   b Compare your ideas with the class. Find out who agrees with you and if anyone has answers to your questions.

9 a Read the information box. Then prepare the short section from the presentation below.

When preparing a short presentation, think about the following:
- where you will pause – mark the pauses with a /
- which word(s) you will emphasise in each section between pauses – underline the word(s)
- how you can vary the pace of what you say – write 'fast' or 'slow' over the section
- if you will vary the tone of what you say – draw an arrow up or down at the end of the section

OK. So, that's the outline. Now, turning to my own thoughts, I found the programme really fascinating. It made me think a lot about my own education and upbringing. Overall, I suppose the programme was more focused on boosting girls' self-esteem, because it's women who suffer inequality later in life, but what I liked most was that the experiment also benefited boys. I've since seen one of the mothers being interviewed and she commented on how her son was better behaved and nicer to his sister as a result of the changes at school.

   b Work in pairs and take turns to read out the section. Can you suggest any ways your partner might improve their delivery?

Speaking

10 a Plan a short presentation on one of the topics in Exercise 4a or one of the topics below. Think about how you will explain the structure and use signposting.
- a documentary series you've watched
- a documentary film or programme
- a lecture or presentation you've watched online
- a presentation you've seen at a conference or at university
- a non-fiction book you've read
- a research-based article in a journal

   b Work in pairs. Take turns to give your presentations and ask questions.

 For more practice go to your Workbook or app.

Go online for the Roadmap video.

Time of your life

> **Goal:** talk about a range of people you know
> **Grammar:** defining and non-defining relative clauses
> **Vocabulary:** describing different age groups

Reading

1 **Work in groups. Look at the photos. Discuss the questions.**

   1 How many people in the different age groups do you talk to on a regular basis?
   2 How do you know the people?
   3 Which group do you find it easiest or most difficult to talk to?
   4 What sort of things do you talk about with each group? If they are different things, why?

2 **Read an article about new ways of dealing with a growing problem. Answer the questions.**

   1 What's the problem?
   2 What's caused it?
   3 What solutions are being put forward?

3 **Decide which of the ideas are suggested in the article.**

   1 Extended families have become uncommon in many countries.
   2 People are working longer hours than they did fifty years ago.
   3 A lot of senior citizens don't want to cause problems for their children.
   4 Technology can often help people deal with feelings of isolation and loneliness.
   5 *The Growing Season* highlights the benefits of the young and the old mixing more.
   6 The Singaporean government is investing heavily in new care homes for senior citizens.

4 **Work in pairs and discuss the questions.**

   1 Why do you think there are high rates of loneliness among young people?
   2 What do you think of the different projects in the text?
   3 What does each age group get out of them?
   4 What else could be done to encourage intergenerational relationships?

Bridging the age gap

In many countries today, it seems hard to believe that there was once a time when it was common for extended families to live together under the same roof. Grandparents would share a house with their offspring, **¹who would generally be working**, and their children's children. In some ways, it was a mutually beneficial arrangement **²whereby children had ready-made carers available** and the oldest members of the family would also be looked after.

There are many reasons **³why this way of living has become less common**. Life expectancy has risen dramatically over the last fifty years, **⁴during which time it's also become more common for family members to move away for work**. This has led to a situation **⁵where children often have less contact with grandparents**.

These social shifts have had major consequences for how we live, **⁶perhaps the most damaging of which is an increase in rates of loneliness**. According to a survey **⁷the UK government commissioned**, almost three-quarters of old people, **⁸many of whom have chosen to live alone**, frequently feel lonely. Perhaps more surprisingly, the group **⁹that reports the second highest feelings of isolation** are teenagers and young people.

In response to this issue, many projects, **¹⁰whose goal is to bring old and young together**, are springing up all over the world. For example, the Providence Mount St Vincent care home in Seattle now incorporates a kindergarten, **¹¹the positive impact of which you can see in the documentary *The Growing Season***. The government of Singapore is also investing two billion dollars to improve the experience of aging. Their plans include housing schemes where different generations are again brought together, not necessarily under the same roof, but in a supportive network within the same development.

Grammar

5 a Look at the relative clauses in bold in the article on page 30. For each one, say:

  a which noun it refers back to.

  b if it defines the noun or if it adds non-essential extra information about it.

  c which relative pronoun, adverb or phrase (if any) introduces the clause.

b Complete the grammar box by adding relative pronouns, adverbs or phrases from the article.

Defining and non-defining relative clauses

Relative clauses refer back to a noun in the previous clause. Sometimes they add essential information that defines the noun, sometimes they add non-essential information.

When a relative clause defines a noun, it is <u>not</u> preceded by a comma.

The care home my grandmother lives in is very expensive.

There are still too many young people
*¹_____ /**that** cannot afford to buy property.*

*It's a scheme **which**/²_____ encourages young people to make a difference.*

We now find ourselves in a situation ³_____ /
***in which** young people are being forced to live at home longer.*

*The reason ⁴_____/**that** we need to invest in this should be obvious.*

Where a relative clause is non-defining, and adds non-essential information, it is preceded by a comma.

We stayed with my grandmother, ⁵_____ is still mentally very sharp.

The show, ⁶_____ main aim is to connect young and old, launched last month.

He's got special educational needs, the most serious
⁷_____ is his dyslexia.

She sings in a choir with thirty other kids, all
⁸_____ are very talented.

Diagnosis can take years, ⁹_____ parents have to support their kids as best they can.

6 a 🔊 **4.1** Listen to the sentences. Notice how we pause slightly before the non-defining relative clauses.

  1 My sister Ana, whose husband you met yesterday, is having a party.

  2 Andrew's mother, who I've never really liked, is staying with us.

  3 The twins are five now, which is a lovely age, really.

  4 There are twenty other people in the class, all of whom are older than me.

  5 Old people face many problems, most of which don't get addressed.

b Listen again and repeat.

7 Rewrite each pair of sentences as a single sentence. Start each sentence with the underlined words.

  1 <u>My grandmother</u> still lives on her own. She's 96 now.

  2 <u>He</u> gave me good advice. I can't remember any of it!

  3 <u>My uncle</u> gave me £100. I've already spent most of it!

  4 She wouldn't do that. <u>There's no reason</u> for it.

  5 <u>I've got loads of cousins</u>. I hardly ever see most of them.

  6 <u>They've lived there since 2012</u>. The area has changed a lot during that time.

8 Write four sentences about some people, places or things you know using different relative clauses.

 Go to page 142 or your app for more information and practice.

Vocabulary

9 Work in pairs. Look at the photos in Exercise 1 again. What is good/bad about being these ages?

10 Match comments 1–7 with follow-up comments a–g. Check you understand the words in bold.

  1 My grandad's stroke left him **in a bad way**.

  2 My friend, Maya, is struggling a bit at school.

  3 My nephew is a **promising** singer.

  4 My neighbour's almost 90, but she's still very **sharp**.

  5 My son's very **mature for his age**.

  6 My daughter **lacks confidence** a bit.

  7 My sister won't do things she doesn't want to do.

  a He acts on his own **initiative** quite a bit.

  b She's still quite **insecure** about her appearance.

  c He's got real **potential**.

  d He's **paralysed** down one side.

  e She's got a real stubborn **streak**.

  f She's really **on the ball**.

  g She was recently diagnosed with **dyslexia**.

11 Think of a question you might ask in response to the comments in Exercise 10.

 Go to page 159 or your app for more vocabulary and practice.

Speaking

PREPARE

12 a 🔊 **4.2** Listen to someone describing three people they know. How or why do they know each person?

b Choose three people you know well or a little. Decide what to say about your relationship with them.

SPEAK

13 a Work in pairs. Talk about the people you chose.

b Who has the most intergenerational relationships?

Develop your listening
page 89

4B Fashion icon

A	Iris Apfel

> **Goal:** answer a questionnaire about clothes and fashion
>
> **Grammar:** noun phrases
>
> **Vocabulary:** clothes and fashion

Vocabulary

1 **Work in groups. Discuss the questions.**

   1 How important are clothes and your appearance to you? Why?

   2 How often do you shop for clothes? Where do you usually go?

   3 Is there anyone that you think dresses really well?

2 a **Look at the categories below. Add two words from the box to each category.**

> a blouse   a bob   a bracelet   a cap   faded
> flowery   laces   ripped   a strap   stripy   a stud
> wavy

Patterns	checked
Accessories	a pendant on a chain
Clothes	tights
Parts of clothes	a buckle
Styles of clothes	flared
Hair	dyed

  b **Work in pairs and compare your answers. Then try to think of more words that could be used to describe the photos. Add them to the correct category in Exercise 2a.**

3 **Decide if the comments are positive or negative about what people are wearing and why.**

   1 It really brings out the colour of your eyes.

   2 The colour's a bit loud and it clashes with the jacket.

   3 It's the kind of thing my dad would wear.

   4 It's not exactly subtle.

   5 I think it looks quite trendy and you wear it well.

4 a 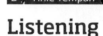 **4.5 Listen and notice that when we stress *quite* before an adjective, it makes the statement sound less certain.**

  b **Listen again and repeat.**

5 **Work in pairs. Look again at the photos. Which of the clothes do you like? Would you wear any of them? Why/Why not?**

📱 Go to your app for more practice.

B	Tinie Tempah	C	Coco Chanel

Listening

6 🔊 **4.6 Read the questionnaire. Then listen to four people speaking and decide which question each person is answering.**

> **Are you a potential fashion icon?**
>
> a Do you have a favourite piece of clothing?
>
> b What would be your 'best'/most formal clothes?
>
> c Is there a dress code where you work? What clothing might be disapproved of?
>
> d How many different hairstyles have you had? When?
>
> e What would you have been wearing five or ten years ago? Has it changed much?
>
> f What accessories do you have? Do you wear any regularly?
>
> g Do you use many beauty or grooming products? What for? How long would it usually take you to get ready?
>
> h What were the last two pieces of clothing you bought? Are you happy with them? Why/Why not?
>
> i When was the last time you dressed up? What for?

7 **Listen again and decide which speaker:**

  a is careful to look after something.

  b regularly uses products to style their hair.

  c has inherited something from a relative.

  d has considered repairing something.

  e feels or felt embarrassed.

  f is or was criticised.

8 **Work in pairs and discuss the questions.**

  1 Do you think men and women think differently about fashion? Why/Why not?

  2 What do you think of the dad's reaction to his daughter cutting off all her hair?

  3 Did your parents ever complain about your fashion choices?

  4 Do you know anyone who finds it difficult to throw things away? Give examples.

Grace Jones D   Mary Quant E

Grammar

9 a 4.7 **Work in pairs. Try to remember which words and phrases were added to the underlined nouns to define them more clearly. Then listen and check.**

1 I had to go to <u>the Clios</u>, _____ for <u>people</u> _____ .
2 I actually only possess one <u>dress</u> – a _____ thing _____ from my grandma.
3 I have a _____ <u>shirt</u> _____ a few years ago.
4 Then I had it long and natural. Then it was _____ <u>hair</u> _____ .
5 I use a _____ <u>wash</u> _____ .

b **Read the grammar box and add one example from Exercise 9a to each section. More than one answer is possible for some sections.**

Noun phrases

We make noun phrases by adding information before and after a noun. Look at the words in bold in the examples.

Before the main noun you can add:
• adjectives – usually opinion before fact
*a **lovely knee-length** dress* / **1** _____
• another noun that describes what it's for, what it's made of, etc.
*a lovely knee-length **party** dress* / **2** _____

After the noun you can add:
• an explanation, for example, of a proper noun
*Jimmy Choo, **the shoe designer*** / **3** _____
• a phrase starting with a preposition to describe the noun.
*Jimmy Choo, the shoe designer **from Malaysia*** /
*a belt **with a big silver buckle*** / **4** _____
• a relative clause
*the dress **(which/that) I wore the other day*** /
5 _____
• a relative clause starting with an *-ed* verb form
*a pair of jeans **ripped at the knees*** (= which are/were ripped) / **6** _____
• a relative clause with an *-ing* verb form
*the guy **wearing a blue shirt***
(= who is/was wearing a blue shirt) / **7** _____

10 a **Complete the sentences with noun phrases using the words in brackets. The main noun is underlined.**

1 Dr Martens are *<u>iconic mid-calf-length boots, originating in Munich in the 1950s.</u>*
   (iconic / in the 1950s / originating in Munich / mid-calf length / <u>boots,</u>)
2 The boots have _____ .
   (with foot injuries / created to provide comfort / a special / for people / <u>sole</u>)
3 _____ went on to develop the boots for use in industry.
   (in Northampton in the UK, / a shoemaker / <u>Bill Griggs,</u>)
4 In the 1960s, the boots became a _____ and since then, the boots have been in and out of fashion.
   (for punks / fashion / <u>accessory</u>)
5 In 2003 the company almost went bankrupt, but it is now booming again thanks to _____ .
   (in the boots / from the Asian market, / renewed / which has been growing rapidly / <u>interest</u>)

b **Can you think of any other fashion items that were made popular in one country and then spread round the world? What happened?**

11 **Work in pairs. Write five different noun phrases with these words as the main nouns.**

a holiday   Coco Chanel   dress   film   man

Go to page 142 or your app for more information and practice.

Speaking

PREPARE

12 **Think of your own answers to the questionnaire in Exercise 6. Then add one question of your own.**

SPEAK

13 a **Work in pairs. Interview each other using the questionnaire and your own question.**

b **How similar are you when it comes to fashion? Use the Useful phrases to help you explain.**

Useful phrases
We're quite similar in lots of ways, I guess.
We both like …
Neither of us like …
We don't have that much in common.
We're quite different in many ways.

Develop your writing
page 122

A | B

> **Goal:** rank things that have most influenced you
> **Language focus:** prepositions 1
> **Vocabulary:** influences and identity

Vocabulary

1 **Look at the photos and discuss the questions.**

1 What can you speculate about the people's lifestyles?

2 Do you know anyone who lives like this?

3 What might the appeal of each lifestyle be?

4 How might people get into these lifestyles?

2 **Complete the blog posts about influences and identity with the words in the boxes. Then underline the complete phrases as in the example.**

> ~~emphasis~~   impacted   meaningful   rebelled
> stand out

I come from a very conventional family, and there was a lot of ¹*emphasis on* looking nice, finding a good husband, that kind of thing, and I really ²_____ against that. To begin with, it was just things like dyeing my hair so I'd ³_____ from the crowd, but then I read *No Logo* by Naomi Klein, which ⁴_____ on me in a major way. It really made me realise how important it was to do something ⁵_____ with my life. **Tara**

> blessing   equals   influential   pointless
> relevant

I used to hate school. I felt I was useless at most subjects and that it was ⁶_____ to even try and do well because I was bound to fail. Then when I was about fourteen I got a new English teacher, and she was incredibly ⁷_____ in my life. She was the first teacher I'd had who treated us all as ⁸_____ and who tried to make what she was teaching ⁹_____ to our lives. It was a real ¹⁰_____ for me and changed my life. **Mirko**

> gratitude   invaluable   leading   rubbed off

I often feel like I was born to do what I do. I'm a performer by nature! My mother was a ¹¹_____ figure in the art scene here, and my dad was a writer. All of that ¹²_____ on me as I was growing up, in that I loved everything to do with the arts. When I left school, I started working in a theatre, which was a really ¹³_____ experience. It shaped the direction I then headed in and so I owe a real debt of ¹⁴_____ to the people there. **Elena**

3 **Work in pairs and discuss the questions.**

1 Have you ever owed a debt of gratitude to someone?

2 What is the most invaluable piece of advice/information you have been given? Why?

3 Who has been the most influential person in your life?

4 What two things does your place of study/work put a lot of emphasis on? Do you agree with them?

Go to page 159 or your app for more vocabulary and practice.

Reading

4 **Read the article and tick the claim the writer makes.**

1 Captain Jack was going to a party when she first saw him.

2 University for her was a bit of a waste of time.

3 The creativity of others has influenced her.

4 Scientists are certain to find the genes that make Captain Jack dress as a pirate.

5 **Work in pairs. Why were the times, numbers and dates in the box mentioned? Read again and check.**

> 19th-century   for years   over half   a week later
> over the years   five percent

Rohini Harijan has her sense of self shaken up

I'll never forget the first time I encountered Captain Jack as it's not every day you see someone in full 19th-century pirate dress. To say he stood out from the crowd would be an understatement. When he first passed me on the street, I assumed he must be on his way to a fancy-dress party, but then a week later I saw him again in town, carrying shopping bags, wearing the same outfit.

When I mentioned this to a friend, she said he was a well-known local character, who'd been amusing and confusing folk for years. We speculated about what the appeal of such a lifestyle might be, and how you end up becoming so eccentric, which started me thinking about what it is that makes any of us what we are. Like many of you, probably, my parents have been incredibly influential in shaping who I am, but I also owe a debt of gratitude to the teachers who had faith in me and saw my potential. My university education was invaluable, too, and I'm sure all the films, music and books I've consumed over the years have also rubbed off on me.

However, if the book I'm currently reading is right, I may be overestimating the impact of all of these factors. In *Blueprint: How DNA Makes Us Who We Are*, the American scientist Robert Plomin claims that the key to understanding who we are lies in our genes. Personality is often thought to be mainly the product of our environment, yet according to Plomin, what's in our DNA accounts for over half of all psychological differences, while families and schools account for just five percent.

Of course, none of this means they've found the gene that makes you decide to live life as a pirate. Yet!

6 Work in groups. Discuss how big an influence on personality you think genes have and how much impact you think our environment has. Explain your ideas.

Language focus

7 a The underlined words all appear in this lesson. Add the missing prepositions.
  1 My parents always put a lot of <u>emphasis</u> _____ education.
  2 I've always been <u>useless</u> _____ making decisions.
  3 I've just always been quiet and shy _____ <u>nature</u>.
  4 Growing up in the countryside as an only child probably <u>accounts</u> _____ my private nature.

b Add the underlined words and prepositions to the language focus box. Can you think of three more items you could add to each category?

Prepositions 1

1 Some verbs are often followed by particular prepositions.
  benefit from, participate in, _____
2 Some adjectives often go with particular prepositions
  addicted to, keen on, _____
3 Some nouns often go with particular prepositions in particular contexts.
  belief in, dedication to, _____
4 Lots of short phrases start with prepositions.
  in debt, on purpose, _____

8 a 4.8 Listen and write what you hear. Notice how prepositions are linked to the words that come before and after them.

b Listen again and repeat.

9 Complete the gaps with one or two words and the word in brackets.
  1 When I was younger, I used to _____ skateboarding. (crazy)
  2 I got into the film industry _____ really. It wasn't something I'd planned. (accident)
  3 I'm a bit _____ my big brother, because he enjoys quite a luxurious lifestyle. (jealous)
  4 I was a bit _____ during my teens. It must've been a nightmare for my parents. (control)
  5 I used to have a job which started at 6 and I just got _____ of getting up early. (habit)
  6 In the end, we split up because her parents really didn't _____ the relationship. (approve)
  7 My geography teacher was the first person to have _____ my abilities. (faith)

10 Work in pairs. Take turns using a phrase in the box to say a sentence about the subjects below.

benefit from	capable of	emphasis on	faith in
fed up with	for obvious reasons		in my (20)'s
on a (daily) basis	succeed in		terrified of
the key to	without doubt		worry about

  • my character   • my future
  • my life now   • my friends and family

📱 Go to page 142 or your app for more information and practice.

Speaking

PREPARE

11 Order the things in the box from most influential (1) to least influential (8) on your life. Then add two more things that have had an impact on you.

work	education	film	parents	politics
fashion	music	religion		

12 🔊 4.9 Listen to a man telling a friend about things that have influenced his life. Answer the questions.
  1 What are the six influences the friends talk about?
  2 Have the influences always been positive?

SPEAK

13 Work in groups. Compare your lists in Exercise 11. Use the Useful phrases to help you.

Useful phrases
I guess the single biggest influence on my life so far has been …
At the age of 14, I started getting really into …
I think it's shaped the way I think about …
It meant a huge amount to me when I was growing up.
It never really did much for me.

Develop your reading
page 102

Check and reflect: Units 3 and 4

1 a Complete the sentences with the adjectives in the box.

> bitter   chilly   crisp   glorious   humid
> miserable   soaked

1   It started pouring down and we got absolutely _____ .
2   The sun was out and it was a clear, _____ winter morning.
3   They'd been predicting rain, but it was absolutely _____ the whole time we were there.
4   You might want to take a coat. It's a bit _____ out there.
5   It gets very hot and _____ in the summer, so you may want to visit later in the year.
6   Make sure you wrap up warm. It's absolutely _____ out there today!
7   It was cold and wet, just _____ the whole time we were there.

b   Use three of the adjectives in Exercise 1a to describe weather you've had recently.

2   Complete the sentences using the verbs and structures in brackets.

1   Apparently, this Friday _____ the hottest April day ever. (predicted / be)
2   According to the forecast, it _____ a bit over the weekend. (going to / brighten up)
3   I _____ in May, and was wondering what the weather's like then. (future continuous / visit)
4   I've been looking at the forecast and it _____ fine and dry when we arrive. (expected / be)
5   We _____ a barbecue tomorrow, but they said there might be a storm. (supposed to / have)
6   It's going to be nice until Friday and then it _____ over the weekend. (set / change)
7   We _____ to rent a little cottage up in the mountains for a few weeks. (present continuous / hope)

3 a   Match the sentence halves.

1   After a long legal battle, the judge awarded
2   They're promising to crack down on
3   It's claimed that the new laws will dramatically restrict
4   His lawyer persuaded him to plead
5   They've been accused of breaking
6   She denied
7   They somehow managed to get him to testify

a   the terms of the agreement.
b   petty crime.
c   all the charges.
d   custody of the children to the mother.
e   for the prosecution.
f   guilty to all charges.
g   people's rights.

b   Work in pairs. Discuss why four of the things in Exercise 3a might happen.

4   Choose the correct alternatives.

1   I'd advise you *don't stay / not staying / not to stay* there if at all possible.
2   I really would recommend *talking / to talk / you to talk* to a lawyer about it.
3   At least they've admitted *that they made / to make / make* a mistake.
4   We want to assure you *for doing / to do / that we're doing* all we can to catch those responsible.
5   The government promised *increase / to increase / increasing* spending, but little has changed.
6   They've apologised *posting / for posting / for to post* rude comments on their social media sites.

5 a   Rewrite the parts of the sentences in italics using *hardly*.

1   We should have got better tickets. I *couldn't see very much* from where we were sitting.
2   She broke her leg last year and she *hasn't played much* since then.
3   *Almost none* of the runners who started the race actually managed to finish.
4   I used to go skiing all the time, but nowadays I *don't go very often*.
5   I had a really good workout, but the next day I *couldn't even walk properly*!

b   Complete the sentences by adding *even* in the best gap.

1   It was so cold out there that _____ I couldn't _____ feel _____ my hands.
2   It was _____ embarrassing because _____ my little brother _____ finished before I did.
3   That wasn't a foul. _____ I didn't _____ touch him _____ !
4   She was great _____ last year, but I think she's _____ playing _____ better this year.
5   I was _____ so excited when I got the tickets, I didn't _____ care how much they'd _____ cost!

6 a   Complete the sentences with the best word or phrase. The first letter is given.

1   The club have just signed a major s_____ deal with a big oil company.
2   She was d_____ from the competition after failing a drug test.
3   They had almost 80 percent p_____ in the game, but they somehow still lost 1-0.
4   The club have been accused of paying b_____ to referees.
5   He was sent off for t_____ b_____ to the referee.
6   I can't believe they gave a penalty for that. Everyone could see she d_____ !
7   They were neck and neck as they started the final l_____ , so it was a really exciting finish.
8   You deserved to win. You played some amazing s_____ in the final set.

b   Tell a partner about sports and news stories using three of the words or phrases.

7 Complete the sentences with the correct relative pronouns. Sometimes no pronoun is needed.

1 I work with twenty people, none of _____ have health insurance.
2 What was the hospital _____ you had your operation in?
3 The main reason _____ I stopped eating meat is because I don't like the taste.
4 It's an area _____ the disease is not uncommon, so be careful!
5 She's the kind of person _____ relaxes you when you enter the room.
6 I read about a girl _____ arm won't stop growing!
7 What's the name of that dentist's _____ you had your teeth done?

8 a Complete the definitions with one word. The first letter is given.

1 If you are p_____ in part of your body, you can't move that part.
2 If someone is in a bad w_____ , they're sick, unhappy, or in a serious condition.
3 If you act on your own i_____ , you are good at making independent decisions.
4 If you're a bit i_____ , you're not confident about yourself and unsure of your abilities.
5 If someone is on the b_____ , they are quick to understand things.
6 If someone has a s_____ mind, they're intelligent and notice things quickly.

b Choose three words to describe people you know.

9 Add the words in the box to the groups they go with.

| checked   dyed   faded   loud   ripped |

1 _____ hair/T-shirt
2 _____ jeans/the sleeve on my jacket
3 _____ jeans/colour
4 _____ colours/pattern
5 _____ shirt/suit

10 Complete the sentences with the past participle or *-ing* form of the verbs in the box.

| make   rip   sell   tie   wear |

1 He was wearing a long white coat _____ up with a belt.
2 She was wearing old blue jeans _____ at the knees.
3 Who's the guy over there _____ the purple suit?
4 He was wearing a 'Make our country great' cap _____ in China.
5 I saw the same coat _____ for over £500 online the other day.

11 a Complete the sentences with the pairs of words in the box. You will need to decide which order to use the words in.

| emphasis/rebelled   influential/equals invaluable/gratitude   pointless/meaningful stand out/impacted |

1 My work experience was _____ . I owe everyone there a debt of _____ .
2 My English teacher was very _____ in my life. She always treated us all as _____ .
3 My family placed a lot of _____ on discipline and I _____ against that.
4 I want to do something _____ with my life. I don't want to get stuck in a _____ job.
5 Punk _____ on me a lot. It made me want to _____ from the crowd.

b Work in pairs. How many sentences are true for you?

12 Complete the sentences with the words in the box and the correct prepositions.

| accident   benefit   capable   debt   useless |

1 I've always been _____ remembering names.
2 You're quite _____ making your own decisions.
3 I discovered her shop _____ and fell in love with it.
4 I was lucky enough to _____ a free education.
5 After university, most people end up seriously _____ .

13 Put the words in italics in the correct order to complete the sentences/questions.

1 What I *some / context / first / is / will / do / provide*
2 After that, I *problem / reasons / explain / will / for / the / this*
3 I will then *solutions / go / forward / some / to / on / put*
4 So what *article / about / is / exactly / the /* ?
5 I'd like *discussion / open / up / for / it / to*

Reflect

How confident do you feel about the statements below? Write 1–5 (1 = not very confident, 5 = very confident).

- I can talk about the weather and plan activities.
- I can discuss legal cases and consequences.
- I can talk about sports events and news stories.
- I can give a short presentation.
- I can talk about a range of different people.
- I can answer questions about clothes and fashion.
- I can discuss things that have influenced me.

For more practice go to your Workbook or app.

Go online for the Roadmap video.

5A On the move

> **Goal:** take part in a discussion on commuting
> **Grammar:** continuous forms
> **Vocabulary:** commuting

Vocabulary

1 **Work in pairs and discuss the questions.**

1 What do you think has happened in each of the photos?
2 What problems might this lead to?
3 How long does your journey to work/class take?
4 Do you go by public transport? If so, what's it like?
5 What do you usually do on your journey?

2 🔊 **5.1 Listen to some travel news on the radio. Put the stories in the order you hear them.**

a a suspicious package
b a pile-up
c delays on the railway
d roadworks

3 **Work in pairs. Can you remember how many of the things in the box are mentioned in the stories in Exercise 2? Listen again and check your ideas.**

> the all-clear   a bypass   crawling   debris
> diversions   evacuated   flowing freely   hold-ups
> northbound carriageway   a power failure
> a replacement bus service   a roadblock
> shed its load   a tailback

4 **Choose four things from Exercise 3 that are connected with experiences that you have had while travelling. Tell your partner about them.**

> *I recently drove past a lorry that had shed its load and there were hundreds of pineapples all over the road!*

📱 Go to page 160 or your app for more vocabulary and practice.

Listening

5 🔊 **5.2 Listen to the next part of the radio programme with a discussion on commuting. Which of the following are mentioned?**

1 a criticism of how animals are transported
2 the claim the UK has the longest commute times
3 a job that exists in Tokyo
4 a story about someone falling ill on their commute
5 concern about how much time people spend working
6 a blog someone is writing about their commute
7 someone holding a party on the way to work
8 not wanting a serious discussion early in the morning

6 **Listen again and take notes on each point mentioned in Exercise 5.**

7 **Work in pairs and compare your ideas. Then discuss the questions.**

1 Would you like to read or take part in something like the commute blog mentioned? If so, why?
2 Would you like to join a book club? If so, what book would you suggest? If not, why not?
3 In what other ways could commuting be made more social or creative?

Grammar

8 a **Read the grammar box on page 39. Then try to complete the sentences from the radio programme using the verbs in brackets in a continuous form.**

1 You _____ to afternoon radio with me, Angela Hassan. (listen)
2 After the break, the phone lines will be open and we _____ whether we've reached breaking point with our daily commute. (discuss)
3 I've got bad news, I'm afraid, for those who _____ to get home on the M79 motorway this evening. (try)
4 Queues _____ and there's already a tailback of about three kilometres. (form)
5 People _____ something more productive than just staring into space. (can do)
6 It worries me that wifi now means that our daily lives _____ by work. (increasingly / take over)
7 No, I _____ about doing something creative. (talk)
8 I _____ the same train for about two years and I'd see the same people a lot of the time. (take)
9 We ended up talking about a book we _____ . (read)

b 🔊 **5.3 Listen and check your ideas. Then work in pairs and discuss why you think each form is used.**

Continuous forms

We make a continuous form using the verb *be* + verb + *-ing*.

Present continuous
I'm waiting for my train.

Present perfect continuous
I've been commuting for the last six years

Past continuous
I was looking for that.

Past perfect continuous
I'd been thinking about it for a while

Future continuous
I'll be talking to him later.
I'm going to be seeing them tonight.

Modals + continuous
He might be waiting outside.
It's not so bad. It could be raining.
If I'd known, I wouldn't be sitting here right now.

We use the continuous when, at a particular point of time, the action is, was or will be:
* temporary.
* unfinished.

It may also emphasise that an action is repetitive or constant during a particular period of time.

9 a 🔊 **5.4** Listen and write the six sentences you hear. Each sentence is said twice. Notice how the auxiliary verbs are reduced.

  b 🔊 **5.5** Work in pairs and compare what you wrote. Then listen and repeat.

10 Choose the correct alternatives. Where both options are possible, what is the difference in meaning?

I ¹*was cycling/cycled* to work the other day and this guy pulled out in front of me without signalling and I crashed into him. Fortunately, I ²*was wearing/wore* a helmet and I wasn't badly injured, but my bike was damaged. Anyway, the driver got out of his car and had a go at me because I ³*had been scratching/had scratched* his car. He ⁴*was being/ was* very aggressive and I thought he might actually hit me. Fortunately, there was a guy who ⁵*'d been standing/ had stood* nearby waiting to cross the road and had seen the whole thing. Basically, he ⁶*was coming/came* over and backed me up and the driver then got back in his car and just drove off. I contacted the police and it ⁷*'s been/'s being* investigated, but I'm not very hopeful anything will happen. I just feel these kinds of incidents are too common and discourage people from commuting by bike.

11 Work in pairs and discuss the questions.
  1 What are your regular journeys and how long have you been doing them?
  2 Have you experienced any incidents on any of these journeys? If so, what happened and did you learn any lessons from it/them?
  3 Are there any plans to change roads or transport where you live? What consequences do you expect and how will it affect you? If not, what changes would you like to make to improve local transport in your area?

📱 Go to page 144 or your app for more information and practice.

Speaking

PREPARE

12 a Work in groups. You're going to have a similar discussion to the one in Exercise 5. Choose one person to be host. Other group members each choose a topic below to talk about.
  * current travel news
  * a funny thing happened to me on my commute
  * how commuting could be improved
  * working from home rather than commuting
  * the best way to commute
  * your own idea

  b The host should think about how to introduce the show and start the discussion. Other members plan what to say about their chosen topic.

SPEAK

13 The host starts the discussion and introduces the speakers. After each speaker the host comments and invites others to share their ideas. Use the Useful phrases to help you.

Useful phrases
OK. So today we'll be talking about commuting.
We're going to start with …
Has anyone had a similar experience?
That reminds me of a time …
That doesn't bother me so much. What annoys me is …

> Develop your listening
> page 90

5B In the wild

> **Goal:** talk about ways to attract more investment to or protect a place you know

> **Grammar:** participle clauses

> **Vocabulary:** geographical features

A

Vocabulary

1 Work in pairs. Look at the photos of travel destinations and discuss the questions.

    1 Would you like to visit any of the places? Why/Why not?

    2 Are there similar places in your country? Where?

    3 What's good about a National Park? Are there any problems with them? Why?

2 a Which of the things in the box might you find in the places in the photos?

> a glacier   a marine reserve   a marsh   a ridge
> a rocky shoreline   sand dunes   a valley   a waterfall

b Complete the descriptions of two different places using the words in the boxes.

> channel   dunes   mainland   sandy   shoreline

I love my little island and I can't imagine not living by the sea. Most mornings, I walk along the **1**_____ with my dog, looking out across the water. We have a lovely **2**_____ beach and behind that are the **3**_____ , where you're a bit more out of the wind. If I do need to visit the **4**_____ , which is maybe eight or nine miles away, there's a ferry that runs every other day. During the winter, though, it can get quite wild out in the **5**_____ .

> mountainous   pass   ridge   sea level   valley

We sometimes spend the summer in my uncle's place up in the highlands, which is quite a **6**_____ area. Hidden away in its own little **7**_____ , the house is about a thousand metres above **8**_____ and to get there, you have to drive over this steep mountain **9**_____ . We relax in the garden, go swimming in the river, or climb up the mountainside behind the house and walk along the **10**_____ that overlooks the valley.

3 Work in pairs. Use words and phrases from Exercise 2 to describe two places you have visited. Or use the photos on page 167 to imagine a visit.

📱 Go to your app for more practice.

Reading

4 Work in pairs. Read the title of the article. Discuss what you think it might be about. Read and check.

5 Read the article again and answer the questions.

    1 What was the initial research carried out?

    2 How does the writer feel about the findings?

    3 What reasons are put forward to explain the findings?

    4 Why are parents and grandparents mentioned?

    5 What's the significance of the hashtag #PokeBlitz?

Lost words lead to lost world

How good are young people at recognising and naming plants and animals? Wanting to find out the answers to this question, researchers showed hundreds of primary school children cards depicting common species of wildlife, and another set featuring Pokémon characters. Having analysed the data, they published their rather shocking findings in the journal *Science*. It turned out that the kids knew far more names for the characters in the game than they did for things in the natural world around them.

In many ways, of course, this should not surprise us, given the major changes there have been to the way childhood is experienced. The area within which children are allowed to play without supervision from parents has shrunk by more than 90% since the 1970s.

At the same time, online culture has boomed. There's more traffic on the roads, school has become more pressurised, parents are more worried and green space is less available. Taken together, all these factors mean that not only young people but also their parents often see nature as something to watch, to consume … and to ignore. Spending far less time outside than our grandparents did, we now lack the words to describe that natural world and this, in turn, may mean we have less desire to protect and preserve our valleys, hillsides and shorelines.

However, technology doesn't have to be the enemy of nature. Some members of the conservation movement are seeing opportunities in the rise in popularity of geocaching – games which use the GPS software on our phones to hide and find 'treasure', which get people outdoors. One notable example of such games is Pokémon Go, an augmented reality version of the original game. In this version, players go out and 'catch' characters 'hidden' in real world places, and, in the process, may encounter real creatures they're not familiar with. Indeed, images of these real creatures are often shared – and identified – using the hashtag #PokeBlitz.

The game's popularity suggests we need to do more to inspire interest in the natural world. If its user-friendly, hi-tech approach could be used to encourage greater interaction with nature, kids may yet learn to see the world with fresh eyes.

6 Work in groups. Tell each other about the following:

* how good you are at recognising and naming wildlife
* whether you share the writer's optimism about Pokémon Go

Grammar

7 a Choose the correct alternatives.

   a Most mornings, I'll walk along the shoreline with my dog, _looking/looked_ out across the water.

   b _Hiding/Hidden_ away in its own little valley, it's about a thousand metres above sea level.

   c _Analysing/Having analysed_ the data, they published their rather shocking findings in the journal _Science_.

b Work in pairs and discuss the questions about the underlined clauses in Exercise 7a. Then read the grammar box and check your ideas.

   1 Are the underlined clauses the main clauses in the sentences, or do they add extra information?

   2 Which clause has a passive meaning? How do you know?

   3 Which clauses have an active meaning? Why do they have different structures?

Participle clauses

Clauses starting with a participle (-_ing_ or -_ed_ form of verb) are most commonly found in writing, especially in stories. The participle clause can have the same meaning as one starting with _when, while, because_ or _as_.

• The subject of the participle clause is the same as the subject in the main clause of the sentence.

Because we spend less time outside than we used to, we lack words to describe the natural world.

  → **Spending** _less time outside than we used to, we lack words to describe the natural world._

• Participle clauses with a **present participle** (-_ing_ form of the verb) have an active meaning.

When we neared the top of the mountain, we came to a glacier.

  → **Nearing** _the top of the mountain, we came to a glacier._

• Participle clauses with a **past participle** (-_ed_ form) have a passive meaning.

Because the group was based in a mountainous region, it operated very independently.

  → **Based** _in a mountainous region, the group operated very independently._

• We use participle clauses with **perfect participles** (_having_ + past participle) to emphasise that one action happened before another.

As I had climbed the ridge before, I was feeling confident.

  → **Having climbed** _the ridge before, I was feeling confident._

8 a 🔊 **5.8 Listen to six sentences from Exercises 7a and the grammar box. Notice how the two clauses in each sentence are said as separate chunks.**

   b Listen again and repeat.

9 Complete the sentences by putting the verbs in brackets into the correct form.

   1 _____ 2000 metres above sea level, the hotel offers great views across the channel. (locate)

   2 _____ the ridge, we had to stop to let a herd of mountain goats pass us. (climb)

   3 _____ the valley many times before, I was already familiar with the landscape. (visit)

   4 _____ in such a mountainous area, I'm used to the weather changing at a moment's notice. (live)

   5 _____ in 1846, the cottage is only a three-mile walk from a spectacular waterfall. (build)

   6 _____ to reduce development along the coast, the law has helped protect the remaining dunes. (introduce)

   7 _____ across the water to the mainland, I collapsed onto the beach, exhausted. (struggle)

10 Using participle clauses, write three sentences about the places you described in Exercise 3 and what you did there. Share your sentences with a partner.

📱 Go to page 144 or your app for more information and practice.

Speaking

PREPARE

11 🔊 **5.9 Listen to two people describing natural places they know. Answer the questions for each speaker.**

   a What do you learn about the places they describe?

   b Do they want more tourists or greater protection? Why?

12 Think of a place you know that either needs more visitors/investment or greater protection. Decide:

• what there is to see and do there.

• what words you could use to describe its appeal.

• three different ways you could either encourage visitors or increase protection.

SPEAK

13 a Work in pairs. Explain your ideas to each other. Use the Useful phrases to help you.

> **Useful phrases**
> One of the most … things about the area is …
> What makes it really unique is …
> I think the best way to … would be to …
> I can't decide if it'd be better to … or …
> Another way to … would be …

   b Decide which is the best proposal.

> **Develop your writing**
> page 124

5c House or home?

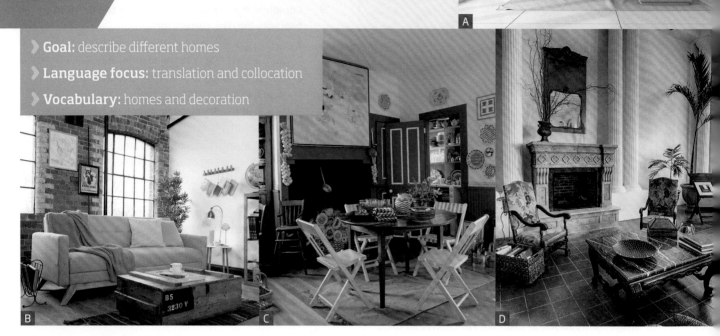

> **Goal:** describe different homes
> **Language focus:** translation and collocation
> **Vocabulary:** homes and decoration

Language focus

1 a Look at the photos. What type of person do you think lives in each place? Which place would you most like to live in? Why?

b Work in pairs and answer the questions.

1 Do you have a different word for *house* and *home* in your language? Do you use them in the same way as we do in English?

2 How can you make a *house* a *home*?

3 Do you know any words in English that don't translate exactly into your language? How do you learn to use these words?

2 Read the language focus box and discuss:
- the benefits of each suggestion.
- which of the suggestions you already do.
- which you might start doing.

Translation and collocation

Many words have a single direct translation from one language to another, but words like *house* and *home* or *make* and *do* may have no direct translation. This can make them difficult to learn and use. Here are some things you can do.

- Record words in a phrase or collocation. (Collocations are combinations of two or more words often used together.)
- Pay attention to the grammar that is connected to the word.
- Translate the whole phrase or collocation.
- Write a separate list of phrases for each word to revise them.
- Make mind maps of these phrases.
- Keep the list or mind map in a folder and add to it when you find new examples.

3 a Complete these mind maps with the words *house* and *home* to make common collocations.

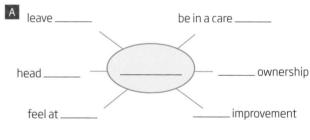

A
leave _____
be in a care _____
head _____
_____ ownership
feel at _____
_____ improvement

B
a friend's _____
_____-warming party
go round to their _____
_____ hunting
do up my _____
wake up the whole _____

b Add one more example to each mind map.

4 a Cover the mind maps and complete the questions.

1 What's the average age people _____ home in your country? Is that the ideal age?

2 How common is home _____ compared to renting in your country? Is that a good thing?

3 Are there many _____ homes for old people or children in your city? Are there enough?

4 Have you ever been to a house-_____ party? Whose? What happened?

5 How often do you go _____ to friends' houses? When? What for?

6 Are there many home _____ or design shows on TV in your country? What happens in them?

b Work in pairs. Ask and answer the questions.

Go to page 144 or your app for more practice.

Reading

5 Read the blog post about home improvement shows. How do you think the author would answer the last question in Exercise 4a?

> If you turn on the television, there seems to be a home improvement show on every channel. You know the ones I mean, where couples discuss whether to buy a half-a-million-pound dream home, or we follow their progress as they transform an old farm house into a dream mansion.
>
> There was a time I would have been grabbed by one of these programmes – greedy for the gorgeous design and envying the choices these people could make – but I have finally kicked the habit. I realised the programmes were all beginning to feel the same. Fitted kitchen with an island – tick; polished concrete flooring – tick; floor to ceiling window overlooking fields or water – tick; spacious living room, the size of a small town square – tick. And it's filmed with those long, loving close-ups of the shiny surfaces without a bit of dust in sight, all accompanied by inspiring music.
>
> These shows are, in effect, only about buildings and buying stuff, when really what's interesting is how we make a house a home. Often, that's not to do with design, but comes down to the people and the clutter that surrounds them, whether it's the random photos and ornaments we have or the kids and pets that scratch and stain even the most stylish furniture.

6 Which of these statements do you think the author would agree with?

1 People spend too much money on their houses.
2 I'm not interested in design.
3 Design programmes are a bit addictive.
4 A lot of modern design has become a bit boring.
5 I couldn't live in an untidy home.
6 You can tell a lot about a person from their home.

7 Work in pairs. How far do you agree with the statements in Exercise 6?

Vocabulary

8 Complete the descriptions with the words in brackets in the correct place.

1 They live in this _exclusive_ block of flats that looks out over the beach. I can't imagine what it is _____! They also have a lot of _____ furniture and a cupboard full of _____ plates. (antique, china, ~~exclusive~~, worth)

2 His office is a tip and full of _____ . There are _____ of magazines on the floor, a broken coffee maker, various cups and awards on the _____ . And these dusty old _____ over the windows. I don't know how he can work in there. (blinds, clutter, bookshelves, stacks)

3 She's got African _____ on the shelves from when she lived in Kenya and the _____ are filled with framed _____ and letters of thanks from clients. (walls, certificates, ornaments)

4 They have quite a _____ living room, which has these big glass doors that slide open on to this _____ little patio with _____ plants and a barbecue. It's lovely in the summer. (pot, shady, spacious)

5 Their place always looks _____ ; there are never any toys or clothes in sight. They have all these _____ cupboards and if you open them, everything's all _____ arranged and every surface is _____ and shiny! (fitted, neatly, polished, spotless)

9 a 5.10 Listen and write down six phrases. Notice how *of* is reduced.

b 5.11 Work in pairs and check what you wrote. Then listen and repeat.

10 Work in pairs. Discuss the questions about the descriptions in Exercise 8.

1 Which words and phrases can you use to describe the rooms?
2 What kind of people do you think live in or use the places described?
3 What can you tell about the peoples' interests or lives based on the descriptions?
4 Which words can you use to describe your own home?

Go to page 160 or your app for more vocabulary and practice.

Speaking

PREPARE

11 Think of two different homes you know well. Then answer the questions.

1 Whose homes are they?
2 Where are they?
3 What are they like generally?
4 What do you like most about the place (if anything!)?
5 Are there any particular things you've noticed?
6 Do they reflect the life or interests of the people who live there?

12 a 5.12 Listen to two people describing homes that they know well. Take notes.

b Work in pairs and compare your notes. What information do the speakers give to answer the questions in Exercise 11?

SPEAK

13 a Take turns to tell your partner about the homes you chose in Exercise 11. Comment and ask questions to find out more. Use the Useful phrases to help you.

> **Useful phrases**
> One thing that really strikes you when you go in is …
> The main thing I remember about it is that …
> One thing I really love is …
> How big is it? How many rooms do they have?
> How long have they been living there?

b Decide which home sounds the most interesting and why.

Develop your reading
page 104

5D English in action

> **Goal:** make suggestions about what to do in an area

> **Vocabulary:** hosting guests

Vocabulary

1 **Work in pairs. Discuss what's happening in the pictures and answer the questions.**

   1 What other things might be good or bad about being a paying guest in someone's house?

   2 What might be good or bad about being a host and letting out a room in your house?

   3 How could you find guests or a host?

   4 Do you know anyone who hosts people or has been a paying guest? How was it?

2 a **Decide what the words in bold mean in 1–10 below.**

   1 Is the room **en suite** or will I have to share a bathroom?

   2 There's a **communal** garden outside that you can use.

   3 I'm not sure if I'm doing something wrong or not, but the toilet doesn't seem to **flush**.

   4 I'll email you a receipt once the payment has **cleared**.

   5 If you do use the kitchen, please try not to **set off** the smoke alarm.

   6 Do you know what the **dimensions** of the room are?

   7 I can sort you out a parking permit for £10 a day – **payable** on arrival.

   8 You need to stick the rubbish in the black bin and use the **recycling bins** outside.

   9 Do you have a **safe** where I could put my valuables?

   10 It's quite chilly. Do you have a spare **duvet** we could use?

2 b **Look at sentences 1–10 again. Answer the questions.**

   1 Which things are said/written by a guest (G) and which by a host (H)?

   2 Which things are said/written during the booking process (D) and which after the guest has arrived (A)?

3 **Work in pairs and discuss the questions.**

   1 What other things in a house or building might be communal, apart from a garden?

   2 What would you normally do if your toilet at home didn't flush?

   3 How long do payments usually take to clear? Why might they not clear?

   4 How might you set off a smoke alarm? A car alarm? A burglar alarm?

   5 Do you know the dimensions of any of the rooms where you live?

   6 What else might be payable on arrival?

   7 What are five things you might keep in a safe?

   8 What's the opposite of 'It's quite chilly'? What might you need in that case?

Listening

4 🔊 **5.13 Listen to a conversation between a host and a guest. Which four things do they talk about? In what order?**

   a a good place to go out   **e** avoiding problems

   b getting around   **f** where they work

   c crime in the local area   **g** where to eat

   d photography   **h** reading

5 **Tick the sentences that are true in the conversation. Then listen again to check.**

   1 The local area is busy and full of people who are enjoying themselves.

   2 There's an amazing Chinese restaurant nearby.

   3 The host recommends phoning to reserve a table before visiting Dotori.

   4 The arts centre used to be a factory.

   5 It doesn't cost anything to go to the Friday night event.

   6 The guest is impressed by what the area has to offer.

   7 There's an all-night bus service.

   8 If you're coming back late at night, you can just grab any taxi on the street.

   9 There's no iron the guest can use.

6 a **Work in pairs and complete the sentences from the conversation in Exercise 4. The first letters are given.**

   1 If you're into Korean or Japanese food, c_____ o_____ Dotori on the main road. It's a m_____ .

   2 It depends a bit on the day, but I think it'd probably be w_____ to.

   3 You really o_____ to go and have a look at Factory.

   4 I guess your b_____ b_____ would be to just get the 154 bus, to be honest.

   5 Any later than that and it's a_____ to just get a cab. M_____ s_____ you get a licensed one, though, preferably.

   6 Yes of course, but p_____ ask me first – just in case I need it.

b **Read the Useful phrases box and check your ideas.**

You said you wanted somewhere quiet.

C

Useful phrases

Advising and suggesting

If you're into … , (you might want to) check out …
It's a must.
You really ought to …
It'd (probably) be wise (to …)
Your best bet would be to …
Make sure you …
Preferably/Ideally, …
There's no harm in –ing.
It's advisable to …
You'd be well advised to …

Note that *It's advisable to/ You'd be well advised to* are a bit more formal than the other examples.

7 Complete the sentences with the words in brackets. Add any other necessary words.

1 I know you're only here for two days, but do _____ visit the castle. It's worth it. (make)

2 You _____ come again, ideally in the summer when the weather's better! (ought)

3 You _____ take out comprehensive travel insurance before you come. (advised)

4 To be honest, I doubt you'll be able to get tickets, but _____ trying. (harm)

5 If you're into dance music, you _____ a club called Volt. It's amazing. (check)

6 Don't miss the Jardin de Majorelle whatever you do. _____ . (must)

7 If you're coming from the main station, your _____ get the 147 and then walk. (bet)

8 Out in the countryside, _____ carry some cash, just in case. (advisable)

9 It gets really busy there, so _____ get there early, preferably before eight. (wise)

8 🔊 5.14 Listen and write the six sentences you hear. Which word is in every sentence?

9 a Read the information box. Then listen again to the sentences in Exercise 8 and repeat.

Changing sounds of words in speech
The sounds of words vary a lot when heard at different speeds and with different words around them. This is especially true for grammar words like *would*.

b Match the sentences you wrote in Exercise 8 with descriptions a–f.

a On its own, *would* sounds like /wʊd/.

b It blends with the following word, e.g. with *you* = /wʊdjə/.

c It loses the *d*, e.g. before *be* = /wʊbiː/.

d It is reduced to *d* and can blend with the next word, e.g. before a word beginning with a vowel like *ask* = /dɑːsk/.

e It is reduced to a /ə/ sound, e.g. between *it* and *be* = /ɪtəbiː/.

f It disappears completely!

Speaking

PREPARE

10 a Imagine you have a paying guest coming to stay. Make a list of things you want them to know about.

- their room
- your house/flat
- house rules
- the area
- places to visit
- places to avoid

b Choose items from the Useful phrases box and write five sentences to welcome your guest.

SPEAK

11 a Work in pairs. Student A is the host and Student B is the guest. Roleplay a conversation using this pattern.

b Change roles and roleplay again.

Host	Guest
Welcome your guest. Ask about journey and offer food/drink	Comment and accept/ refuse.
Give a guided tour of the house/flat. Explain the house rules.	Ask any questions. Ask about the local area.
Describe the area. Make suggestions and give advice.	Comment and ask extra questions. Ask questions about the centre of town.
Explain where (and where not to) go.	

12 What's the best thing about your host's place? Why?

For more practice go to your Workbook or app.

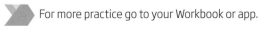

Go online for the Roadmap video.

6A A difficult business

> **Goal:** talk about businesses and the economy

> **Grammar:** adverbs and adverbial phrases

> **Vocabulary:** successful and failing businesses

HOW CAN BUSINESSES SURVIVE IN THE 21ST CENTURY?

1 _____

Over recent years, a few companies have come to dominate our economies, with several being valued at around one *trillion* US dollars and having an annual turnover larger than the GDP (total value of goods and services) of a medium-sized country. It is difficult to imagine a world without these companies, but then there were plenty of giants in the past that are now seen as 'dinosaurs' or that have shrunk quite dramatically. So, what are the threats today's executives need to look out for if their companies are to avoid dying out?

2 _____

Whether they're driven by greed or fear, some companies grow ever bigger by taking over their rivals until they become a monopoly. I don't know if you ever played the game Monopoly when you were younger, but it always ended in tears in our house – with my parents angrily telling my brother not to be a bully. Real life is not so different; governments have forced companies to be broken up in the past – or have taken direct control of them. There's no reason why this couldn't happen again to some of today's giants.

3 _____

A lot of businesses have been made irrelevant by rapidly expanding companies selling a new technology. For example, companies selling camera films were hit hard by digital cameras, but then in turn digital camera sales dropped sharply because of smartphones. Perhaps if these companies had branched out into other areas, they might have faced less risk and been more sustainable.

4 _____

Having said that, branching out has its problems too. On the one hand, if one part of the business fails, all may not be lost as the entire company isn't affected. On the other hand, broadening your offer can mean you lose focus. Competitors then gain an edge in your core market and end up forcing you out.

5 _____

Sometimes it just takes one person to do the wrong thing. In 1995, the second oldest bank in the world – Barings – found itself facing bankruptcy because one of its traders, Nick Leeson, had secretly made deals, which were then affected by a recession in Japan, resulting in a £1.6 billion loss for the bank.

Reading

1 **Work in pairs and discuss the questions.**

1 What companies and brands do you respect the most or least? Why?

2 What can make a brand stronger or weaker?

3 Which of the factors below are most or least important when choosing a company or brand? Why?

| company reputation | price | product quality |
| recommendations | reviews | service quality |

2 **Read the article and match headings a–e with paragraphs 1–5.**

a Taking too much on

b Bad management or dishonest behaviour

c Too much power

d Failure to keep up with new developments

e Things don't necessarily last forever

3 **Which of the points 1–6 are made in the article?**

1 Many companies are now more powerful than the countries they operate in.

2 Even big companies can fail.

3 It's not always wise for a company to just keep growing.

4 New technology creates as many jobs as it destroys.

5 The best way for a company to survive is to spread its business over different areas.

6 You can't always predict or control the risks you'll face.

Vocabulary

4 **Complete the descriptions of different businesses with the words in the box.**

focus/edge	monopoly/broken up
struggling/management	sustainable/branch out
turnover/valued	undercut/board

1 Our local department store closed down because online stores _____ their prices and the _____ didn't invest enough.

2 One huge company controls both production and distribution. Basically, it's a _____ in this country. A lot of people would like it to be _____ .

3 The restaurant's _____ because of a mixture of rising costs and poor financial _____ . Apparently, they redecorated when they didn't need to.

4 With the boom in technology, they've expanded very rapidly. They've doubled their _____ in the last year and the company's _____ at 30 million dollars now.

5 It's taken advantage of a new trend and its business is booming. I'm not sure how _____ it is though, unless they _____ into other areas.

6 They were doing well, but I think they lost _____ and allowed their competitors to get an _____ over them.

5 Work in pairs and discuss the questions.

1 What might the board of a company do to protect it?

2 What is good or bad about a monopoly?

3 What is good or bad about a company branching out?

4 How can one company get an edge over a competitor?

 Go to page 161 or your app for more vocabulary and practice

Grammar

6 6.1 Look at sentences 1–3. Listen to the complete sentences and rewrite them.

1 There were plenty of giants that are now seen as 'dinosaurs' or that have shrunk.

2 It always ended in tears – with my parents telling my brother not to be a bully.

3 They wasted a lot of money redecorating when they didn't need to.

7 a Work in pairs. Discuss what kind of information the extra words add to the sentences in Exercise 6.

b Read the grammar box and check your ideas.

Adverbs and adverbial phrases

Adverbs add information about where, when and how something happens. Adverbial phrases are short phrases which act as adverbs, e.g. *in the morning, at the corner.*

The position of adverbs and adverbial phrases can be flexible, but for each type, one position may be more common. Different types include:

• **when** the action happens: beginning or end of the clause.

*They've doubled their turnover **in the last year**.*

• **where** the action happens: end of the clause, but before time adverbs.

*The company started operating **in the US** at the end of the 19th century.*

• **the strength or speed** (degree) of the action: immediately after the main verb.

*expanded **very rapidly** / dropped **sharply***

• **the way** (or manner) the action is done: immediately before the main verb.

*My mum would **angrily** tell my brother not to be a bully. He had **secretly** made multi-million-pound deals.*

• **our opinion** of the situation including how likely/true it is: the beginning of the clause or before the main verb.

***Apparently**, they wasted a lot of money redecorating. They have **obviously** misunderstood the main point.*

• Remember adverbs can also modify adjectives or other adverbs.

***incredibly** large / **quite** dramatically*

8 a 6.2 Listen to adverbs 1–4 said three times at different speeds. Notice how *-ly* and *-ally* get shortened in fast speech.

1 apparently 3 literally

2 generally 4 supposedly

b 6.3 Listen and write the sentences you hear.

c Listen again and repeat.

9 a Complete the sentences by adding the adverbials in brackets in their most common positions. Sometimes, more than one position is possible.

1 The economy has been growing *quite slowly over the last few years*. (quite / slowly / over the last few years)

2 There are thousands of jobs on offer, but they are poorly paid. (literally / generally / pretty)

3 They're the smartest people around, but I think they are incompetent. (supposedly / personally / fairly)

4 I'd work for the rest of my life, but I'm not terribly ambitious. (happily / for this company / admittedly)

5 These companies led their markets, but they have now shrunk or disappeared. (in the past / dramatically / completely)

b 6.4 Check your ideas with a partner. Listen to two possible answers for each sentence.

10 Work in groups. Discuss three of the things in the box using a variety of adverbs and adverbial phrases.

banking	a celebrity	the economy	families
the housing market	your home town	a sports team
the transport system	unemployment

 Go to page 146 or your app for more information and practice.

Speaking

PREPARE

11 Work in pairs. Think of an example of a business that is doing well and a business that is not doing so well.

SPEAK

12 a Discuss the following questions about each company in Exercise 11.

1 Why do you think they're doing well/badly?

2 What threats are they currently facing?

3 What threats might they face in the future?

4 What opportunities do they have to expand?

5 What are some important things they could do next?

b Change partners and compare your ideas.

> Develop
> your
> reading
> page 106

> **Goal:** decide on the best kind of event for your town/city to host
> **Grammar:** further passive constructions
> **Vocabulary:** hosting events

Reading and vocabulary

1 **Work in groups. Discuss the questions.**

   1 Can you think of any places that have hosted big sporting, cultural, or business events? When were the events held?

   2 Which kind of event are you not interested in? Why?

   3 Have you attended any of these kinds of events? When? How was it?

   4 What might be good or bad about a city staging events like these?

2 a **Quickly read the article about hosting events and answer the questions.**

   1 What did the city of Montreal host?

   2 Was the experience good or bad for the city?

   b **Read the article again and complete it with the words in the box.**

bid	boycott	catalyst	corruption	estimate
grants	infrastructure	transformation		

When a city's **¹_____** to host a **prestigious** event such as the Olympics is successful, it's hoped that at the very least, the city's **profile** will be raised. Potentially, of course, such events can act as a **²_____** for social and economic change and even bring about a complete **³_____** of the urban area. The events can provide a real **boost** to the local economy: multi-million-pound **⁴_____** become available, the local government **commissions** top architects to build exciting new buildings and large numbers of new visitors are attracted to the region. The resulting profits and higher tax revenue can then be spent on more social and cultural projects. Everybody wins.

At least that's the theory. For Montreal in Canada, however, the reality was very different indeed. As the Olympic host back in the 1976, the city found itself barely able to get the necessary **⁵_____** built in time, and ended up with a bill thirteen times higher than the original **⁶_____** ! This left the city paying off the debt for the next thirty years. There was also widespread **⁷_____** and millions of dollars were rumoured to have been stolen by individuals with links to the construction industry. Finally, to make matters even worse, there was a **⁸_____** by twenty-five African countries, who were protesting about the inclusion of New Zealand in the games, after their rugby team had broken an international ban to compete in a sporting event with South Africa.

3 **Choose the correct definition for the words in bold in the article.**

   1 prestigious
      a respected and admired b hard to get and expensive

   2 profile
      a outline or shape   b public image

   3 boost
      a improvement   b fall

   4 commission
      a design   b officially ask for

4 **Work in pairs and discuss:**

   1 the infrastructure needed for a city to host a major event.

   2 other reasons for a boycott of a major event.

   3 two other things that can be commissioned.

   4 a prestigious university and a prestigious award.

   5 other catalysts for change in a city.

   Go to your app for more practice.

Listening

5 🔊 **6.5 You're going to hear a report about a city that has changed a lot in the last few years. Listen and answer the questions.**

   1 What is the name of the city that has changed?

   2 What started the change?

   3 What did the city host in 2018?

   4 What effect did hosting the event have?

   5 What other benefits of hosting major events are mentioned?

6 **Listen again and make notes. Why were the things below mentioned?**

corruption	a campaign	climate change
a waste of money	local residents	

7 **Work in pairs and discuss how Palermo avoided the kinds of problems that Montreal experienced and in what ways *failing* to win bids for events like Manifesta might still be positive.**

Grammar

8 a Read the sentences and underline the six passive constructions. Do you know who does each action? Is it important to know?

1 As a result of this transformation, the city was rewarded by being named Italy's capital of culture in 2018.

2 If invested wisely, this money can put places firmly on the map.

3 … Manifesta, which is considered to be Europe's most prestigious art festival.

4 It's hoped that, at the very least, its profile might be raised.

b Match the passive constructions in Exercise 8a with a–e in the grammar box.

Further passive constructions

We use passives when we want to focus on who or what an action affects. Most tenses can be made passive by using the appropriate form of *be* + a past participle. Passives can also appear in the following contexts:

a After modal verbs

We form passives after modal verbs using *be* + a past participle.

*Profits **can be invested** in cultural projects.*

b As -*ing* forms

We use -*ing* passives after prepositions.

*The city partied for days **after being awarded** the Olympic Games back in 2019.*

c In reporting

In some writing, we often use the passive form of reporting verbs + infinitive with *to* or a *that* clause.

*The Olympics **is** often **said to be** the place for countries to prove their greatness*

To emphasise something happened **earlier**, we use a reporting verb + a perfect infinitive (active or passive).

*He **is rumoured to have stolen** millions.*

*Millions **were rumoured to have been stolen**.*

d In reduced relative clauses and *if* clauses

When we use passives in relative clauses, we can leave out the relative pronoun and the verb.

An article ~~which was~~ published online provided evidence of widespread corruption.

We sometimes do the same with an *if* clause.

If needed, we could provide support.

e In combination with another passive construction

*The stadium really **has to be seen** to be believed.*

9 a 🔊 6.6 Listen to five sentences and write down what you hear. Notice how *to have* is often just said as /tuːwəv/.

b Work in pairs and compare what you wrote. Then listen again and repeat.

10 Complete the sentences with the correct active or passive form of the verbs in brackets.

1 The 2026 World Cup will _____ (hold) in three countries: the US, Canada and Mexico, after their joint bid _____ (beat) Morocco's proposal to host it.

2 It's too late now to start worrying about the campaign not _____ (be) successful.

3 The city _____ (choose) to host the event will _____ (receive) a grant of over £5 million.

4 The mayor eventually _____ (resign) after _____ (accuse) of corruption.

5 It _____ often _____ (argue) that hosting the Olympics _____ (benefit) the host city.

6 The stadium _____ (believe / cost) over £1 billion.

7 They _____ (not / consider) any bids _____ (receive) after the deadline last month.

8 The income _____ (generate) by the event _____ (expect / spend) on a wide range of sports projects.

11 Work in pairs. Choose one of the newspaper headlines below and write a paragraph for an article.

1 **WORLD CUP BID CORRUPTION SCANDAL**

2 **HIGH-PROFILE CAMPAIGN SEEKS TO STOP EVENT**

3 OLYMPIC BID RECEIVES BOOST

4 **FESTIVAL CATALYST FOR TRANSFORMATION**

 Go to page 146 or your app for more information and practice.

Speaking

PREPARE

12 Look at the different events in the box. Think about what would be good or bad about hosting each one and which would be most suitable for your town/city.

> a major sports tournament   a film festival
> a music festival   a food festival

13 🔊 6.7 Listen to someone presenting an idea for an event. Find out what kind of event is mentioned and why they think it would be a good thing to host.

SPEAK

14 a Work in pairs. Present your idea of the most suitable event to your partner and discuss whether you agree. Use the Useful phrases to help you.

Useful phrases

I think that one way it'd benefit the town is by …
Another good/bad thing about it is that it'd …
Personally, I'd be opposed to that idea because …
I don't have strong feelings about it either way.
On top of all that, it'd … / it wouldn't …

b Tell the class which event you think would be most suitable. Take a vote on the best option.

> Develop your listening
> page 91

6c ▸ Going out

Goal: talk about events you have been to

Language focus: word grammar and patterns (*expect, surprised*)

Vocabulary: talking about arts events

Reading and vocabulary

1 **Work in pairs. Look at the photos. Which of the arts activities in the box can you see? Discuss the questions below.**

> a cabaret   a circus   a community arts project
> a small gig   an indie film   an open-mike night
> a photographic exhibition   a poetry reading
> stand-up comedy

1 Which of the arts events in the box have you been to? Why/Why not?
2 Which of these events would you go to? Why/Why not?
3 Which of them have you taken part in?
4 Do the arts get much public funding in your country? How do you feel about that?

2 **Read the article about the Adelaide Fringe festival. Answer the questions.**

1 What are fringe festivals?
2 In what ways has Adelaide Fringe festival changed in recent years?

From their origins as spaces for experimental and alternative performances, fringe festivals have now become the new normal. Every year, almost 20 million people see approximately 170,000 performers at the 250 fringe festivals around the world. The Adelaide Fringe is now 60 years old and has become the largest arts festival in the Southern hemisphere, and only second globally to the Edinburgh Festival Fringe.

The Adelaide Fringe is an open-access festival. In other words, anyone who can pay the registration fee (currently between A$210 and $395) can put on an event at venues varying from boats, church halls and community arts centres to circus tents and large theatres. Almost three million people attend during the four weeks of the festival, generating well over A$15 million dollars in ticket sales.

However, while ticket sales have boomed in recent years, many performers struggle simply to break even. Some spend thousands of dollars at the festival only to find that even getting positive reviews may not guarantee a profit. In fact, some now argue that the festival has become too big and too commercial. They say it is now dominated by three central venues putting on big names from mainstream stand-up and cabarets, instead of the more experimental and indie productions. Some would like the organisers to create two distinct festivals, one dedicated to stand-up, the other to more varied arts events.

At the moment, though, the festival is resisting such changes as it goes against their open-access philosophy. They argue that they already help artists with grants of up to A$4000 and that, in the end, festival-goers themselves will decide how things develop.

3 **Work in pairs. Can you remember what the numbers refer to? Read again to check.**

> 20 million   250   60   A$395   A$4000
> second   thousands   three   three million   two

4 **Work in pairs. Discuss the questions.**

1 Would you like to go to the Adelaide Fringe festival? Why/Why not?
2 Do you know any other festivals that include similar things? Where and when are they held?

5 **Check you understand the words in bold. Then match the descriptions with the events in Exercise 1.**

1 The first guy on stage was **out of tune** – he sang so badly! But the woman after that had a great voice.
2 Some of the acts were pretty **mediocre**. I mean, if all you're doing is just juggling, it has to be really amazing.
3 Her work is a mixture of **portraits** of farming populations and the landscapes they live in.
4 It was a low-budget horror. It was really **intense** and quite scary. However, some of the acting was a bit **over-the-top**.
5 It was a bit of a **disappointment**. It was quite amusing in parts, but I was expecting to laugh out loud.
6 It was this **folk duo** in a club in town – a guitarist and a singer. They were absolutely amazing.
7 She was reading from her new book in the **literary** strand of the festival. Some of her stuff is so **moving**.
8 It was really **fast-paced**. There were loads of different **acts** – and some of them were pretty **outrageous**!
9 It's a **collaborative** project that involves local schools and an artist-in-residence.

6 **Choose two of the topics below to talk about. Then discuss your ideas with a partner.**
* someone you know who has a good/bad singing voice
* someone you know who can do circus tricks
* something you thought was mediocre, intense, moving or outrageous
* a famous duo you like

 Go to page 161 or your app for more vocabulary and practice.

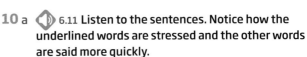

Listening

7 🔊 6.10 **Listen to a conversation between two people talking about a fringe festival.**

1 What kind of events have they been to?
2 Did they like them? Why/Why not?
3 Which event did they disagree about? Why?

8 a **Listen again. Complete the sentences with the missing words and phrases.**

1 I just expected _____ , I suppose.
2 I'm just surprised _____ here.
3 They _____ I expected.
4 I was expecting _____ – you know, _____ , so it was just a surprise.
5 I _____ expect it _____ – but if you see it …
6 I _____ expect it _____ and so rude! Some of it was so over-the-top!

b **Work in pairs. Discuss what they were talking about in each case.**

Language focus

9 a **Work in pairs. What patterns do you notice around the words *expect* and *surprise*?**

b **Read the language focus box. Match each sentence in Exercise 8a with a pattern a–f in the box.**

Word grammar and patterns (*expect, surprised*)

Simple grammatical patterns include whether a word is followed by a noun, a preposition or an *-ing* form of the verb.

Some words, for example *expect* and *surprised*, are often associated with other patterns.

• ***Expect*** often goes with comparatives and patterns with *so* and *such*.

a comparative + *than/as* + *I expected*
b *expect* + noun/pronoun + infinitive with *to* + comparative
c *expect something* + comparative
d *not* + *expect* + noun/pronoun + infinitive with *to* + *so* + adjective/adverb
e *not* + *expect* + noun/pronoun + infinitive with *to* + *such* + noun

• ***Surprised*** often goes with a clause beginning with *how*.

f *surprised* + *how* + adjective/adverb

10 a 🔊 6.11 **Listen to the sentences. Notice how the underlined words are stressed and the other words are said more quickly.**

1 It really wasn't as scary as I was expecting.
2 You'd expect there to be far more people, wouldn't you?
3 I suppose I was expecting something a bit more experimental.
4 I didn't expect there to be so much audience participation.
5 I wasn't expecting it to be such a long film.
6 I was surprised how many people walked out halfway through.

b **Listen again and repeat.**

11 a **Think about the things in the box. What examples can you think of where they were better or worse than you expected and why? Write some reasons with *expect* and *surprised*.**

a place you visited   an event you went to
a course you did   a film you saw

b **Work in pairs and discuss your ideas.**

📱 Go to page 146 or your app for more information and practice.

Speaking

PREPARE

12 You're going to roleplay a discussion at a fringe festival. Student A: Turn to page 170. Student B: Turn to page 172. Follow the instructions.

SPEAK

13 a **Work in groups. Imagine you are at the festival. Ask each other what events you have seen and discuss them. Use the Useful phrases to help you.**

Useful phrases
Are you enjoying the festival?
What have you seen so far?
So did I! What did you think?
Oh right. What's that?
What was it like? Was it any good?

b **What was the most popular event in the class?**

Develop your writing
page 126

Check and reflect: Units 5 and 6

1 Complete the sentences with the nouns in the box.

> all-clear   carriageway   debris   diversion   failure
> load   service   tailback

1 A lorry shed its _____ on the main road, causing long delays.
2 The traffic lights aren't working. I think there's been a power _____ .
3 There's been a serious crash on the southbound _____ .
4 There was a problem on the line, so we had to take the replacement bus _____ .
5 Drivers on the M6 motorway have been given the _____ following an accident earlier today.
6 Sorry I'm so late. The main road was closed so I had to make a bit of a _____ .
7 There was a big crash earlier and they're still clearing all the _____ off the road.
8 We were OK, but there was a huge _____ in the other direction.

2 Complete the sentences using the best continuous form of the verbs in brackets.

1 I'd offer you a lift, but my car _____ at the moment. (repair)
2 Are you around next week? I _____ in your area, and it'd be great to see you again. (work)
3 We should phone and check they've heard the news. I mean, they might still _____ for us at the station. (wait)
4 It _____ all night so the traffic was even worse than usual that morning. (snow)
5 She saved my life. I wouldn't _____ here today if she hadn't pulled me out of my car. (sit)
6 Sorry I didn't answer your call earlier. I _____ . (drive)
7 I'm going to be late. There's been an accident on the motorway and we _____ just _____ along for hours now, so … (crawl)

3 Complete the sentences with the best word. The first letter is given.

1 We tried to cross the mountain p_____ , but it was blocked by snow.
2 We rented a little cottage hidden away in a little v_____ .
3 They've created a big m_____ reserve, which they hope will protect hundreds of water birds.
4 The beach was quite r_____ . I would've preferred a sandy one myself, but the kids liked it.
5 It's quite a remote island. There's only one ferry a day to and from the m_____ .
6 I usually take my dog for a walk along the s_____ most mornings. I love living by the sea.
7 I'm from a little village in a m_____ part of the country. It's hard to get to.
8 There are fears that the g_____ might start to melt, resulting in rising sea levels.

4 Complete the sentences using a participle form of the verbs in the box.

> base   build   check   live   look   visit

1 _____ in Switzerland, we are known for our high standards and competitive prices.
2 _____ the forecast, I was surprised to find myself driving through pouring rain and gales.
3 _____ in Australia, I'm used to 18-hour flights. It's normal if we want to get to most places!
4 _____ in the 14th century, the castle has recently been restored to its former glory.
5 _____ Rome many times before, I was keen to explore a different side of the city.
6 _____ out over the mountains, the hotel is perfect for a relaxing break from city life.

5 a Complete the questions by adding *house* or *home*.

1 Is there much _____ ownership in your country or do most people rent?
2 Do you know anyone who's done up their _____ recently? How has it changed?
3 How do you feel about the idea of living in a care _____ when you're old?
4 What do you think is the best age to leave _____ ? Why?
5 Where do you feel most at _____ ? Why?
6 Do you know anyone who's _____ -hunting at the moment? How's it going?
7 How often do you invite people round to your _____ ?
8 Have you ever got back late and woken up the whole _____ ?

b Work in pairs. Ask and answer four of the questions.

6 Look at the objects in the box. Which object is each sentence 1–8 below about?

> an antique carpet   blinds   a block of flats
> bookshelves   a certificate   a china plate
> a cupboard   a pot plant

1 I was awarded that when I completed my Spanish course at college.
2 I usually get one of my neighbours to water it when I'm away.
3 To be honest, I prefer them to curtains. They just look more modern.
4 They're so full I've ended up with stacks and stacks on the floor as well.
5 I love that one on the sitting room floor by the fire. Where did you get it?
6 I bought it when I was on holiday, but my son dropped it and it broke!
7 It's one of the most exclusive places to live in the whole neighbourhood.
8 We had it fitted when we moved in. It's pretty spacious inside – it holds all my shoes and clothes!.

7 a Match verbs 1–6 with words and phrases a–f.

1 break up   a your annual turnover
2 lose   b the company at £10 million
3 double   c focus
4 value   d into other areas
5 undercut   e a monopoly
6 branch out   f your competitors

b Work in pairs. Who or what might do each of the things in Exercise 7a? Explain why.

8 Complete the sentences by putting the adverbs and adverbial phrases in brackets in the best gap.

1 Our turnover has _____ increased quite dramatically _____ . (in the last year)
2 _____ One of their competitors wants to _____ buy them. (apparently)
3 Their products are amazing, but _____ they're _____ expensive. (incredibly)
4 _____ Benetton was started _____ in the 1960s. (in Italy)
5 I heard that the board have _____ agreed _____ to sell. (secretly)
6 We've _____ expanded _____ over the last few years. (very rapidly)

9 a Complete the definitions. The first letter is given.

1 If a country invests in its i_____ , it builds new roads, airports, transport systems, and so on.
2 A b_____ is a kind of protest where you refuse to take part in an event or buy or use a particular product.
3 If you c_____ someone like an architect, you formally ask them to do a piece of work for you.
4 If there's widespread c_____ , there's a lot of illegal or dishonest behaviour by people in power.
5 If an area experiences a complete t_____ , it changes a lot - and for the better.
6 If an event raises the p_____ of a place, it increases the attention the place gets.
7 If an event is extremely p_____ , it's respected and admired because it's so important.

b Choose three words to describe things that have happened in your town/city.

10 Complete the sentences using the best passive form of the verbs in brackets.

1 Luckily, most of the city _____ have survived the earthquake. (report)
2 Damascus _____ widely _____ be the oldest continuously inhabited city in the world. (believe)
3 More should _____ in schools and education. (invest)
4 After _____ some money by the government, they've started doing up the old town. (give)
5 An email _____ by this newspaper suggests the board knew about the problem. (see)
6 Millions of dollars _____ by corrupt local officials over recent years. (rumour / steal)
7 Cappadocia is an amazing place. It has to _____ . (see / believe)

11 Which descriptions are positive, which are negative and which are neutral?

1 It was pretty mediocre.
2 It was very entertaining.
3 It was an open-mike night.
4 It's quite fast-paced.
5 They were both really out of tune.
6 It was very moving.
7 It's a collaborative project.
8 It was a real disappointment.

12 Complete the sentences with one word.

1 It was much bigger _____ I'd expected.
2 I really didn't expect it to be quite _____ a disappointment.
3 I didn't expect _____ to be so many people there.
4 I was surprised _____ professional they were.
5 I wasn't expecting the gig to be _____ cheap.
6 I preferred the first guy. The second person wasn't _____ funny.

13 Match the sentence halves.

1 If you're into jazz, you might want to
2 It'd probably be wise
3 Make sure
4 Your best
5 There's no harm
6 Getting decent travel insurance is

a you leave a review online.
b bet would be take a cab.
c check out The Vortex.
d in trying.
e a must.
f to book in advance.

Reflect

How confident do you feel about the statements below? Write 1–5 (1 = not very confident, 5 = very confident).

- I can take part in a discussion about commuting.
- I can discuss tourism and underdeveloped parts of the country.
- I can describe different homes.
- I can give advice and make suggestions about what to do in an area.
- I can talk about business and the economy.
- I can decide on the best kind of event for my area to host.
- I can talk about events I've been to.

For more practice go to your Workbook or app.

Go online for the Roadmap video.

7A ⟩ Ups and downs

> **Goal:** tell stories about recent experiences and comment on them

> **Grammar:** adding comments using *must* and *can't*

> **Vocabulary:** life's ups and downs

Vocabulary

1 Work in groups. Look at the pictures and discuss the questions.

   1 What life events do the pictures show? What other important life events can you think of?

   2 What usually happens at each of these kinds of events in your country?

   3 Which events have you been to recently?

2 a Do the words and expressions in bold in the sentences refer to birth, death, marriage, family and home, career, or study?

   1 My son finally completed his **doctorate** in Public Health this summer.

   2 They've tried to **make a go of it**, but it's been hard and they're now having a **trial separation**.

   3 They had a big **falling-out** after the reading of the will because one of them **inherited** everything.

   4 His mum passed away two years ago and he's still **coming to terms with it**.

   5 He decided to **make a clean break** and return to his **native** Poland.

   6 They moved away because the firm he works for **relocated** to a much smaller town.

   7 It was their **golden anniversary** this year and we had a big **get-together** to celebrate.

   8 My partner and I finally decided to **tie the knot**. The big day is going to be in November.

   9 My last child **flew the nest** last year to go to uni.

   10 She **arrived** five weeks **premature**, but she's feeding well and gaining weight.

  b Work in pairs and check your ideas. Discuss whether the situations in Exercise 2a describe positive or negative experiences, or both. Explain why.

3 a Complete the questions with words from Exercise 2a.

   1 Do you know anyone who's tied the _____ recently?

   2 What is the best age to _____ the nest? Why?

   3 Do you know anyone who's ever _____ lots of money?

   4 Do you know anyone who has a newborn baby? When did it _____ ?

   5 Do you know anyone who's ever celebrated a golden wedding _____ ?

  b Work in pairs. Ask and answer the questions in Exercise 3a.

📱 Go to your app for more practice.

Listening

4 🔊 **7.1** Listen to three conversations. Are the speakers talking about a friend, family member or celebrity? What events are discussed?

5 Listen again. In which of the conversations (1, 2 or 3) are each of the following mentioned?

  a something being delayed

  b a party

  c an argument

  d a potentially embarrassing situation

  e saving up

  f a chance meeting

  g a way of avoiding difficulties

  h an expensive plan

  i an enormous change

6 Work in pairs and discuss whether it is better to:

  1 come from a really big family or a small one. Why?

  2 work with family members/friends or with people you're not close to. Why?

  3 have a big expensive wedding or do it cheaply. Why?

  4 have a quiet life or have fame and fortune. Why?

Grammar

7 a Look at extracts 1–5 from the conversations. Can you remember what speaker A was commenting on in each case?

1 A: Wow! That **must've been** nice.
   B: Yeah, it was.

2 A: That **must get** awkward.
   B: Well, I've developed survival strategies over the years, you know.

3 A: I know. It **must be** tough …
   B: Yeah.

4 A: As you say, it **can't be** easy …
   B; Yeah, no, it doesn't appeal to me.

5 A: That **can't have been** much fun.
   B: I know, right.

b Read the grammar box and choose the correct alternatives.

Adding comments using *must* and *can't*

We often use *must* and *can't* to comment on what we are hearing.

A: I can't even remember all their names.
*B: That **must** get awkward.*
A: Hopefully, she'll stop this time.
*B: Well, it **can't** be easy.*

• Use **¹**must/can't to suggest the idea in our comment (e.g. *get awkward* or *be easy*) is very likely.
• Use **²**must/can't to suggest the idea in our comment is very unlikely.
• To comment on the present, use *must* or *can't* + infinitive without *to*.
• To comment on the past, use *must* or *can't* + *have* + past participle.
• We **³**generally/don't usually respond to these comments as if they were questions.
• We **⁴**generally/don't usually repeat the modal verb in the comment; we say something about the real situation.
A: That must have been nice.
B: Yes, it was.

8 a 7.2 Listen to the comments. Notice that we often don't hear the /t/ in *must* and *can't*.

1 You must find that quite tough.
2 That must get pretty dull on occasion.
3 That must've been fascinating.
4 I guess that can't be avoided.
5 You can't be very happy about that.
6 That can't have been an easy decision to make.

b Listen again and repeat.

9 Complete the conversations by adding one to four words in each gap.

1 A: My grandparents had a big get-together to celebrate their golden wedding anniversary.
   B: Oh really? *That must've been* nice.
   A: Yeah, it _____ . I _____ a lovely time.

2 A: My firm relocated last year, so now I have to commute two hours each way to work.
   B: Seriously? _____ much fun for you.
   A: It _____ . I'm exhausted!

3 A: My kids have all flown the nest now.
   B: _____ a bit weird.
   A: Well, _____ can _____ sometimes, yeah, but I'm slowly getting used to it.

4 A: He was working full time and doing a doctorate.
   B: Seriously? _____ easy for him.
   A: No, I _____ . I think he found it a real struggle.

5 A: The baby was six weeks premature.
   B: Gosh! That's quite early. You _____ through quite a mixture of emotions.
   A: I _____ . I was very happy when she arrived, but really anxious, too. Anyway, everything's fine now.
   B: _____ a relief.
   A: _____ . We're really enjoying getting to know her.

10 Work in pairs. Have conversations like the ones in Exercise 9. Take turns to start, using sentences 1–4.

1 I decided to make a clean break of things and start again.
2 She's had a baby boy. He was born last Friday.
3 I get to travel quite a lot for work.
4 My sister works in a big bank dealing with investments.

📱 Go to page 148 or your app for more information and practice.

Speaking

PREPARE

11 a Think about six positive and/or negative pieces of news to talk about that have happened to you, people you know, or celebrities in the past year.

b Decide how you are going to introduce each piece of news. Use the Useful phrases to help you.

Useful phrases
Hey. Did I tell you about … ?
I'm not sure if I've told you or not, but …
I don't know if you know, but …
Did you hear what happened with … ?
Did you see that thing (in the paper) about …?

SPEAK

12 Talk to different students and share your news. Try to continue the conversations.

Develop your writing
page 128

7B Is it news?

A TRANSPORT STRIKE ENTERS THIRD WEEK
B MIXED REACTION TO NEW EXHIBITION
C CITY LIFT THE CUP

> **Goal:** talk about the impact of news stories and events

> **Grammar:** second, third and mixed conditionals

> **Vocabulary:** talking about the news

Vocabulary

1 Work in groups. What kind of news are you most or least interested in?

2 a Work in pairs. Read the definitions. Which words and phrases in bold can you use to talk about the news stories in the photos?

1 If something **causes outrage** it means lots of people are shocked and angry about it.

2 News that **causes controversy** leads to a serious debate, with strong feelings on different sides.

3 If news **triggers violence** or **riots** or an **election**, it makes these things happen.

4 When news **is widely welcomed,** lots of people are satisfied with the result.

5 When news **creates excitement** it means people are happy and enthusiastic about it.

6 When something **leads to resignations** it means people agree to give up important jobs.

b Can you think of news stories that caused the effects described in Exercise 2a?

3 Complete the sentences with the correct form of the collocations in the box.

> a contributing factor   expose a cover-up
> get through to the semi-finals   impose tariffs
> a major breakthrough   massive coverage
> an offensive comment   withdraw from the treaty

1 The inquiry into the disaster has uncovered evidence that poor safety regulations were _____ .

2 In the article they _____ . Apparently, the directors knew all about the stories of wrongdoing within the company, but made sure the stories didn't come out.

3 He made _____ about women on social media, which was then widely shared.

4 They've announced they're going to _____ on workers' rights.

5 They've decided to _____ on imports of steel.

6 They _____ of the World Cup for the first time.

7 The break-up of the band got _____ on the media here. It was really big news.

8 They've announced _____ in gene therapy.

4 Work in pairs. Which do you think is the most and least important piece of news in Exercise 3a? Why?

📱 Go to page 162 your app for more vocabulary and practice.

Reading

5 Read the article about news. Decide the best summary of the main argument.

a Most of the important things that happen in the world are never reported.

b The more viewers news channels try to attract, the less serious the news becomes.

c Events that have the biggest long-term impact don't always make the headlines.

6 a Read the article again and mark the ideas.

! This surprises me.　　　**✓** I agree with this.

? I don't understand this.　**✗** I disagree with this.

b Work in pairs. Compare how you marked the article.

Why some stories never became front-page news

What exactly is news? That's the question I've been asking myself ever since I read Jacques Peretti's book *The Deals that Made the World*. In it, he argues that much of life as we experience it now – from using cards instead of cash, to food and dieting or how we work – is the way it is because of specific business meetings and agreements. His point is that even though these deals don't get much coverage when they happen, they do end up having major consequences.

For example, in the 1990s, the management consultants McKinsey started selling a strategy that emphasised the 'war for talent'. It focused on continuous assessment of staff, leading either to higher pay or losing your job, depending on your results. Peretti argues that if they <u>hadn't come up with</u> this approach, we <u>would have</u> less insecurity at work these days and executive pay <u>wouldn't have increased</u> so much. And yet, this didn't make headlines at the time. Similarly, who reported the first email being sent, or the invention of the World Wide Web? Hardly anyone is the answer!

A contributing factor here has surely been the development of our 24-hour news cycle and the way that stories grow. These days the news media prefers to cover stories that are violent and/or relatively unimportant. Dramatic scenes attract more viewers than pictures of people negotiating a treaty or involved in scientific research; and in between the reports, the channel needs lots of opinions. And while commenting on science requires expertise, almost anyone can have a view on a presidential tweet, a band's break-up or the significance of an election result. Of course, if something causes outrage or wild enthusiasm, that's an even better story, which is not something likely to happen when people in suits decide a new management strategy.

D | SECOND MINISTER ARRESTED IN FINANCIAL SCANDAL

Grammar

7 a Look at the underlined forms in the article. Decide which refer to:

1 the past.
2 the present.
3 a completed action.
4 a consequence of the action.

b Read the grammar box and choose the correct alternatives.

Second, third and mixed conditionals

Second conditionals usually refer to the present and third conditionals refer to the past.

Mixed conditionals use parts of second and third conditionals together in the same sentence.

We often use past forms in the *if*-clauses of conditional sentences to talk about **1***real/imagined* situations or actions.

- **2***Past simple/Past perfect* forms in the *if*-clause refer to the present.

*If there **weren't** constant news updates …*

- **3***Past simple/Past perfect* forms refer to the past.

*If scientists **hadn't needed** to share information …*

- The other half of the sentence (the main clause) usually contains *would, might* or *could* to refer to the imagined situation.

- *would/might/could* + verb/*be -ing* refers to the **4***past/ present*.

*society **would be** very different today*
*we **couldn't communicate** in the way we do now*
*we **might not be discussing** this if …*

- *would've/might've/could've* + past participle refers to the **5***past/present*

*… it **wouldn't have happened**.*
*… they **might not have been invented**.*

We often refer only to the consequence because the situation is clear and doesn't need re-stating.

*Safety regulations **should've been** better. The fire **might not have happened** then and we **wouldn't be having** this inquiry now.*

8 🔊 **7.3 Listen and notice how the modal verbs do not have the main stress in the sentences. Repeat what you hear.**

1 We should've protested. We might've stopped it.
2 It must've been awful. I'm not sure I could've coped.
3 I should do something to help. It's what he would want.
4 They must be worried. They wouldn't have gone to the police otherwise.

9 Write conditional sentences based on sentences 1–6 using the notes in brackets.

1 His arrest led to the true story coming out in the open.
   (he / arrest / the true story / might / uncover)
   If he hadn't been arrested, the true story might not have been uncovered.

2 We didn't expect to do so well.
   (no-one / be surprised / we / go out / in the first round)

3 I think they won the election partly because of the success of the national team.
   (they / win / the election / the national team / do / so well)

4 I think we avoided a disaster because of the way the president reacted.
   (it / be / a disaster / the president / react differently)

5 The problem didn't start when they imposed tariffs. If anything, things are actually better now!
   (there / be / tariffs now, things / go / even more badly)

6 We're experiencing problems like this because of the cuts they've been making.
   (we / might / experience / problems like this / they / cut back so much)

10 a Think of two mistakes you (or people you know) have made in recent years and two actions that have had a positive result. Write a conditional sentence for each.

b Work in pairs. Share and discuss your sentences.

 Go to page 148 or your app for more information and practice.

Speaking

PREPARE

11 a Work in pairs. Make a list of five big news stories you remember from the last few years.

b Work on your own. Think of the impact of each story.

12 🔊 **7.4 Listen to two people discussing a news story. What was the story and what impact did it have?**

SPEAK

13 a Work in pairs and compare your stories from Exercise 11. Use the Useful phrases to help you. Do you agree on the impact each one had?

Useful phrases
It's had a huge impact.
It's already more or less been forgotten.
If it wasn't for that, …
If it hadn't happened, …
I'm not sure it'll last.

b Which of the stories had the greatest and least impact on you personally? Why?

> **Develop your listening**
> page 92

7c ⟩ A show of hands

⟩ **Goal:** take part in a debate (on issues around voting)

⟩ **Language focus:** phrases to show the relationship between ideas

⟩ **Vocabulary:** voting and elections

Listening

1 **Work in groups and discuss the questions.**

1 Why might people have a vote in these situations?

> at home   at school   at work   with friends
> on TV   in the area or country they live in

2 Can you think of other places or situations where people might vote?

3 Have you ever voted? When and what about?

2 🔊 **7.8 Listen to four students having a discussion about voting in elections. Answer the questions.**

1 What is the main issue they're discussing?

2 Which of the following ideas do they also mention?

- compulsory voting
- voter turnout
- a different system
- online voting

3 a **Work in pairs. Can you remember what the speakers said about 1–5?**

1 three things you can do at 16

2 three things the government decides which affect under-18s

3 three ways 16-year-olds aren't yet involved in economic issues

4 an argument you could make to support the idea ten-year-olds should get the vote

5 the number of people who vote

b **Listen again and check your ideas.**

4 **Work in groups. Which do you think were the best ideas in the discussion? Why?**

Language focus

5 a **Look at the extracts from the discussion. Can you remember the missing words of the phrases?**

1 And g_____ a_____ t_____, it just seems crazy that you then have to wait two more years ...

2 Yeah, maybe ... b_____ t_____ a_____, if you're 16, you won't own your own house yet.

3 ... a_____ y_____ economic issues often play a key role in elections.

4 Fair enough, but e_____ s_____, it still seems pretty unfair to me.

5 Then i_____ s_____ o_____ a_____ t_____, they say that letting younger people vote is a bad idea.

6 H_____ s_____ t_____, though, who would be able to vote?

b 🔊 **7.9 Listen and check your ideas.**

6 **Complete the language focus box with the phrases from Exercise 5a.**

Phrases to show the relationship between ideas

These are some of the different phrases used in spoken English.

- Some phrases are used to refer to a previously mentioned condition or fact about something.

Bearing (all) that in mind
Taking (all) that into account
Considering (all that)

1 _____

- Some phrases introduce a statement that seems surprising after what has just been said, or make what has been said seem less true or incorrect.

Despite (all) that / ² _____
But all the same

3 _____
4 _____
5 _____
6 _____

7 a 🔊 **7.10 Listen to the phrases in the language focus box said at different speeds. Notice how the consonants at the end of a word link with the vowel sounds at the start of the next word.**

b 🔊 **7.11 Listen to the phrases and repeat.**

8 a Match comments 1–8 with responses a–h.

1 The right to vote is a core principle of all democracies.

2 He's not a very inspiring candidate.

3 I just feel, like lots of other people, that it doesn't make any difference who I vote for.

4 They've spent way more on their campaign than the other parties and the media's in their favour.

5 I think there are a lot of lies spread on social media in order to stir up hatred.

6 Apparently, lots of postal votes end up getting lost in the mail.

7 If we have another referendum, the 'yes' vote will win this time around.

8 I think it's really important to make yourself heard and have your say.

a **Even so**, I still can't see anyone else I'd rather vote for.

b Well, **given that**, it's not surprising that so few people vote these days.

c **And yet** millions of people still choose not to exercise that right.

d Well, **bearing that in mind**, maybe it's time to do long-distance voting online instead.

e Maybe, **but then again**, it could equally well end up with exactly the same result as before.

f Yeah, **but in spite of all that**, the election's still looking very close, actually.

g So do I. **Having said that**, though, I don't think voting makes you a better person or anything!

h So **taking that into account**, maybe we need tighter controls on how it's used.

b 🔊 7.12 Listen and check your answers.

c Work in pairs. Practise saying the comments and responses.

9 a Look at the quotes below. How do you feel about each one?

1 *I have an idea about voting. How about on every ballot, we include 'None of the above'?* **Jesse Ventura**

2 *Voting is how we participate in civic society [...]. It's the way we teach our children – in school elections – how to be citizens and the importance of their voice.* **Loretta Lynch**

3 *Voting gives us an opportunity to choose from options that were chosen for us.* **Mokokoma Mokhonoana**

4 *History shows us that people often make mistakes [...] and in the end, they pay a heavy price for it!* **Mehmet Murat Ildan**

5 *Someone struggled for your right to vote. Use it.* **Susan B. Anthony**

6 *The best argument against democracy is a five-minute conversation with the average voter.* **Winston Churchill**

b Work in groups and discuss the quotes in Exercise 9a. Use phrases from the language focus box to help you respond to comments.

📱 Go to page 148 or your app for more information and practice.

Vocabulary

10 a Read the facts about voting and elections. Check you understand the words in bold.

1 Switzerland has **held** almost 200 **referendums** in the last twenty years. However, the results are not always fully **implemented**.

2 Over the last 25 years, the average global **voter turnout** rate has dropped by more than 10%.

3 When results in voting areas are very close, there are often **recounts**. In Britain in 1966, there were seven recounts when Sir Harmar-Nicholls won in Peterborough by just three votes.

4 Germany and Belgium have **electoral systems** that means a party rarely wins an absolute majority. These countries often have a **coalition** government.

5 After winning the 1982 election, Paul Biya was **re-elected** president of Cameroon four times.

6 You can **cast your vote** in some very strange places. In the UK, a train carriage, a caravan and even someone's front room have all been **polling stations**.

7 In the US, a group known as The Yippies once **nominated** a pig called Pigasus as a presidential candidate. It was not clear what was in his **manifesto**!

8 Women in Liechtenstein **had no say in** elections until they finally won the right to vote in 1984.

9 In the 1927 election in Liberia, Charles D.B. King won **re-election** with around 240,000 votes. However, the election must have been **fixed** as there were only 15,000 registered voters!

b Work in pairs. Have you heard of similar cases?

📱 Go to page 162 or your app for more vocabulary and practice.

Speaking

PREPARE

11 Turn to page 170 and read the statements. Decide how far you agree with each one and why. Which two do you feel most strongly about?

SPEAK

12 a Work in groups. Choose two topics you all feel quite strongly about. Discuss your ideas. Use the Useful phrases to help.

Useful phrases
All I'm saying is …
(I think that's) fair enough.
I can see where you're coming from (with that).
I hear you (but …)
I'm not sure I get what you mean.

b Did you come to an agreement on either of the topics? Tell the class.

Develop your reading page 108

English in action

> **Goal:** give a presentation with visuals

> **Vocabulary:** explaining statistics

Listening 1

1 **Work in groups and discuss the questions.**
 1 Look at the photo below. How similar or different is housing where you live?
 2 How affordable is housing for most people?
 3 Have prices gone up or down recently?
 4 Is it more common to rent or buy? Why?
 5 Do you think there is enough new housing?
 6 Which part of your town/city would you most like to live in? Why?

2 a 🔊 **7.13 Listen to the start of two presentations. Which one goes with the graph and which with the photo? Take notes on what the speakers say about each.**

 b **Work in pairs and compare your notes.**

3 **Read the Useful phrases 1 box. Can you remember which phrases the speakers used in each presentation? Listen again to check your ideas.**

> **Useful phrases 1**
>
> **Explaining what the visual is about.**
> The graph/pie chart/photo (here) shows …
> This is a photo of …
> (We may mention the time and place)
>
> **Summarising the overall trend or core message**
> As you can see, (the main trend is upward).
> I think it illustrates (a number of points regarding) …
>
> **Highlighting some key features of the visual**
> The first and perhaps most obvious point is …
> It signifies …
> You will also notice that …
> From then on …, increasing by …
>
> **Providing a comparison**
> Just as a comparison, …
> That's the equivalent of …

Vocabulary

4 **Which descriptions 1–12 could be used to describe graphs and charts A–F?**

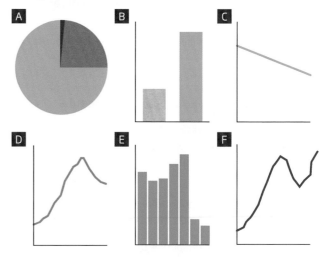

 1 The number is predicted to **fall steadily** over time.
 2 An **insignificant number** never use the service.
 3 The price has **recovered** to previous levels.
 4 The market has **crashed**.
 5 It **reached a peak** before **dropping off**.
 6 The **vast majority** are satisfied.
 7 The market has **bounced back**.
 8 Shares have **rocketed**.
 9 It **fell back** after its high.
 10 There is likely to be a **gradual decline**.
 11 There's been **a sharp rise**.
 12 There's been **a serious slump** in uptake.

5 a Write examples of recent trends and changes in areas such as sports, fashion, the economy, unemployment, politics or your own ideas. Use phrases in bold from Exercise 4.

There was a slump in share prices last year, but they've bounced back since then.
Support for the Green Party has risen steadily.

b Work in pairs. Compare your sentences and explain your ideas.

Listening 2

6 a 7.14 Listen to the next sections of the two presentations and take notes.

b Work in pairs. Discuss what causes and effects of the situations in each place were mentioned.

7 a Look at the Useful phrases 2 box. Then try to complete the extracts from the presentations, using between three and five words in each gap.

   1 The rising accommodation prices have been _____ factors.

   2 … and finally, government policy has, in different ways, _____ this trend.

   3 The increases in property prices are _____ and have _____ . Many people simply can't afford to get on the property ladder.

   4 It is clearly an unsustainable situation, but _____ ? Let's look at some possibilities.

   5 _____ , it's unsurprising that nearly 50 percent of households in the suburbs of Sydney own two or more cars.

   6 _____ increased congestion, which has been getting consistently worse in the city over the last ten years.

   7 … it _____ within Sydney who walk or take public transport must suffer more noise, pollution, and slower services.

   8 _____ what to do? Should we control the development or manage their consequences?

   9 _____ now.

b Listen again and check your answers.

Useful phrases 2

Explaining causes
account for (much/30 percent) of the rise
be down to (a number of factors/the government)

Explaining effects of the main trend
cause (concern/tensions)
mean that (people must suffer/there are shortages)
lead to (increased homelessness/a slump)
give rise to (protests/congestion)
As a consequence, (prices rose sharply)

Signposting the end of the section and what you will talk about next
What should we do/should be done?
The question is (what should be done/what's causing this?)
Let's turn to that now.
Let's look at some possibilities.

---

8 Use phrases from the Useful phrases 2 box to talk about the causes and effects of two of the following:
- falling house prices
- the rising number of people going to university
- life expectancy increasing
- global warming

9 a 7.15 When we give a presentation, we vary the pace of our speech, pausing or slowing down for emphasis. Look at the presentation below then listen and mark:
- the section said at a <u>normal</u> pace.
- the section which is said at a <u>slower pace</u>.
- a clear pause //.

'The increases in property prices are causing huge concern and have given rise to protests. Many people simply can't afford to get on the property ladder or live independently – because the average salary has failed to keep pace with housing costs. Salaries have risen by an average of just £10,000 over the same period of time. That means a flat which cost around four times the average salary in 1998, now costs around fourteen times the typical income. Yes, you heard that right fourTEEN. …'

---

b Work in pairs. Prepare the next section of another presentation. Take turns to read it out. Tell your partner what they did well.

… As you can see, the houses are organised in rows – often in cul-de-sacs like this, where the road goes nowhere. Developments like this tend to be entirely residential. There are no schools, no banks, and few, if any, shops. You will also notice that there aren't even any footpaths. Not one. In other words, the development has been built in a way that requires people to use a car.

As a consequence, it's unsurprising that nearly 50 percent of households in the suburbs of Sydney own two or more cars. That means half of these houses you see here will have multiple cars – but then, how else is the family to get around?

Speaking

10 a You're going to give a presentation using a visual to a partner. Choose one of the visuals on page 171 and decide:
- the theme of the visual.
- the main points you want to make.
- the causes and effects you want to talk about.
- any other points to include.

b Work in pairs and take turns to present your visual. After your partner's presentation, ask questions.

For more practice go to your Workbook or app.

Go online for the Roadmap video.

Jobs for life?

> **Goal:** roleplay a conversation about what you do
> **Grammar:** complex questions
> **Vocabulary:** describing what your job involves

Reading

1. **Work in pairs. Look at the photos and discuss the questions.**
   1. What do you think each of the jobs involves?
   2. Do you think these jobs are dying out? Why?
   3. What jobs are dying out where you live? Why?
   4. Can you think of any modern jobs that didn't exist when you were young?

2. a **Look at the title and sub-title of the article. How do you think they might be connected to question 4 in Exercise 1?**

   b **Read the article and check your ideas. Explain the subtitle, and what Dan Klyn does for a living.**

3. **Read the article again. Are the sentences true (T) or false (F)? How do you know?**
   1. Dan doesn't enjoy explaining what he does.
   2. Most people have heard of information architects.
   3. People can sometimes be a bit scared to say they don't understand what his job involves.
   4. Most new jobs exist because of technological developments.
   5. Getting young people ready for the jobs of the future requires a new approach to education.
   6. Most people want to know all about what his job involves.

4. **Work in groups and discuss the questions.**
   1. Have you heard of any of the other new jobs Dan Klyn mentions? What do think they might involve?
   2. Do you agree that we need to rethink the way we train young people for the world of work?

WHAT EXACTLY IS IT THAT YOU DO?

Dan Klyn explains why he avoids small talk at parties.

Like many people in the modern world, I dread meeting new folk at social events because I know that sooner or later someone will ask me what I do for a living. Don't get me wrong. It's not that I'm ashamed of my profession or anything like that. It's just that I know that when I announce the fact that I'm an information architect, most people won't have a clue what that means. Sure they've heard the words before, but never together and so they usually look nervously at each other, their eyes asking, 'What do you suppose that even means?' before eventually finding the courage to ask: 'Right. An information architect. OK. Um . . . . so what exactly is it that you DO?' and 'How was it that you got into THAT?!'

At the heart of the problem lies the fact that many of us do jobs that simply didn't exist when we were at school. We're data scientists and YouTube content creators, we're social media managers and drone operators. Obviously, almost all these jobs exist because of rapid advances in the fields of robotics, artificial intelligence, biotechnology, and so on, and these trends are likely to continue. Kids entering their teens today may well be asking their teachers 'What do you think would be a good thing for me to study?', but coming up with a sensible answer is made far more complicated when you know that over half of these kids will end up doing things that aren't yet on our radar! Clearly, this requires rethinking the way we train our young people for the world of work.

Oh, and in case you're still wondering what exactly it is that I do, by the way, the simple answer is my job is to make information clear and appealing to the people who use it. I develop user experiences and I build bridges – bridges between digital content and users, between corporate strategy and tactics, and between research and practice. However, if I try to explain this any more, it usually kills the conversation stone dead!

Grammar

5 a **Find versions of questions 1–4 in the article on page 62. Then do A and B below.**

1 What does that even mean?
2 What exactly do you do?
3 What would be a good thing for me to study?
4 How did you get into that?

A Look at the form of the questions you found in the article. Divide them into two groups.

B How are the forms of the questions in the article different to those in 1–4?

b **Read the grammar box and check your ideas.**

Complex questions

• We add emphasis to the question word using:
question word + *be* + *it* + *that* clause.
It's similar to a cleft sentence. We often use this structure if we are surprised or confused.
What *(exactly)* ***is it*** *that you do?*
How was it *that you got into that?*
• We focus on the person and their opinion using the pattern:
question word + *do you* + *think/suggest/recommend,* etc.
What ***do you suppose*** *that even means?*
What ***do you think*** *I should study?*

6 a 8.1 **Listen to the questions said at different speeds. Notice how the underlined *that* becomes reduced when the questions are said more quickly.**

1 Who was it <u>that</u> you spoke to?
2 Where was it <u>that</u> you went to university?
3 Why was it <u>that</u> you decided to study that, then?
4 What exactly is it <u>that</u> that involves?
5 Why did you think <u>that</u> that would work?

b 8.2 **Listen to the questions and repeat.**

7 **Rewrite the basic questions as complex questions. Use the words in brackets.**

1 Who told you about the job in the first place?
_____ ? (was)
2 What were you reading when I saw you the other day?
_____ ? (that)
3 When will you hear if you've got onto the course?
_____ ? (suppose)
4 What should I do if I want to get into that field?
_____ ? (recommend)
5 Who'd be the best person to ask?
_____ ? (reckon)
6 What did that guy want?
_____ ? (it)

8 a **Write a possible answer to each of the questions in Exercise 7.**

b **Work in pairs. Student A: Say an answer. Student B: Say the question. Then change roles.**

Go to page 150 or your app for more information and practice.

Vocabulary

9 **Match the verbs in the boxes with the phrases below.**

collaborate   ~~devise~~   facilitate   head up   mend   monitor

1 *devise* online games for school kids / new environmental strategies
2 _____ broken machinery / high-end watches
3 _____ the progress new people make / levels of stress and sickness
4 _____ the management team / a consultancy firm
5 _____ on nationwide projects / with other designers
6 _____ discussions in conflict situations / team-building workshops

assemble   delegate   fit   log   oversee   submit

7 _____ all calls / deliveries on the system
8 _____ some work to my assistants / responsibility to my team
9 _____ the project / the recruitment process
10 _____ flatpack furniture / all the documents needed
11 _____ a regular report / a claim for travel expenses
12 _____ fire alarms in offices and factories / locks

10 **Work in pairs. Look at the activities in Exercise 9. Tell your partner about any of the things that:**

1 you do.
2 people you know do.
3 you'd never do.
4 you'd like to try.

Go to page 163 or your app for more vocabulary and practice.

Speaking

PREPARE

11 **Work in pairs. You're going to roleplay a conversation at a party. Student A: Go to page 172. Student B: Go to page 173.**

12 8.3 **Listen to a conversation at a party. What information does Mo give in response to the questions in Exercise 11?**

SPEAK

13 **Roleplay the conversation. Ask the questions in Exercise 11 and in the Useful phrases box. Try to keep the conversation going.**

Useful phrases

How long have you been doing that?
Is it something you see yourself staying in?
How do you get on with the people you work with?
How do you keep up with new developments?
Isn't it very stressful?

Develop your listening
page 93

8B Sleep well

> **Goal:** talk about sleep and insomnia
> **Grammar:** auxiliary verbs
> **Vocabulary:** sleep

Vocabulary

1 **Work in pairs. Look at the pictures and discuss the questions.**

1 What do you think is happening in each one?
2 How would you feel in each situation?
3 What do you think the characters might say or do next?

2 **Complete sentences 1–10 with the correct form of the words and phrases in the box.**

> be a night owl   be an early riser   be out like a light
> can't stop yawning   have a lie-in   have a little nap
> have a sleepless night   nod off   snore loudly
> suffer from jet lag

1 I never _____ . I just sleep on the plane and I always feel great the next day.
2 Can you tell me what happened at the end of that film? I must have _____ for a minute or two!
3 A: You look awful.
   B: Yes, I know. I _____ – the neighbours had a party and the music kept me awake all night.
4 The great thing about being on holiday is that you can _____ whenever you feel like it. Yesterday I had two in the afternoon!
5 Every Sunday morning I _____ – it's the only day when my alarm clock doesn't go off at 7 a.m.
6 I couldn't sleep last night because my aunt _____ in the other room.
7 A: Am I boring you?
   B: Sorry! I slept really badly last night and now I _____ .
8 Ana _____ – she gets up every day at 6 a.m.!
9 _____ or do you prefer to go to bed early?
10 I was so tired I couldn't keep my eyes open – I went to bed and I _____ .

3 a **Use your own ideas to link the phrases from Exercise 2 into twos or threes.**

> *suffer from jet lag* → *have a sleepless night* → *have a little nap*

b **Work in pairs. Compare your ideas and explain your choices.**

> *If you're **suffering from jet lag** after a really long flight, you might **have a sleepless night**, and then the next day you might **have a little nap** in the afternoon – to catch up on some sleep.*

Go to your app for more practice.

Listening

4 🔊 **8.6 Listen to three conversations. Which two sentences (a–f) go with each conversation?**

a They're in a hotel.
b They are students.
c They are colleagues.
d Someone fell asleep at work.
e Someone overslept.
f Someone has an unusual sleep pattern.

5 **Listen again to the conversations. Answer the questions.**

1 a What's causing the man's sleepless nights?
   b Why was he embarrassed?
2 a Why does the woman think her friend's suffering from jet lag?
   b Is her friend worried about her sleep?
3 a Why was the woman having a nap?
   b What two solutions does the man offer for stress?

6 **Work in pairs and discuss the questions.**

1 What do you think is the best way for working parents to deal with having a new baby?
2 Have you ever suffered from jet lag or had sleepless nights? What happened?
3 What do you get stressed by? How does it affect you? How do you deal with it?

Grammar

7 a Work in pairs. Look at extracts 1–7 from the conversations. Can you remember what comments or questions each of the underlined auxiliaries refer to?

1 I <u>am</u>. I'm exhausted.
2 I wish I <u>had</u>!
3 I <u>would</u> if I could, but there's nowhere to have one.
4 I know. So <u>am</u> I.
5 I <u>am</u>! I mean, not right this moment.
6 I <u>did</u>. I must've slept through it.
7 I probably <u>will</u>. I mean I want to …

b 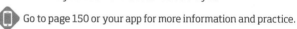 8.7 Listen to the exchanges and check.

8 Complete the grammar box using auxiliary verbs from Exercise 7a. Why are the auxiliaries in the replies sometimes different from the verbs in the comments or questions?

Auxiliary verbs

Auxiliary verbs are used with other verbs to make different tenses. They are *be*, *do*, *have* and modal verbs. When we use modal verbs (we only ever use them as auxiliaries) they add extra layers of meaning.

We often use auxiliary verbs on their own when we respond to comments or questions from other people. They avoid repeating a verb or verb phrase.

Depending on what the speaker means, these can relate to the verb in the comment:

A: **You look** *(well).*   *B:* I¹_____

A: **You must've been** *(delighted).*   *B:* I was.

A: **Can't you** *(have a nap at lunchtime)?*   *B:* I²_____ if I³_____ .
B: I **do** … but it's not enough.

A: **You should've** *(set your alarm).*   *B:* I⁴_____
B: If I **had** …

A: **Shouldn't you be** *(studying)?*   *B:* I⁵_____

A: **Do you** *(have trouble sleeping)?*   *B:* I **used** to.

A: **Have you been** *(to Paris)?*   *B:* I wish I⁶_____

A: **Are you going** *(out tonight)?*   *B:* I probably⁷_____
B: I **might**.

A: **Did you** *(get an early night)?*   *B:* No, but I should've.
B: I **would've**, but …

9 a 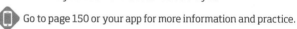 8.8 Listen to the sentences. Notice that we stress the auxiliary verbs to show contrast. In sentences 1–4, an auxiliary is added for emphasis.

1 I do like it. There's just too much of it.
2 It found it difficult, but I did do it in the end.
3 I did try to do it, it just wasn't good enough.
4 It is going to happen, but I do worry about it.
5 It is good, but I've seen better.

b Listen again and repeat.

10 Complete the conversations with a pronoun and an auxiliary verb. Some auxiliaries are negative.

1 A: It must be difficult to get a full night's sleep living so near to the airport.
   B: _____ to begin with, but I soon got used to it.
2 A: Maybe you shouldn't drink coffee at night.
   B: _____ . It must be something else that's stopping me sleeping.
3 A: Can you call me if I'm not up by 8?
   B: _____ if I'm still here.
4 A: I'm a bit of a night owl, so I start work later.
   B: Really? I wish _____ too. I hate getting up early.
5 A: I overslept. _____ , too?
   B: No, I've got the day off. Didn't you set an alarm?
   A: I thought _____ , but I guess _____ .
6 A: They should provide space at work for people to take a nap.
   B: But how much work would be done if _____ ?
   A: Actually, _____ already at other places and it's improved productivity.

11 Work in pairs. How many ways can you think of to respond to the sentences and questions using different auxiliaries?

1 Do you ever have trouble sleeping?
2 Sleep is a fascinating subject.
3 Would you take part in sleep research?
4 Did you go out last night?
5 Have you seen the doctor about it yet?

Go to page 150 or your app for more information and practice.

Speaking

PREPARE

12 Go to page 174 and answer the sleep quiz. Think of experiences that help you to explain your answers.

13 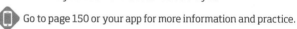 8.9 Listen to a discussion about whether it's healthier to be a night owl or an early riser. What answer do they give and what does it depend on?

SPEAK

14 Work in groups. Discuss the questions from the sleep quiz. Use the Useful phrases to help you.

Useful phrases

Maybe the best thing to do is to …
It's something to do with (your body clock).
If I remember rightly …
As far as I understand it, … I think you're right.

Develop
your
writing
page 130

8c ▶ Food for thought

> **Goal:** talk about food and cooking
>
> **Language focus:** complex comparatives
>
> **Vocabulary:** food and cooking

Vocabulary

1 Work in pairs and answer the questions.

   1 Who does the cooking in your house?

   2 What kinds of things do they/you cook?

   3 Do you know anyone who doesn't eat certain kinds of food? Why not?

2 Match the pictures with the verbs in the box below.

> blend   dip   drain   grate   grill   peel   roast
> simmer   sprinkle

3 a Complete the phrases with the verbs in Exercise 2.

   1 _____ until smooth / the mixture into a paste

   2 _____ the pasta, but keep the cooking water / the tofu and dry it

   3 _____ some sugar on top / chopped herbs over it

   4 _____ the potatoes / the meat in the oven

   5 _____ the cheese into a bowl / the carrots and add

   6 _____ the potatoes and cut into large pieces / the banana and slice it

   7 _____ the peppers until the skin blackens / the meat over a low flame

   8 _____ the bread into melted cheese / the chicken in the egg mixture

   9 _____ very gently for ten minutes / over a low heat

b Work in pairs. Think of a dish you have prepared recently (or that someone you know has). What was the dish? Which of the actions in Exercise 3a were used?

📱 Go to page 163 or your app for more vocabulary and practice.

Reading

4 a Work in pairs and discuss the questions.

   1 What kind of foods do vegetarians/vegans avoid?

   2 Who do you think it would be easier to prepare a meal for, a meat eater or a vegan? Why?

b Read the blog post and recipe. How does the author answer the questions in Exercise 4a?

Going vegan

My girlfriend first went veggie when she was ten, which is young, but she cared about animals so much that she couldn't imagine eating them. When she left home at 18 she decided to go the whole way and turn vegan. You might think that making a few small changes to your diet would make life only a little bit more complicated. But no: the move from vegetarian to vegan makes things way more complex. Cutting out dairy products and eggs can mean cooking becomes way more time-consuming (assuming you like to eat well, of course!). Eat meat and you can just grill a quick steak and maybe roast some potatoes. Go vegan and life is nowhere near as easy. In order to have a fully balanced diet, your meal needs much more thought and preparation. But I have to say my girlfriend has really opened my eyes to how good vegan food can be! So to help those of you who've only recently converted, here's one of our favourite recipes: peppery purple soup.

Ingredients

2 red onions	3 cups vegetable stock
1 red cabbage	2 cups almond milk
1 large apple	2 tablespoons balsamic vinegar
2 tablespoons olive oil	salt and pepper to taste
4 thyme leaves	

Method

1 Peel and slice the onions. Peel the outer layers of the red cabbage then slice into thin strips. Grate the apple flesh.

2 Put a large saucepan on a medium heat and add the olive oil. Once hot, throw in the onion, cabbage and apple. Add the thyme.

3 Cook for around 4 minutes. Then add the stock, milk and vinegar and put the lid on. Simmer for 10–15 minutes until the red cabbage is soft. Blend until smooth.

4 Serve it topped with fresh apple slices. Add salt and pepper to taste.

5 a Work in pairs. Look at the list of ingredients only. Work together to remember the recipe.

b Read the recipe again to check.

6 Work in groups and discuss the questions.

   1 Do you agree that being able to cook well is more important if you don't eat meat?

   2 How easy would it be for you to go vegan?

   3 How do you feel about the fact the blogger's girlfriend went vegetarian when she was ten?

   4 Do you agree that if you care about animals it's impossible to eat them?

Language focus

7 a **8.10 Listen to two friends discussing an attempt to cook the dish in the blog post. How did it go? Why?**

b Listen again. Complete extracts 1–4 with three or four words.

1 A: How was it?
B: Nowhere _____ it sounded!

2 Exactly. Nothing _____ the one on the blog!

3 Well, _____ stylishly presented, that's for sure.

4 The equipment they use is _____ expensive than yours.

8 Complete the language focus box with words and phrases from Exercise 7b and the blog post.

Complex comparatives

We can use lots of different words and phrases before comparatives to show degree.

To say a bit more
a tiny bit/a ¹_____ *bit/a bit more* complicated
(just) a touch nicer

To say a lot more
much more complex
²_____ more expensive
³_____ easier
ten/fifty/a ⁴_____ *times better*

To say a bit less
not ⁵_____ *as* complicated/easy (as …)
a tiny bit/a little bit/a bit/a touch less complex/
less nice than …

To say a lot less
⁶_____ *near as* difficult/simple (as …)
⁷_____ *like as* tasty/filling (as …)
much/a lot/miles/way less expensive than …
ten/fifty/a hundred times less greasy than …

9 a **8.11 Listen to the sentences and write what you hear. Notice that when we speak at normal speed, it can be difficult to hear the word *as*.**

b **8.12 Listen to the sentences and repeat.**

10 Rewrite the sentences using the words in brackets.

1 The vegan food served these days is miles better than it used to be.
The vegan food served back then _____ . (nowhere)

2 The food here is way cheaper than it is back home.
The food back home _____ . (nothing)

3 It wasn't as easy to cook as I thought it would be.
_____ I thought it would be. (ten / complicated)

4 These portions are much bigger than I'm used to.
These portions _____ than I'm used to. (way)

5 The food was probably a touch better last time we were there, but it was still great.
The food _____ it was the last time we ate there, but it was still great. (quite)

6 Her new recipes are boring compared to her old ones.
Her old recipes _____ her new ones. (miles)

11 a Write at least five comparisons using structures from the language focus box about one or more of the following topics.
- the food in two different places you've eaten in
- the food in two different countries you've been to
- the food that two different people you know cook
- a dish you've tried in at least two different places

b Work in pairs and discuss your ideas.

Go to page 150 or your app for more information and practice.

Speaking

PREPARE

12 Think of a dish that you cook well (or someone you know cooks well). Make a note of the ingredients and the recipe. Alternatively, look at the ingredients on page 174 and create a dish.

SPEAK

13 Work in groups and share your dishes. Respond using ideas from the Useful phrases box.

Useful phrases

So how long does it take to cook, all in all?
How many times have you cooked it?
Is it easy to get all the ingredients?
And how many people will that serve?
It sounds delicious. Actually, I sometimes cook something similar.

Develop your reading
page 110

67

Check and reflect: Units 7 and 8

1 a Complete the sentences with the best word. The first letter is given.

1 We agreed to a trial s_____ , so we're living apart at the moment.

2 He i_____ the family business when his father passed away last year.

3 It must be a bit strange for them now that all the kids have flown the n_____ .

4 After being together for years and years, they've finally decided to tie the k_____ .

5 We usually have a big family get-t_____ sometime around New Year.

6 Apparently, I was tiny when I was born. I arrived three weeks p_____ .

7 It's our wedding a_____ on Friday, so we're going away for the weekend.

8 I don't really talk to my brother. We had a big f_____ -out a couple of years ago.

b Use three words and phrases from Exercise 1a to talk about people you know.

2 Rewrite the words in italics using *must/can't*. Make any other changes necessary.

1 *I don't think he's* feeling very well. I'm sure he would be here otherwise.

2 I'm jealous you got to see inside the temple. *I bet that was* fascinating.

3 They have parties every single night? *I'd find that* really annoying.

4 She's working as a lawyer now, so *she's bound to be* making good money.

5 *I'm guessing that wasn't* an easy decision to make.

6 Some things in life *are just impossible to avoid.*

3 a Match verbs 1–6 with a–f to make collocations.

1	expose	a	tariffs on imports
2	make	b	to the final
3	impose	c	an offensive comment
4	get through	d	a riot
5	announce	e	a cover-up
6	trigger	f	a major breakthrough

b Work in pairs. Say what the causes and results might be of four things in Exercise 3a.

4 Correct the mistake in three of the underlined clauses.

1 I'd be rich by now if <u>I took that job I was offered.</u>

2 We would've won if <u>the referee hadn't awarded a penalty</u> for that dive.

3 You <u>won't be in this mess</u> if you'd listened to me.

4 He <u>wouldn't be working</u> for this company if his dad wasn't on the board!

5 If they withdrew from the treaty, <u>it'd have a huge impact</u> on the economy.

6 If <u>he's honest</u>, he would've handed the bag in to the police.

7 I wouldn't have taken the train if <u>I wasn't so terrified of flying</u>.

5 Choose the correct alternatives. In one sentence, both options are possible.

1 *Considering/Bearing in mind* they're a new party, they've done well so far.

2 It was a very close result. *In spite of that/Taking that into account,* there should be a recount.

3 I don't like some of their policies, but *even so/what's more* I'm still going to vote for them.

4 *Given/Despite* their good record on environmental issues, they will get my vote again.

5 He's been accused of lying. *Then again/Despite that,* it's hard to see who's 100 percent honest.

6 She's young, good on social media and *considering all that/on top of all that,* she talks sense.

6 a Complete the sentences with the nouns in the box.

election	manifesto	polling	referendum
system	turnout	vote	

1 In our electoral _____ , each party gets a percentage of seats based on the national vote.

2 It'd be better if you could vote from the age of 15. Voter _____ would be much higher.

3 I read somewhere that they're using the local swimming pool as a _____ station for this election.

4 The government have been accused of trying to fix the last _____ .

5 Casting your _____ should be made compulsory.

6 They're going to hold a _____ to decide whether all books should be sold at a fixed price.

7 In their _____ , they're promising to increase the minimum wage by 20 percent.

b Which of the ideas in Exercise 6a do you think are good? Why?

7 Put the words in the correct order to make questions.

1 you / how / about / heard / us / it / that / was?

2 would / good / visit / to / think / where / a / place / do / you / be?

3 that / spoke / you / was / who / it / to?

4 stayed / you / was / that / where / it?

5 that / exactly / it / what / do / you / is?

6 that / work / did / think / why / you / would / that?

7 suppose / you / means / even / do / that / what?

8 Choose the correct alternatives.

1 The system *submits/monitors* the movement of ships in the Mediterranean Sea.

2 I usually pay for things myself and then *submit/facilitate* an expense claim once a month.

3 We're currently *devising/collaborating* on a new project with some German scientists.

4 We specialise in *mending/fitting* cars and motorbikes.

5 She is the one that *delegates/heads up* the Latin American marketing team.

6 We're looking for someone to *fit/assemble* new locks on all our warehouses.

9 a Complete the questions with the words in the box.

jet lag   lie-in   light   nap   nod off   riser
sleepless

1 When was the last time you were out like a _____ as soon as you went to bed?
2 Have you ever suffered from really bad _____ ? When?
3 How often do you manage to have a _____ ? Until what time?
4 Do you know anyone who's a really early _____ ?
5 Do you ever manage to have a little _____ in the afternoon?
6 Do you ever _____ on the bus or train? Or at school or work?
7 Can you remember the last time you had a _____ night? What caused it?

b Work in pairs. Choose four questions to ask and answer.

10 Complete the conversations with one word.

1 A: It's a fascinating programme, don't you think?
   B: It _____ be sometimes, but sometimes it's a bit dull.
2 A: Would you be interested in trying it?
   B: Actually, I _____ last year. It really wasn't for me.
3 A: Did you manage to get a lie-in?
   B: No. I _____ have done, but my neighbour's dog woke me up.
4 A: Have you made an appointment to see the doctor?
   B: No, but I _____ if I'm still feeling like this tomorrow.
5 A: You look very well. Have you been away somewhere?
   B: No. I wish I _____ . I've just been working in the garden!
6 A: You should go and see someone about that cut. It looks bad.
   B: I _____ already. I went yesterday and they said it'll be fine.

11 a Complete the definitions with the correct verbs.

1 If you leave a stew to _____ , you leave it cooking on a low heat.
2 If you _____ a banana or a potato, you remove its skin.
3 If you _____ meat or potatoes, you cook them in the oven.
4 If you _____ meat, you cook it under a strong heat.
5 If you _____ cheese, you rub it over a metal tool that cuts it into very small pieces.
6 If you _____ sugar on a cake, you drop sugar evenly on the surface.
7 If you _____ a piece of food into a sauce, you put it in briefly and then take it out.

b How many of the things in Exercise 11a have you done in the last week?

12 Complete the sentences using the words in brackets and up to three other words.

1 They've done the place up. It's _____ it used to be. (ten / nicer)
2 It was _____ I was expecting it to be. (nowhere / expensive)
3 I'd read that the film was really boring, but it was _____ I'd expected. (miles / exciting)
4 The recipe made it sound easy, but it was _____ it looked. (way / complicated)
5 They were OK, but _____ the ones my mum usually makes. (nothing / tasty)
6 The food was a disappointment. It wasn't _____ the last time we ate there. (anywhere / good)
7 He makes a great curry although it's _____ I'm used to. (touch / spicier)
8 It tasted nice, but it wasn't _____ I'd hoped. I was still hungry after the meal! (quite / filling)

13 Decide if each sentence describes an upward or a downward trend.

1 There's been a sharp rise in the number of people leaving the country.
2 Trust in the company has now recovered to previous levels.
3 The graph shows that prices have rocketed.
4 You'll notice that there's been a serious slump in sales.
5 As you can see, there's been a gradual decline over recent years.
6 The share price has completely collapsed.
7 Since the start of the year, we've bounced back.
8 Sales have been dropping off since the CEO left at the beginning of this year.
9 The pound's value has fallen back sharply since the news broke.

Reflect

How confident do you feel about the statements below? Write 1–5 (1 = not very confident, 5 = very confident).

• I can comment on and tell stories about recent experiences.
• I can talk about the impact of news stories and events.
• I can take part in a debate (on issues around voting).
• I can give a presentation.
• I can talk in detail about what I do.
• I can talk about sleep and insomnia.
• I can discuss vegan food and cooking.

For more practice go to your Workbook or app.

Go online for the Roadmap video.

9A Feelings

> **Goal:** tell better stories and anecdotes

> **Grammar:** *not only* and *no sooner/as soon as*

> **Vocabulary:** feelings

Vocabulary

1 **Work in groups and discuss the questions.**

1 What's happening in each of the photos? How do you think the people are feeling?

2 Do you show your emotions much? Do you talk about them? Is that a good or bad thing?

3 Can you think of any situations where it's good or bad to show your feelings?

4 What kind of things (if any) upset you, cheer you up or embarrass you?

2 **Look at the pairs of words. In each case, decide which (if any) suggests a stronger feeling or emotion.**

1 ashamed / embarrassed

2 tired / exhausted

3 shaken up / traumatised

4 pleased / ecstatic

5 overwhelmed / surprised

6 disappointed / appalled

7 angry / furious

8 hilarious / funny

3 **Work in pairs. Match the groups of words and phrases a–h with the pairs of words in Exercise 2. Explain your reasons.**

a dead on my feet / collapse / hit a wall

b blind panic / a bit tearful / calm your nerves

c jump for joy / have a huge grin / get the news

d put my foot in it / go red / feel a bit foolish

e lash out / scream with rage / lose it

f crack up / rolling around / pull their leg

g so grateful / couldn't take it in / lost for words

h disgusting behaviour / tut / write to complain

4 **Choose two of the photos. Use words and phrases from Exercises 2 and 3 to describe them.**

📱 Go to page 164 or your app for more vocabulary and practice.

Listening

5 **You're going to hear four stories connected to smartphones and social media. First, work in pairs and discuss the questions.**

1 Have smartphones improved your life? Why/Why not?

2 Is social media more of a good or bad thing? Why?

6 a 🔊 **9.1 Listen to the stories and answer the questions.**

Story 1 Why was the speaker shaken up?

Story 2 Why did the speaker feel a bit overwhelmed?

Story 3 Why did the speaker feel slightly ashamed?

Story 4 Why did the speaker feel quite embarrassed?

b **Work in pairs. Compare your ideas. Explain how each story is connected to smartphones or social media.**

7 **Are the statements true (T), false (F) or not mentioned (NM)? Listen again and check.**

Story 1

a The incident happened before the play started.

b A lot of people were badly injured.

Story 2

a They received more money than they needed.

b She didn't run the marathon in the end.

Story 3

a The shop called the police.

b The speaker was embarrassed about getting into a fight.

Story 4

a Quite a few people were angry about the noise.

b The speaker decided to leave the opera house after the incident.

8 **Work in pairs. Discuss the stories you heard.**

1 Would you have felt the same as each of the speakers? Why/Why not?

2 Tell your partner about similar stories you have about:
- successful social media campaigns.
- riots and arguments connected to sales.
- people taking selfies or filming at an inappropriate time.

Grammar

9 a Work in pairs. Look at sentences 1–4 below and discuss:
- the position of the words in bold.
- why we might start sentences with negative adverbs like *not only* or *no sooner*.
- the grammar structures that follow the words in bold.

1 Some people were **not only** smiling and laughing, but actually taking selfies … and even posting on Facebook!
2 **Not only** had I not recognised the sound of my own phone, but I'd actually worked myself up into a temper.
3 There was a mad rush **as soon as** the doors opened.
4 **No sooner** had I pressed 'send' than it was getting retweeted.

b Read the grammar box and check your answers.

---

not only and *no sooner/as soon as*

not only
- We often use *not only* to link two actions/feelings that are surprising, especially the second one. The second action/feeling is often introduced with *but* and sometimes includes the words *actually* or *even*.

*Some people were **not only** smiling and laughing, **but actually** taking selfies.*

- We can add extra emphasis by starting a sentence with *not only* and putting the auxiliary verb before the subject (inverting).

***Not only were some people** smiling and laughing, but they were actually taking selfies.*

(= People were smiling and laughing and they were also taking selfies.)

- When there is no auxiliary verb or main verb *be*, we use *do, does,* or *did*.

***Not only did** we raise enough money for my son, we had enough to establish a foundation.*

no sooner/as soon as
- We use *as soon as* to link an action with an immediate reaction or consequence.

*There was a mad rush **as soon as** the doors opened.*

- We can add extra emphasis by starting with *no sooner* and inverting the subject and the auxiliary verb.

***No sooner had I** pressed 'send' than it was re-tweeted.*

(= As soon as I had pressed send, it was getting re-tweeted.)

We often start sentences with *not only* and *no sooner* when we want to make stories more exciting.

---

10 a 🔊 9.2 Listen to the sentences. Notice how we stress the underlined words and use intonation to show what surprised us.

1 Not <u>only</u> did he not apologise, he <u>actually</u> <u>laughed</u> at me.
2 Not <u>only</u> did she get <u>in</u>, she won a <u>scholarship</u>, too.
3 As <u>soon</u> as I said it, I <u>knew</u> I'd said the <u>wrong</u> <u>thing</u>.
4 No <u>sooner</u> had they started <u>using</u> it than they managed to <u>break</u> it.
5 No <u>sooner</u> is he <u>home</u> than he's making a <u>mess</u> everywhere.

b Listen again and repeat.

11 a Write complete sentences using the prompts.

1 no sooner / told her / I realised / put my foot in it
2 not only / expensive / it didn't work properly
3 the kids / not only / making a mess / disturbing the other passengers / on the plane
4 not only / people / cheering / actually jumping for joy
5 no sooner / the plane / in the air / the engine caught fire

b Work in pairs and compare your answers. Choose two sentences and discuss what you think happened before and after each one.

12 a Write two replies to each of the questions, one with *not only* and one with *no sooner*.

1 So did they say sorry?
   ***Not only** did they apologise, but they **also** gave me $500 compensation!*
   *Yeah, but **no sooner** had he done that than he managed to insult me again!*
2 So did you get an interview?
3 So did he offer to help you with the move?
4 So did you speak to their parents about their behaviour?
5 So what happened next?

b Take turns to read the questions and respond. Try to continue each conversation.

📱 Go to page 152 or your app for more information and practice.

Speaking

PREPARE

13 You're going to tell a story. Choose one of the feelings or emotions in Exercise 2 and make notes. Your story can be:
- something true that happened to you.
- something that happened to someone you know.
- something you've seen on social media.
- something you invent.

SPEAK

14 Work in pairs and tell your stories. Ask questions or respond as your partner tells the story. Use the Useful phrases to help you.

> **Useful phrases**
> A few years ago, I had this (frightening) experience.
> What happened was …
> Imagine if I'd …
> You must've been (exhausted).
> No way! You're kidding, right?

Develop your listening page 94

9B Habits

> **Goal:** describe other people's habits and how you feel about them

> **Grammar:** *will* and *would* for habits; *I wish + would*

> **Vocabulary:** describing people and their habits

Reading

1 a Work in pairs. Look at the habits in the pictures and put them in order from best (1) to worst (5).

b Change partner and compare your ideas. Discuss whether there are any bad habits you would like to stop or any good habits you would like to develop.

2 Read the blog post quickly and answer the questions.

   1 What does *a leopard can't change its spots* mean?

   2 Why does the writer <u>not</u> like this phrase?

Don't you just hate that phrase 'Well, a leopard can't change its spots' whenever someone disappoints us by falling back into bad old habits? Sayings like this make it seem as if our character and behaviour are fixed by nature with no hope for change, but is it actually true?

In the past, some psychologists believed that 'by the age of thirty the character has set like plaster and will never soften again' as William James put it, but more recent science shows how flexible – or plastic – our brains are. Examples of people undergoing profound change are all around us. Children experience all manner of changes before they reach puberty. Watching our first child being born or loved ones die will often bring about radical changes in the way we view the world and the way that we behave. Some people become more cautious with age, others seem to be set free by it! The reality is that we all change throughout our lives and even the most damaging habits can be broken – given enough patience, support and guidance.

Which is the point. I'm not saying change is easy – simply that it can, and does, happen! When we take the view that it's impossible to change our behaviour, it's usually because we find it easier to say 'I am who I am' than to keep questioning our own actions and take responsibility for our behaviour.

---

3 Which of the points 1–5 does the writer make in the blog post?

   1 People accuse the writer of not changing bad habits.

   2 People sometimes try to justify boys' bad behaviour as something natural.

   3 William James argued that behaviour became fixed with age.

   4 Changing the way we think and act isn't unusual.

   5 People should make more effort to give up bad habits.

4 a Write down five events in life that you think have the biggest impact on how people behave. Think about what kind of changes each event often brings about.

b Work in pairs. Compare your lists and explain your choices.

Grammar

5 9.5 Listen to two people talking about a former colleague. Answer the questions.

   1 What changes do they describe in the colleague?

   2 What caused the changes and what were the results?

   3 How do the speakers feel about these changes?

6 a Look at extracts 1–5 from the listening and answer the questions.

   1 *... he was the kind of guy who'd take the lift to go up one floor and have junk food for breakfast, lunch and dinner.*
     Is this talking about single actions or repeated ones?

   2 *... he won't even wear leather ... these days.*
     Is this a general habit or a plan for the future?

   3 *I'll sometimes go a week without any meat at all, ...*
     Is this a promise about the future?

   4 *I just wish they would keep it to themselves.*
     What do the people actually do?

   5 *I wish you wouldn't see the worst in things all the time.*
     How does the speaker feel about this habit?

b Read the grammar box and check your ideas.

will and *would* for habits; *I wish + would*

- We can use *will/won't* to talk about repeated actions or habits in the present.

I'm not a huge sports fan, but I'll watch the World Cup if it's on.

I do work hard, but I won't normally bring things home from the office at the weekend.

Note that in both sentences above, we can use the present simple instead with no real change of meaning.

- We use *would/wouldn't* (or *would never*) to talk about repeated past actions or habits.

When we first met, he'd always bring me flowers.

He'd never/He wouldn't (ever) offer to help.

Note that in both sentences above, we can also use the past simple or *used to* + verb without any real change of meaning.

- We use *I wish you/he/she/it*, etc. + *would/wouldn't* to talk about annoying habits that we would like to change.

I wish she'd stop going on about her job. It's so boring!

I wish you wouldn't keep interrupting me when I'm talking. It's very rude!

7 a **9.6 Listen to the sentences. Notice that when spoken at normal speed, we can hardly hear *would* and *will* at all.**

1   When I was a kid, I'd play the piano for hours after school most days.

2   My dad would take me fishing every Saturday when I was young.

3   I wish he'd help round the house a bit more.

4   He'll always get up early and go out for a run.

5   She'll usually get what she wants.

b **Listen again and repeat.**

8 **Complete the comment below about the post in Exercise 2. Use the verbs in the box with *would, wouldn't, will* or *won't*.**

take	complain	do	miss	relax	stay	study

Great post! I couldn't agree more. Up until she was about 15 my sister used to be really lazy. She **1**_____ never _____ any homework and some days she **2**_____ even _____ a pen or a notebook to class. She always used to get bad marks and no-one ever really expected much of her. How wrong we all were, though. She's 18 now and doing really well at school. Most days, she **3**_____ behind in the library for a couple of hours after class. She **4**_____ never _____ any lectures and she **5**_____ ever _____ about the workload she's got. It's been a remarkable change. To be honest, I sometimes wish she **6**_____ a bit more and take it easy. I know I shouldn't say this, but I do kind of wish she **7**_____ quite so hard. It's starting to make me look like the lazy one!

9 **Think of three habits you have now (or once had) and how they annoy people you know. What do people wish you would do? Tell a partner.**

 Go to page 152 or your app for more information and practice.

Vocabulary

10 a **Match 1–10 with follow-up comments a–j.**

1   My sister's so **cynical**.

2   My gran's always seemed very **content** with her life.

3   My daughter never gives up – she's very **determined**.

4   She has a very **dry sense of humour**.

5   She can be very **intense**.

6   My dad's always been pretty **liberal**.

7   My granddad was a very **modest** sort of chap.

8   Everyone said he was a very **charming** man.

9   He was a very **demanding** child.

10   Her husband was such a **controlling** man.

a   I mean, you'll never hear her complaining or anything.

b   She'll usually see the worst motives in everything.

c   Once she's decided to do something, she'll do it!

d   She's so emotional! I wish she'd **lighten up** a bit.

e   She'll always look dead serious when she's joking.

f   He was certainly **a smooth talker**. He could sell you anything.

g   He'd constantly **whine** if he didn't get attention.

h   He'd always need to know where she was going.

i   He'd always let me stay out late and have friends over.

j   He'd never boast, even though he was very talented.

b **Work in pairs. Discuss which words in bold describe more positive/negative characteristics.**

11 **Choose words in bold in Exercise 10a to describe people you know now or once knew. Work in pairs and compare your ideas. Give examples.**

 Go to your app for more practice.

Speaking

PREPARE

12 **Think about someone you know who has really changed/hasn't changed at all. Think about:**

1   their habits in the past and now.

2   why and how they've changed/haven't changed.

3   anything you still wish they'd do – or wouldn't do. Why?

SPEAK

13 **Work in pairs. Tell your partner about the person. Use the Useful phrases to help you.**

Useful phrases

She's much better than she used to be.

If anything, he's getting worse!

I just find it really annoying.

It really drives me mad!

Have you told him/her how you feel about it?

> Develop your writing
> page 132

9c All the rage

> **Goal:** talk about trends
> **Language focus:** making new words
> **Vocabulary:** trends

Vocabulary

1 Work in groups and look at the photos. Discuss:

1 which things you see a lot of where you live.
2 which used to be more popular.
3 which things you've never seen.
4 what you think about them.

2 a Read the sentences. Check you understand the words in bold. Which show something is getting lower, and which show something is getting higher?

1 The number of trendy coffee shops has **soared** over the last couple of years.
2 The size of the average family has **shrunk** quite dramatically since the seventies.
3 Sales of razors have **slumped** by 15 percent.
4 The cost of renewable energy has **plunged** over the last decade.
5 Two of the biggest supermarkets here have recently **slashed** the price of petrol.
6 Standards in our schools have **slipped** a lot since I was a kid.
7 There's been a **dip** in university applications in the last couple of years.
8 There's been a real **hike** in the price of tickets for major sporting events.
9 Since 2016, there's been a **surge** in the number of British people applying for Irish passports.
10 There's been a steady **decline** in teenage smoking this century.
11 There's been an **epidemic** of fake news on social media over the last few years.
12 There's been a recent **explosion** of apps that have been brought out to support mental health.

b Work in pairs and discuss the questions.

1 What do you think are the three most significant changes in Exercise 2a? Why?
2 What might be the causes of these trends?
3 What might be the results?

Go to page 164 or your app for more vocabulary and practice.

Reading

3 a You're going to read an article about trendspotters. What do you think they do? Which industries do you think they might work in?

b Read the article and check your ideas.

4 Read the article again and answer the questions.

1 How does technology create the need for trendspotters?
2 What's the most valuable talent that trendspotters possess?
3 How do they help in fields like fashion and marketing?
4 How do online dictionaries differ from print ones?
5 What does the author say is significant about the word *trend?*

We live in a fast-changing world. Information technology is advancing at a remarkable pace and what is fresh and innovative today may easily become outdated and commonplace tomorrow. Given this, many professionals struggle to make predictions about the trends that will come to dominate their fields in the years to come. Businesses complain that consumers are increasingly likely to change their minds – and their shopping habits – without any obvious reasons and a general panic develops. This is where the trendspotter comes in.

On a basic level, trendspotters do what the name suggests – they spot new fashions, ideas and activities that are becoming popular. However, there's far more to it than that. Many trends come and go without making any major impact. What top professionals in the field do is consider society as a whole. They look for the shifts in mood and mindset that will have a lasting effect, and identify consumer trends that capture this zeitgeist. And they get very well paid for doing so!

The function of trendspotters is more obvious in some industries than others. In the fashion world, their experience and observations on the street help forward-looking clothing companies set next season's trends. While in marketing, knowing which new platforms all the kids are using can be the difference between survival and slow death. But trendspotting is also essential to some fields of work that perhaps you might not immediately think of – such as creating dictionaries!

New words pour into the language all the time and deciding which of the thousands of new creations should end up in print is the job of professional lexicographers. While many online dictionaries often just crowdsource definitions and examples, words only get into official dictionaries such as the *Oxford English Dictionary* when they are used by enough people who all agree they mean the same thing. Lexicographers research how – and how frequently – new items are used, and in doing so, they often uncover interesting trends. For example, just a few years ago, the use of the word *trend* as a verb started soaring – and it's been trending ever since!

Language focus

5 Work in pairs. Match the words in bold in 1–6 with definitions a–f.

1 They managed to **crowdsource** $100,000 to start up their business.

2 The job of a trendspotter is to capture the **zeitgeist**.

3 They're a hot new band most definitely on the **up**.

4 The children's **edutainment** market is growing fast.

5 Reading on social media what all my friends are doing just gives me terrible **FOMO**.

6 It's a brilliant novel – completely **unputdownable**.

a video games, TV programmes, and so on that are intended to be both educational and entertaining

b the general mood or quality of a particular time

c get information or money from lots of people by asking anyone to contribute (usually via the internet)

d so exciting you don't want to stop reading

e a feeling that you are missing out on exciting events

f rise

6 a Look again at the words in bold in Exercise 5 and the words around them. How do you think they are pronounced?

b 9.7 Listen and repeat what you hear.

7 Look at the language focus box. Match the words in bold in Exercise 5 with the ways of making new words a–f.

Making new words

There are six main ways of making new words.

a Derivation

The most common way of making a new word is to add a prefix or a suffix to words that already exist.
*The coffee there was completely **undrinkable**.*
*I'm sort of **busyish**, but not crazy busy.*

b Conversion

Taking a word from one word class and using it in another, so a noun may start being used as an adjective or a verb.
*Once Friday night is here, we can go out and **party**.*
*You can **verb** almost any noun in English.*

c Abbreviations

A short form of a longer word or phrase.
ETA (= estimated time of arrival)
uni (= university)

d Loanwords

Words taken from one language and used in another.
karaoke (= from Japanese)   yoga (= from Sanskrit)

e Compounding

Words formed by putting two *complete* words together. The first word is like an adjective describing the second.
a trendspotter   a technology startup

f Portmanteau words

Words formed by combining *parts* of two other words.
brunch (= a meal eaten in the late morning so it's a combination of breakfast and lunch)

8 Look at the words in the box. Which can be used both as nouns and verbs?

decline	dip	epidemic	explosion	hike	plunge
shrink	slash	slip	slump	soar	surge

9 Work in pairs. Answer the questions.

1 Which nouns in the box can also be verbs?

2 Which nouns in the box can you combine with other nouns to make compound nouns?

3 Which nouns in the box can we add a prefix or suffix to?

balloon	elbow	eye	friend	Google	Hoover
impact	taxi	workshop			

Go to page 152 or your app for more information and practice.

Speaking

PREPARE

10 Make notes on at least three trends that you have noticed where you live. Choose from these areas or your own ideas.

- changing eating and drinking habits
- social media and internet use
- lifestyle choices and free-time activities
- clothes, hair and fashion
- ways of getting around
- advertising and marketing
- changes to cultural attitudes
- shopping and consumer culture

11 9.8 Listen to a discussion about one of the trends in Exercise 10. Answer the questions.

1 Which trend do they talk about?

2 Do the speakers follow the trend?

3 Why do they think the trend is happening?

SPEAK

12 Work in groups. Compare recent trends you have noticed. Use the Useful phrases to help you. Discuss:

1 what you think has caused each one.

2 whether you think they will remain popular.

3 how you feel about them.

Useful phrases

I think it's basically a reaction against …
I see it as a reflection of …
I can't see it lasting, to be honest.
I'm (not really) a big fan of it.

13 What do you feel the most significant trend is? Share your ideas with the class.

Develop your reading
page 112

9D > English in action

> **Goal:** manage informal conversations
> **Vocabulary:** colloquial and idiomatic language

Listening 1

1 **Work in pairs and discuss the questions.**

   1 When might it be useful or important to be able to have informal conversations?

   2 Who's the most sociable person you know? How do they make friends and start conversations?

   3 Think of three people you know from different backgrounds or ages. Are there any topics you talk about more or less with each of them? How might each conversation begin?

2 9.9 **Listen to the start of three conversations. Match each conversation with one of the following:**

   a drawing attention to a problem

   b asking about the other person's life

   c mentioning the time since they last met

   d commenting on the weather

   e talking about sports team or other interests

   f commenting on the news

3 a **Complete the Useful phrases 1 box with category headings a–f in Exercise 2.**

  b **In each conversation, the speakers use two phrases from the box. Can you remember which ones? Listen again to check.**

Useful phrases 1

1 _____
Miserable day!
Turned out nice, hasn't it?
Gorgeous weather!

2 _____
That's just typical!
I don't believe it!

3 _____
You must be pleased/a bit depressed at how United are doing.
Did you see the race on Sunday?
You like opera, don't you?

4 _____
Hello stranger!
Long time, no see!
It's been ages!

5 _____
What've you been up to?
How's work/business/the family?
What's up?

6 _____
This [news story] is great/a disaster, isn't it?
Did you see this business about (news story)?

---

4 **Work in pairs. Start similar conversations using the phrases in the Useful phrases 1 box. Try to continue the conversations.**

5 9.10 **Listen to the first conversation in full. Find out:**

   1 how well the speakers know each other.

   2 where they are.

   3 three topics they mention.

6 a **Try to complete the sentences from the listening with three words in each gap. Contractions, such as *don't*, count as one word. Listen again and check.**

   1 Still, it's probably _____ you did, what with the way the trains are.

   2 Getting to work _____ !

   3 _____ or frozen tracks at this time of year, can they?

   4 _____ of that yet.

   5 _____ my breath.

   6 _____ ! Here it comes.

  b **Work in pairs. Discuss what each sentence 1–6 is referring to.**

Vocabulary

7 **Replace the colloquial and idiomatic language in bold in 1–6 with definitions a–j.**

   1 A: It's **a good job** you're here. You can help me shift all this stuff.

      B: Marvellous! Just what I wanted to do, spend my afternoon **chucking out** rubbish.

   2 A: I'm seeing a few of my **uni mates** tonight. Do you fancy coming?

      B: Yeah, I'd **be up for** that.

   3 A: Did you know your ex is tying the knot? And apparently, a move to Australia is **on the cards**.

      B: Really? Well, **touch wood**, I'll never have to see him again!

   4 A: How come you're in such a bad mood?

      B: I don't want **go into** it now. Let's just say I had a **rubbish** day.

   5 A: They were all **going on** about the boss and saying how hard it is to work under her.

      B: Well, she might not be here much longer. Apparently, she might **get the chop**.

a hopefully	**f** be fired
b lucky	**g** like to do
c terrible	**h** complaining
d likely to happen	**i** throwing away
e discuss	**j** university friends

8 Work in pairs. Discuss how many of the expressions:

   1 you've heard before. In what situation?

   2 you would like to try and use.

   3 you would never use. Explain why.

9 a Read the information box. Say the examples.

> **Elision**
>
> In normal speech, we often miss out sounds and in some cases, pronouns, auxiliary verbs and other grammar words as well.
>
> What have you been up to? → What you been up to? →
> /wɒtʃəbɪnʌptə/
>
> It sounds a right mess. → Sounds a right mess. →
> /saʊnzəraɪmes/

  b 🔊 9.11 Listen and write down the five phrases you hear. Note that you might not hear every word. Then work in pairs and compare what you wrote.

  c Practise saying the five phrases.

Listening 2

10 🔊 9.12 Listen to the two other conversations from Exercise 2 in full. For each conversation find out:

  a where the speakers know each other from.

  b what topics they cover in the conversation.

11 Look at the sentences from the conversations. Listen again and tick the phrases in the Useful phrases 2 box that were used to respond to them.

   1 I managed to avoid the chop, but now I'm doing the job of two people.

   2 The bottom line is she's on the mend now.

   3 Yeah, and I'm going to be a bridesmaid!

   4 I've got my sights set on an Iron Woman event now.

   5 That's my evening done for.

   6 You're a lifesaver!

   7 The boss just said he needs all that stuff he asked us for tomorrow morning.

   8 He did, but he was wrong.

> **Useful phrases 2**
>
> **Agree something is bad**
> It's a joke!
> Typical!
>
> **Comment on something good.**
> Good stuff!
> Nice one!
>
> **Sympathise**
> What a pain!
> Phew!
>
> **Show surprise or disbelief**
> No way!
> Good grief!
> Seriously?
>
> **Accept thanks**
> No worries.
> Don't be silly.
>
> **Show difference**
> Rather you than me!
> Suit yourself.
>
> **Change the subject**
> Talking of which …
> Oh, speak of the devil.
>
> **Ending conversations**
> Anyway, I've got to dash. See you later.
> I'd best be off. Speak again soon.

12 a Choose two phrases from the Useful phrases 2 box you could use to respond to each of the sentences 1–6.

   1 I've got to work late.

   2 We're off camping this weekend.

   3 That's so sweet of you.

   4 They said they'll sort it tomorrow.

   5 Simone's said she's going to pick up the tab.

   6 Look at the state of this place!

  b Work in pairs. Take turns to say one of the sentences in Exercise 12a, and respond to it. Try to continue the conversation in each case.

Speaking

13 You're going to have informal conversations. Choose four of the topics in the box. Think about how to introduce the topics and which phrases you might use.

| work | a celebrity | the weather | family | TV/film |
| politics | a holiday | a social event | sport | |

14 a Work in pairs or small groups. Start and continue a conversation. Talk about the topics you chose and find opportunities to use your phrases.

  b Repeat the activity, using different phrases/topics.

> For more practice go to your Workbook or app.

Go online for the Roadmap video.

10A Eureka!

› **Goal:** report on and discuss science
› **Grammar:** prepositions 2
› **Vocabulary:** science

Grammar

1 **Work in pairs and discuss the questions.**

1 What do you think is happening in each of the photos?
2 Do you know anyone who works in or studies science? What do they (want to) do?
3 Did you enjoy studying science at school? Why/Why not?
4 What do you think have been the most important scientific discoveries of recent times?

2 🔊 10.1 **Listen to a short conversation. Which is the best summary for what the man explains?**

1 How he became a physicist.
2 What his mother does for a job.
3 Why he doesn't get on with his mother.
4 Why he doesn't want the same job as his mother.
5 How his mother is helping him find a job.

3 a **Work in pairs. Add the missing prepositions to extracts 1–8 from the conversation.**

1 What field of physics does she work?
2 ... but to be honest, it usually goes my head.
3 It's not something you've ever been interested doing?
4 ... having your mum there to help you?
5 ... you know, I'd get frustrated and it'd often end in an argument ...
6 Plus, there were other subjects I was just better.
7 She used to make the odd comment, but you know, it wasn't something she went on.
8 In the end, she's more concerned that I find something I'm happy.

b **Listen again and check your answers.**

4 **Read the grammar box and choose the correct alternatives.**

Prepositions 2

Prepositions are followed by a noun, pronoun or ¹*-ing/infinitive* form of a verb.
*It's not something you've ever been interested **in doing**?*

• Some prepositions are used with specific verbs, adjectives or nouns or are part of a fixed phrase.
*It just goes **over my head**.*

• In spoken and informal written English, a preposition connected to a question word or relative pronoun goes ²*before the question word or relative pronoun/at the end of the clause*.
*What field of physics does she work **in**?* rather than
In what field of physics does she work? (more formal)
*There were subjects that I was better **at**.* rather than
There were subjects at which I was better. (more formal)

• Both prepositions and adverbs can combine with verbs to form phrasal verbs. When a verb is followed by a preposition, the object of the verb ³*usually/never* goes between the two.
*I guess that's why I **went down** a different track.*

• However, when a verb is followed by an adverb, the object of the verb can come between them.
*We're still trying to figure **it** out.*

• Some prepositions and prepositional phrases can join two parts of a sentence. Notice the *-ing* form that follows.
*I didn't understand it, despite my mum **trying** to explain.*

5 a 🔊 10.2 **Listen to the phrases. Notice how the prepositions are reduced or not fully stressed.**

1 What are you doing at the moment?
2 They're leaving very early in the morning.
3 We're still waiting for the results.
4 I'm trying to listen to this.

b **Listen again and repeat the sentences.**

6 a **Sentences 1–6 contain mistakes according to the rules in the grammar box. Find and correct them.**

1 Do you know for what Marie Curie won the Nobel Prize? Do you know any other Nobel winners?
2 About what was the last science programme you saw?
3 Are you keen science fiction?
4 Could you ever get used to work in a lab all day?
5 Do people think highly scientists in your country?
6 What scientific things would you like to know more about, if you had time to look them into?

b **Work in pairs. Ask and answer the questions.**

 Go to page 154 or your app for more information and practice.

Reading

7 a Work in pairs. Read the title of the article and discuss the questions.

1 Why do you think unusual questions might be important in science?
2 Have you heard of the Ig Nobel awards before?
3 What do you think they might be?

b Read the article and find out:

1 what the Ig Nobel awards are.
2 why they are called Ig Nobel.
3 who Andre Geim is.

8 Read the article again. Then work in pairs and explain what was said about the things in the box.

> ears   saliva   frog   graphene

The Ig Nobel Awards: celebrating the power of an unusual question

The science fiction writer Isaac Asimov once said that the most exciting phrase to hear in science – the one that indicates new discoveries – is not 'Eureka!' but 'That's funny'. Presumably, Asimov meant funny peculiar rather than funny ha-ha, but science can sometimes be both. This is the idea behind the Ig Nobel Awards, which recognise published scientific research that makes you first laugh, but then think. Ig Nobel is a play on the word *ignoble* (an adjective that describes an action that should make you feel ashamed) and on the Nobel Prize, which is awarded for significant achievements in science and literature.

Some questions past winners of Ig Nobel Awards have investigated are: Do old men have big ears? Is human saliva a good cleaning agent? Can you levitate a frog in a magnetic field?

Is investment in such research really worthwhile? Well, the investigation into ears was the first step in getting doctors involved in research. The doctors overcame fears that patients wouldn't want to participate and learnt research techniques. The saliva researchers not only proved that spit was good for polishing, but also identified the main chemical responsible for these effects.

What the long-term benefit of the research will be remains to be seen, but that's the point Asimov makes – scientists rarely start with the idea of a life-changing discovery. Take Andre Geim. He won a Nobel Prize for discovering graphene, a material one-atom thick, but which is stronger than diamond. He calls his work 'search' (rather than 're-search') and his random journey through science all started with a frog floating in the air.

9 Work in pairs. Discuss your opinion of statements 1–4.

1 Investment in any kind of research is a good thing.
2 Awards should not be given to individual scientists.
3 They should publish more research describing experiments that failed.
4 All children are natural scientists.

Vocabulary

10 Complete the sentences with the correct form of the words in brackets.

1 My daughter's at university at the moment. She wants to be a _____ when she graduates. (physics)
2 We need to carry out more _____ work before we can be sure of the results. (experiment)
3 It is _____ possible, but it hasn't been done. (theory)
4 He suffers from a rare _____ disorder. (gene)
5 The creation of a _____ model allows scientists to study things in more detail. (reliability)
6 We'll do a _____ analysis of the data. (statistics)
7 They're _____ this new drug at the moment. (trial)
8 The people were selected at _____ . (randomly)
9 It's an interesting theory, but we've yet to find any clear _____ of it. (prove)
10 We now need to _____ the data according to particular categories. (classification)
11 After an investigation, they were forced to admit that the data was _____ . (invalidate)
12 I'm creating a computer _____ and will let you know what happens. (simulate)

11 Work in groups and discuss the questions.

1 Can you think of anything that is theoretically possible, but hasn't actually been done yet?
2 What are two human features that can be genetic?
3 What things might make research invalid?
4 What are some ways computer simulations can help different kinds of jobs?

 Go to your app for more practice.

Speaking

> PREPARE

12 Work in pairs. Student A: Turn to page 168. Student B turn to page 173.

> SPEAK

13 a Work in groups. Use the Useful phrases and tell each other about the Ig Nobel Award you chose. Discuss:

1 what else you might want to find out about each topic.
2 what uses this research might be put to.

Useful phrases

Maybe the most amazing thing about it all is …
One thing I still don't get is how/why/what …
I guess one major implication is …
Explain it to me again. I don't get it.
What's the point of it, though?

b Which do you think is the most useful research?

Develop your writing page 134

10B A great read

> **Goal:** describe books
> **Grammar:** linking words and phrases
> **Vocabulary:** book reviews

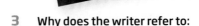

Reading

1 a Choose the alternatives that are true for you.

1 I read *more than/ less than/ about the same amount as* I did five years ago.
2 I prefer reading *digital books/ printed books/ social media posts and comments.*
3 I *never/ hardly ever/ sometimes/ often* read a book the whole way through.
4 I *usually/ rarely/ never* read more than one book at a time.

b Work in groups. Explain your choices.

2 a Read an article about trends in reading. Write one sentence to summarise the main idea.

b Compare your summary with a partner. Which summary do you prefer? Why?

Is reading really dead?

You will, no doubt, be familiar with the argument. We are supposedly experiencing a reading crisis **[1]on account of** the ever-expanding role that technology plays in the life of young people around the world. Many of those who grew up before the arrival of the internet imagine they once inhabited a golden age of literacy, **[2]whereas** kids today are believed to be so addicted to their devices that they won't read at all **[3]unless** sentences come in the form of super short comments on social media! It's a simple story many would like to believe. The reality, however, is far more complex.

Those teens you see staring at their phones may not be texting or uploading selfies; instead, they could well be in the middle of a gripping new thriller delivered via a popular new app where readers see stories unfold in text message form and tap their screens to see more.

It's not just digital reading that's all the rage, though, as the majority of under-25s do actually still prefer printed books. In fact, those in this age group read more than older generations do and, **[4]what's more**, they also read more than the previous generation did at the same age . . . not that you'd know it from listening to parents moan!

So what's causing this unexpected surge of interest in the written word? Well, firstly, young people are more likely to be in higher education or starting out in professional careers than their parents' generation. **[5]Consequently**, much of their reading is done to support their development in these areas. The attachment to physical formats, meanwhile, seems to be **[6]down to** the fact that paper copies can more easily be written on, highlighted and **[7]subsequently** shared with friends.

While you may not hear about all this in the daily news, you can **[8]nonetheless** be sure that reading is still alive and well.

3 Why does the writer refer to:

1 a golden age of literacy?
2 a popular new app?
3 parents moaning?
4 higher education and professional careers?
5 highlighting and sharing books?

4 Work in pairs and discuss the questions.

1 How far do your experiences match the arguments in the article?
2 What other ways can technology promote reading or stop people reading?
3 Does it actually matter if people read less? Why/Why not?

Grammar

5 a Replace the linking words and phrases in bold in the article with the ones in the box so the meaning is unchanged.

| as a result of | as such | due to | if ... don't |
| nevertheless | on top of that | then | while |

b Work in pairs and compare your answers.

6 Complete the grammar box using the linking words and phrases in bold in the article and in the box in Exercise 5a.

Linking words and phrases

Linking words and phrases can be used to show:

Contrast
on the other hand, despite, in spite of, even though, although, however, all the same, _____ , _____ , _____ , _____

Condition
otherwise, provided, providing, so long as, as long as, in case, whether, even if, _____ , _____

Time/order
after that, meanwhile, during, once, as soon as, _____ , _____

Addition
not to mention, as well, not only ... but also, _____ , _____

Cause
due to, owing to, because of, thanks to, _____ , _____ , _____

Result/purpose
so as to, in order to, thus, therefore, _____ , _____

7 a 🔊 **10.3 Listen to six statements about books. Write down what you hear. Notice how words often link where a consonant sound is followed by a vowel.**

b Work in pairs and compare what you wrote. Then listen again and repeat.

8 **Choose the correct alternatives.**

1 I finished it – *whether/ otherwise* or not I actually understood it is another matter!

2 It's an ambitious and well-written thriller, *not to mention/ subsequently* a really gripping read.

3 The book deals with some dark subject matter. *All the same/ As such,* it's probably got quite limited appeal.

4 This book is more serious than her earlier work. *As such/ All the same,* I found it very enjoyable.

5 At the beginning, the main character has just moved to the city *thanks to/ in order to* find work.

6 I discovered this book *not to mention/ thanks to* a friend of mine, who kept telling me how great it was.

7 It was on display in an airport bookshop. *Whether/ Otherwise,* I'd probably never have heard of it.

8 The protagonists were best friends but *as such/ subsequently* fall out badly.

9 a **Complete sentences by adding the names of books or authors, and your own ideas.**

1 On the one hand, I think _____ is _____ , but on the other, I _____ .

2 I really enjoyed _____ , even though _____ .

3 I've generally avoided reading _____ due to _____ .

4 I really love _____ , although I know lots of people really don't!

b Work in pairs and compare your ideas.

📱 Go to page 154 or your app for more information and practice.

Vocabulary

10 **Work in pairs and check you understand the words in bold. Then look at the covers of the books A–F at the top of the page and discuss the questions.**

1 What kind of book do you think each one is?

2 Where and when might each one **be set**?

3 Who do you think the **protagonist** might be?

4 Which of the books would you expect to be **gripping** or **descriptive** or **disturbing**?

5 Which might you expect to have a **twist at the end**?

11 a **Complete each review with the words in the box.**

controversial   descriptive   gripping
protagonist   twist

Life of Pi by Yann Martel

Named after the book's **1**_____ , a teenage Indian boy who ends up trapped on a boat in the Pacific Ocean with a tiger, *Life of Pi* is a **2**_____ adventure story that also deals with big and sometimes **3**_____ themes such as religious belief, truth and loss. Its Canadian author uses highly **4**_____ imagery throughout and there's a remarkable **5**_____ at the end that changes the whole book. It's a really excellent read and if it sounds vaguely familiar, it may be because it was made into a big budget film in 2012.

disturbing   masterpiece   narrator   portrait   set

The Forgotten Waltz by Anne Enright

6_____ in and around Dublin, the capital of Ireland, during the boom years of the first decade of this century, this novel is nothing less than a **7**_____ . At the centre of the story is the **8**_____ , Gina Moynihan, a married woman in her 30s who is struggling to understand how her life has changed in such a damaging and **9**_____ way. The novel is a powerful **10**_____ of Gina and explores the journey of the human heart, the connections that keep us together and the lies that can break us apart. It's beautifully written and stays with you long after you finish reading it.

b Which of the books would you rather read? Why?

📱 Go to page 165 or your app for more vocabulary and practice.

Speaking

PREPARE

12 **Choose two of the following to talk about. Plan what you want to say about each one.**
- a book you think is a masterpiece
- a book you had to read at school
- a book that changed your life
- a book you think is overrated

13 🔊 **10.4 Listen to a conversation about one of the topics in Exercise 12. Which one is it? Find out:**
1 which book they discuss.
2 whether both speakers have read it.
3 what they think of it.

SPEAK

14 a **Work in pairs. Talk about the books you chose.**

b Which book might be most interesting for the class?

Develop your reading page 114

81

10c A good laugh

> **Goal:** tell jokes
> **Language focus:** puns
> **Vocabulary:** talking about humour

Vocabulary

1 **Work in pairs and discuss the questions.**

1 What comedy film or TV show from your country makes you laugh? What's it about?
2 What's your favourite international comedy film or TV show? Why?
3 What comedy films or TV shows do you <u>not</u> like? Why?
4 Who is the funniest person you know? Why?
5 Do you like telling jokes? Why/Why not?

2 **Complete the definitions with the words in the box.**

> black   dry   get it (x2)   irony   practical
> a pun   satire   slapstick   a stereotype
> a straight face   witty

1 _____ is a type of humour where you say the opposite of what you mean. For example, when it's pouring with rain and blowing a gale, you might say 'Lovely weather!'.
2 _____ is a kind of physical comedy. For example, someone falls over or gets soaked.
3 _____ humour is when people find something funny in a very serious situation or make jokes about a difficult topic.
4 If you play a _____ joke on someone, you do something unexpected to make them look silly.
5 _____ is a fixed idea about a kind of person or group of people.
6 _____ is the use of humour to criticise people – especially politicians – or to show how silly or wicked they are.
7 If you keep _____ , you don't smile or laugh when you say or hear something funny.
8 If someone has a _____ sense of humour, they often say things that are the opposite of what they mean, and generally have a serious expression even when they are joking.
9 _____ is a play on words where you use words which have two meanings to make a joke.
10 If something or someone is _____ they are both clever and funny. They make use of plays on words.
11 Someone telling a joke might ask '_____ ?' at the end to see if you understand or when people don't understand they might say 'I don't _____ '.

3 a **Match pictures A–E with types of humour 1–5.**

1 slapstick/a practical joke
2 black humour
3 a pun
4 irony
5 a stereotype

b **Work in pairs. Which joke do you like the best? Why?**

4 **Use words from Exercise 2 to talk about some of the things below.**

* your own sense of humour
  I'd say I have quite a dry sense of humour. People don't always realise I'm making a joke.
* a friend's sense of humour
* comedians you like or don't like
* a time you wanted to laugh but couldn't
* the cartoons

Go to page 165 or your app for more vocabulary and practice.

Listening

5 a **You're going to listen to a radio programme discussing humour. First, discuss the questions.**

1 What makes people laugh?
2 Does it differ between countries or is our sense of humour universal?

b 🔊 **10.5 Listen to the radio programme. What conclusion do the speakers come to about the questions in Exercise 5a?**

6 **Work in pairs. Discuss why 1–6 were mentioned. Listen again and check your ideas.**

1 *Just for Laughs*
2 *Qian Ren 3*
3 What's a panda's favourite food?
4 stereotypes of people from different regions
5 Plato
6 the ontic-epistemic theory

The English are such bad cooks, their speciality is indigestion.

I TOLD YOU I WAS SICK.

Language focus

7 a Work in pairs. Discuss the questions.

1 Why do you think some of the comedies mentioned in the programme are popular worldwide?

2 Do you think your country has a particular sense of humour? If so, how would you describe it?

3 Can you explain this joke made by the presenter's friend, Liam?

I burnt 2000 calories this afternoon ... That's the last time I leave chocolate brownies in the oven while I have a little sleep.

b Read the language focus box and check the explanation of Liam's joke.

Puns

Puns and plays on words usually work in three ways:

• A word has two different meanings.
burn calories = use fat/energy in your body
burn calories = overcook the chocolate brownies containing the calories

• A phrase which is normally used in an idiomatic way is used literally.
*Living near the city centre is **a big plus*** = a common idiomatic way of saying it's an advantage
A: *What's the best thing about living in Switzerland?*
B: *Well, the flag is **a big plus**!* = it's literally a big plus (+) sign.

• Two words sound the same, or almost the same.
A: *Why is ten scared of seven?*
B: *Because seven **ate** nine.* (*ate* sounds like *eight*)

8 a 10.6 Listen and write down the words you hear.

b 10.7 Now listen and write down the complete sentences.

c Work in pairs. Did you write the individual words in Exercise 8a in the same way or in a different way from how you wrote them in 8b? Why?

9 a Work in pairs. Can you explain these jokes?

1 Two fish are sitting in a <u>tank</u>. One looks over to the other and says, 'Hey! Do you know how to drive this thing?'

2 I joined a gym recently and on my first day there I asked one of the instructors if he could teach me some gymnastics. 'How <u>flexible</u> are you?' he replied, and so I said, 'Well, I can't do Tuesdays or Thursdays.'

3 I hate <u>sitting in traffic</u> because I always get run over.

4 I was about to get in my car and drive to work this morning when one of my neighbours asked if I could <u>give him a lift</u>. 'Of course.' I said. 'You're looking great today! You've got a lovely family and I'm sure today's going to be your day!' Then I drove off!

5 I've got a fear of over-engineered buildings. I've got a complex complex <u>complex</u>!

6 A: Knock, knock.
   B: Who's there?
   A: <u>Figs</u>.
   B: Figs who?
   A: Figs the doorbell, it's not working.

7 A: Knock, knock.
   B: Who's there?
   A: <u>Ice cream</u>?
   B: Ice cream who?
   A: Ice cream if you don't let me in!

b Which joke do you think is the wittiest?

Go to page 154 or your app for more information and practice.

Speaking

PREPARE

10 a Student A: Look at the jokes on page 169.
Student B: Look at the jokes on page 170. Choose two that you would like to tell or choose one and a joke of your own.

b Spend a few minutes trying to remember your jokes and preparing how to tell them.

SPEAK

11 a Work in groups. Take turns to tell your jokes and respond. Use the Useful phrases to help you.

> **Useful phrases**
>
> I don't get it.
> That's awful!
> Hmm. I guess it's mildly amusing.
> I think it has maybe lost something in translation.
> That's a cracker!

b Vote on the best joke.

> Develop your listening
> page 95

Check and reflect: Units 9 and 10

1 a **Complete the short conversations with words in the box.**

> ashamed   ecstatic   exhausted   furious
> hilarious   traumatised

1 A: He must've been shaken up by the whole experience.
   B: He was. He was _____ by it!

2 A: You must've been pleased when you heard the news.
   B: I was. I was _____ .

3 A: I bet you were tired by the end of all that, weren't you?
   B: Tired? I was absolutely _____ .

4 A: Was she angry when she found out?
   B: Yeah – _____ !

5 A: It sounds funny.
   B: Honestly, it was absolutely _____ .

6 A: I would've been so embarrassed if that had been me.
   B: I know, right. I was so _____ of myself!

b **Match conversations 1–6 in Exercise 1a with speaker B's follow-up comments a–f.**

a We all just totally cracked up.
b I was jumping for joy.
c I was dead on my feet!
d She totally lost it!
e He went into a blind panic.
f I just felt so stupid to have done that.

c **Think of a time you had two of the feelings in Exercise 1b. Tell a partner how you felt and why.**

2 **Combine the two sentences. Start each sentence with the words in brackets and make any other changes necessary.**

1 I felt pretty foolish. I went bright red, too. (not only)

2 You've been late every day this week. You've missed your deadlines. (not only)

3 My application had been successful. They were also offering me a grant. (not only)

4 She left hospital in the morning. In the afternoon, she was training again. (no sooner)

5 I left university. The very next day, I was offered a job. (no sooner)

6 I got home around five. Almost immediately, I had to go out. (no sooner)

3 **Complete the text with one word in each gap. Negative contractions count as one word.**

When I was a kid, I ¹_____ to go fishing almost every weekend. I ²_____ get up really early – before everyone else in the house – and cycle off to the lake near my house. And then I usually just ³_____ the whole day there. I ⁴_____ normally catch much, but I loved it all the same. I ⁵_____ go every now and then, especially if my son fancies it. My wife always ⁶_____ fun of us when we don't catch anything. To be honest, I wish she ⁷_____ stop doing it.

4 a **Complete the sentences with the best word. The first letter is given.**

1 He's a very s_____ talker. He could persuade almost anyone to do almost anything!

2 My boss is very d_____ . She expects a lot from us and isn't easily pleased!

3 She's always seemed very happy with what she's got, you know – very c_____ with life.

4 She's always been very d_____ . Once she decides to do something, there's no stopping her.

5 He's always very serious. He needs to l_____ up a bit and enjoy life more.

6 She's quite m_____ . She's not one for showing off about her achievements and abilities.

7 My parents were pretty l_____ . They weren't that strict and they gave me a lot of freedom.

b **Choose three sentences from Exercise 4a that describe people you know. Tell a partner.**

5 a **Decide if the sentences describe upwards or downwards trends.**

1 Online sales of non-food items have soared over the last few years.

2 House sales have plunged over recent years.

3 The laptop market has shrunk quite dramatically over recent years.

4 There's been a surge in anti-social behaviour recently.

5 They've slashed funding for libraries recently.

6 There's been a hike in the number of people moving abroad to work.

7 There has been a recent explosion of interest in men's fashion.

b **Work in pairs. Which sentences in Exercise 5a do you think are true for your country?**

6 **Choose the correct definition of the words in italics.**

1 I really don't need feminism *mansplained* to me, thank you!
   a explained using only facts and the fewest words possible
   b explained by a man to a woman in a way that suggests he knows more about it

2 It was a great night. The *craic* was good.
   a fun or enjoyment
   b noise

3 Don't need to know where you're going – idc.
   a It doesn't cost.
   b I don't care

4 We're working on a *telethon* for victims of the earthquake.
   a a long TV programme designed to raise money
   b a marathon race that will be shown on TV

5 They have an amazing *mocktail* list there.
   a meat – including the tail of an animal
   b an alcohol-free cocktail

7 Complete sentences 1–7 with the prepositions in the box.

after   against   in   of   on   out   with

1 The site has improved its security response to recent complaints.
2 I'm absolutely terrified dentists.
3 It's not something I've ever been very keen.
4 Who's looking the baby while you're away?
5 I need time to warm up. I'm a bit of practice.
6 Who did you go there?
7 She's a lawyer famous for her involvement in the fight corruption.

8 Complete the sentences with the correct word. The beginning of the words is given.

1 Let's try an exp_____ . Let's stop using any kind of social media at the weekend.
2 The computer sim_____ conditions for pilots to practise flying in.
3 Many people have expressed doubts about the reli_____ of the results.
4 The explorer Ferdinand Magellan was the first person to pr_____ the Earth is round.
5 The fact that there were a few minor errors shouldn't inv_____ the whole idea.
6 It's a nice the_____ , but I'm not sure it'll work in practice.
7 The collection and clas_____ of the data is going to take weeks.

9 Choose the correct alternatives. Sometimes both options are correct.

1 *Despite/Although* not enjoying his previous book, I decided to give his new one a try.
2 The book was made into a film and *consequently/as a result*, sales soared.
3 You're allowed in to see it *provided/so long as* you have an adult with you.
4 The main character, Jim, is struggling at school. *Meanwhile/Whereas*, his sister is doing well.
5 It's a difficult book for native speakers, *on top of that/not to mention* foreign students.
6 The children keep to the woods and the fields *so as to/in order to* avoid people.

10 a Match descriptions 1–5 with follow-up comments a–e.

1 It's really gripping.
2 It was very controversial.
3 It's an absolute must.
4 There's a twist at the end of the film.
5 It's very disturbing.
a It made a lot of people angry.
b I really didn't see it coming.
c It really holds your attention.
d Honestly, this is *the* film you have to see this year.
e It gave me nightmares for weeks afterwards.

b Work in pairs. Choose words from Exercise 10a to describe books and films you know.

11 a Match the types of humour in the box with descriptions 1–5 below.

irony   a pun   satire   slapstick

1 A funny play that's making a political point.
2 When an actor falls over in a funny way.
3 A playful use of language using words that have different meanings or sound like other words.
4 When a pilot has a fear of heights.

b Work in pairs. Can you think of examples of any of the different kinds of humour?

12 Look at the jokes below. Write the correct spellings of one word in each that is being used in a funny way.

1 Why does the crab never share? Because he's shellfish.
2 Want to hear a joke about paper? I should warn you: it's tearable!
3 What did the grape do when someone stepped on him? He let out a little wine.
4 What did the chess piece say before bed? Knight knight.

13 Match sentences 1–6 with responses a–f.

1 Hey! Long time, no see.
2 That's typical, that is!
3 I'd rather just stay in, to be honest.
4 We have to leave the flat by the end of the month.
5 I'm going to the opera tonight.
6 Hey, did I tell you? I've got a new job.
a Oh, nice one! Well done.
b Seriously? What a pain!
c I know! It's been ages.
d All right. Suit yourself.
e What's up?
f Yeah? Rather you than me!

Reflect

How confident do you feel about the statements below? Write 1–5 (1 = not very confident, 5 = very confident).

- I can tell better stories.
- I can describe other people's habits and how I feel about them.
- I can talk about trends.
- I can manage informal conversations.
- I can report on and discuss science.
- I can describe books.
- I can tell jokes.

 For more practice go to your Workbook or app.

 Go online for the Roadmap video.

Develop your listening

> **Goal:** understand informal discussions
> **Focus:** identifying rhetorical questions

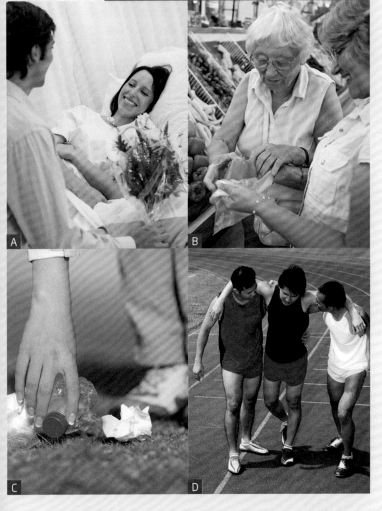

1 a Work in pairs. Describe what is happening in each photo and why.

b Do you ever do good deeds (e.g. helping a stranger, picking up rubbish)? Why/Why not?

2 🔊 1.6 Listen to four informal discussions. What good deeds did the speakers do?

3 Listen again and answer the questions for each discussion.

Discussion 1

1 Where was the rubbish?

2 What, according to the driver, is the problem with the other man?

Discussion 2

3 Why was Lisette feeling a bit down?

4 What did one of the women do to help Lisette?

Discussion 3

5 Why did the man take the rabbit home?

6 Where did he take the rabbit after that?

Discussion 4

7 What problem did the woman in the shop have?

8 What did the man do?

4 a Work in pairs. Can you remember which discussion the extract below is from? In what way is the second question different in purpose to the first?

A: Is he going to sort it out?
B: How should I know?

b Read the Focus box and check your ideas.

Identifying rhetorical questions

Rhetorical questions are questions where the answer is not important or not required. Sometimes the speaker answers the question themselves. We can use rhetorical questions to:

• show a strong emotional reaction.
Are you mad? *That was a stupid thing to do.*

• say you don't know or care about something.
Who cares? *I certainly don't.*

• persuade or influence someone.
That's not a bad deal, ***is it?***

• move a discussion or presentation forward.
So, ***what does this mean for us?*** *Well, firstly…*

5 a Complete extracts 1–6 from the discussions with rhetorical questions a–f below.

1 A: You stopped to pick up rubbish? Why?
B: _____

2 A: … who's got her photocopying and boring stuff like that.
B: She's an apprentice. _____

3 A: Why did you do that?
B: I just wanted to help I guess. _____

4 A: You took it home? _____
B: Maybe!

5 A: What did the checkout guy do?
B: _____ He wasn't going to pay it himself.

6 A: So will she pay you back?
B: _____ It's not the end of the world if she doesn't.

a What could he do?
b What does she expect?
c It's not that strange, is it?
d What's wrong with picking up rubbish?
e Who knows?
f Are you mad?

b Listen again to the discussions and check your answers.

6 Work in pairs. Take turns to say sentences 1–4. The other person should respond with a rhetorical question.

1 I paid for a stranger's flight home once.

2 Why did you give money to that homeless guy?

3 So you've quit your job. What are you going to do now?

4 The boss said no to my request for a pay rise.

7 Work in small groups. What good deeds have you done or witnessed? Why don't people do good deeds more often?

> **Goal:** understand disagreement in a radio interview

> **Focus:** recognising how modifiers can express disagreement

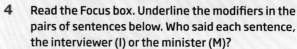

1 Work in pairs and discuss the questions.

1 Look at the building projects in the photos. Which one do you find most interesting or impressive? Why?

2 Are they a good use of money? Why/Why not?

3 Do you know of any big public building projects in your country at the moment? Are these projects behind schedule or over-budget?

2 🔊 **2.9 Listen to an interview with a government minister. Answer the questions.**

1 What is being built?

2 What are the problems with the project?

3 In what way is it not as good as the old one?

3 Choose the correct alternatives to complete the sentences. Then listen again and check.

1 The theatre has been nicknamed The *Castor/Disaster/City* Theatre.

2 According to the minister, the theatre will probably open *later this year/early next year/some time next year*.

3 The old theatre was *demolished/restored/rebuilt*.

4 *The minister/The minister and other people/Other people but not the minister* decided to build a theatre.

5 The first building contractor is *no longer in business/behind schedule/not responsible*.

6 The new theatre will be *less than/exactly/at least* fourteen million euros over budget.

7 The new theatre will be able to hold *two/two and a half/twenty* thousand people.

8 The minister *agrees/doesn't agree/plans* to resign if the theatre is not finished next year.

4 Read the Focus box. Underline the modifiers in the pairs of sentences below. Who said each sentence, the interviewer (I) or the minister (M)?

1 a The old theatre was very outdated.

   b It wasn't that outdated.

2 a You were solely responsible.

   b I was one of the people responsible.

3 a The project is slightly behind schedule.

   b The project is very behind schedule.

4 a It's hugely over budget.

   b It's somewhat over budget.

5 a The capacity of the new theatre will be substantially less that the old one.

   b The capacity will be marginally less.

Recognising how modifiers can express disagreement

There are various ways to disagree with someone and one way is through choice of modifier. Look at these examples from the listening:

A: … you have **no** idea when it will open.

B: Well, I have **some** idea. We hope …

The minister disagrees with the presenter by changing the modifying word from *no* to *some*.

A: You don't sound **very** confident.

B: I'm **quietly** confident.

The minister disagrees with the presenter by changing the modifying word from *very* to *quietly*.

By listening out for how speakers change the modifier, you can tell when they are disagreeing with each other.

5 a Read the start of four conversations. Which word or words do you think the other speaker will change to show disagreement? What different word might the other speaker use?

1 'You haven't emptied the dishwasher. You never do it.'

2 'Hi. Sorry I'm a bit late.'

3 'I've got a rental property you might be interested in. It's slightly over your budget but it's worth it!'

4 'And you're absolutely sure that you didn't leave your laptop on the train, are you?'

b 🔊 **2.10 Listen to some possible answers.**

6 Work in small groups. What building projects do you think your local town should undertake? Why?

> **Goal:** understand a podcast
> **Focus:** recognising fractions and multiples

1 **Work in pairs and discuss the questions.**
1 How much does a university education cost in your country?
2 What sacrifices do you have to make to go to university?
3 In what situations might it not be a good idea to get a university education?

2 a 🔊 3.9 **Listen to a podcast about three students that sued their university in court. Answer the questions about each student.**
1 Why did the student sue their university?
2 What did the student claim the university had done?
3 What did the student want the court to do?
4 What was the result?

b **Work in pairs and check your answers.**

3 🔊 3.10 **Read the Focus box. How do we pronounce the fractions and multiples? Listen and check.**

Recognising fractions and multiples

To summarise data we often use fractions and multiples. It helps to be able to spot these when you are listening.
Fractions: *a half* (1/2), *two thirds* (2/3), *a quarter* (1/4), *four fifths* (4/5)
Multiples (describing a change): *halved* (-50%), *doubled* (x2), *tripled* (x3), *quadrupled* (x4), *increased tenfold* (x10)
Multiples (describing a state): *twice as high, five times more* (*expensive*), *three times as many* (*students*)
Two-thirds of students go on to …
The number of students **increased by half**.
The number of students has **doubled**.
The cost has increased **six times faster** than wages.

4 **Listen to the podcast again. What fractions or multiples do you hear for the facts below?**
1 the number of students in the UK
2 the cost of a university education in the US
3 the number of students getting a first class degree
4 the average salary for UK graduates
5 students who will never repay their student debts

5 **Work in pairs. What do you think of the three students who tried to sue their university? Did any of them have a good case?**

6 🔊 3.11 **Listen to extracts from other podcasts about education and choose the correct answer (a, b or c) to the questions below.**
Extract 1
1 What percentage of 18–24 year olds are in full-time education?
  a around 25% **b** around 33%   **c** around 66%
2 What is the increase during term time in some places in the number of 18–24 year olds?
  a x2   **b** x3   **c** x4
Extract 2
3 What percentage of students in Australia are international students
  a 4%   **b** 25%   **c** 75%
4 How many people are likely to go to university from a city compared to people from a rural area?
  a half as many **b** nearly double the number
  c three times as many
Extract 3
5 What percentage of students work part-time?
  a 20%   **b** 40%   **c** 60%
6 What percentage of students work full-time?
  a 20%   **b** 40%   **c** 60%

7 **Work in small groups and discuss the questions.**
1 How have the following changed recently?
  • the cost of a university education
  • the number of people going to university
  • student debt
  • the number of students going abroad to study
2 Do you think university education should be free for students? Why/Why not?
3 If you were studying at university, would you look for a part-time job? If so, what kind of job?
4 Some universities now offer degrees in non-traditional subjects like e-sports, popular culture and circus studies. Do you think this is a good idea?

> **Goal:** understand casual conversations

> **Focus:** recognising when something is said ironically

1 Work in pairs and discuss the questions.

1 Do/Did you have good discussions with your grandparents? Is there one in particular who you are or were close to?

2 What useful advice have you been given in your life by someone older than you?

2 ◀) 4.3 **Listen to a discussion between a grandmother and her adult grandson. Are the sentences true (T) or false (F)?**

1 He was a well-behaved boy.

2 He swam in the loch (lake) even in winter.

3 He didn't change his mind easily.

4 When he was 14 he came to see his grandmother by himself.

5 His grandmother sent him back home.

6 They saw a lot of each other when he settled down with his girlfriend.

7 He decided to move to Scotland.

8 His grandmother approves of his new girlfriend.

3 Listen again and number extracts a–h in the order you hear them.

a Your mother was happy about that.

b Life was so simple then.

c What a great choice that was!

d She's a smart girl for choosing you!

e There are plenty more fish in the sea.

f That loch in winter was a warm bath.

g Scotland, where the sun shines every day!

h I definitely didn't feel welcome for a while.

4 Read the Focus box and say which four extracts from the conversation in Exercise 3 are ironic.

Recognising when something is said ironically

When we say something ironically we say the opposite of what we mean. For example, the grandmother is being ironic when she says:

Your mother was happy about that, let me tell you!

What she really means is that the mother wasn't happy about it at all. She is using irony to emphasise a point in a slightly amusing way.

When someone says the opposite of what both people having the conversation know to be true, there is a good chance he or she is being ironic.

A: *Could you help me look for my lost contact lens? I lost it in the garden somewhere.*

B: *In the garden? That's going to be easy to find, then.*

The speaker will often use an exaggerated intonation to show that their words are meant ironically.

5 Work in pairs and discuss how much irony is used in your culture. Give examples.

6 ◀) 4.4 **Listen to six short conversations. What do the speakers mean (a or b) when they say sentences 1–6?**

1 'Well, that went well.'
   a It was a good conversation.
   b It was a disastrous conversation.

2 'Oh, yes, wonderful. Have a great time.'
   a I'm happy you guys can spend time together.
   b I'm sad that you're leaving me alone.

3 'Yeah, I thought it was excellent.'
   a I agree. It was a great film.
   b Are you joking? It was awful.

4 'Guess it's my lucky day!'
   a Well, it could have been much worse.
   b Poor me! I hate being at the dentist's.

5 'Oh wonderful.'
   a This is terrible.
   b I actually like the rain.

6 'I haven't got a clue what you're talking about.'
   a I don't understand you.
   b I'm pretending that I don't understand you.

7 Work in pairs and discuss the questions.

1 Are you friends with anyone who is much older or younger than you? Who are they?

2 Would you prefer a close friend who is much older or much younger than you? Why?

3 Why do you think people usually choose friends who are similar in age to them?

> **Goal:** understand public address announcements

> **Focus:** understanding public announcements

Understanding public announcements

Public announcements made on public address systems (PA systems) can be hard to understand because the sound quality is often not good and there is a lot of competing noise. However, certain expressions are very common in public announcements and recognising these often makes the announcement easier to understand. The expressions are usually formal ways of saying something simple, for example:

We are sorry to announce that ... = Unfortunately ...
In the event of an emergency, please ... = If there is an emergency ...

Other commonly heard phrases include:
on behalf of = used when speaking for someone else
please proceed to = please go to
is about to commence = is going to start soon
your belongings = your possessions

1 Work in pairs. Make a list of situations in which you might hear public announcements.

on a train, in a shop ...

2 a ◖ 5.6 Listen to eight public announcements and note where each one happens.

b Work in pairs and check your answers. Then listen again and answer one question for each announcement 1–8.

1 Which train has been cancelled? Why?
2 What do passengers need to do?
3 What should Doctor Issac do?
4 What is the announcer asking people to do?
5 What is the purpose of the announcement?
6 What do customers need to do?
7 What do passengers for this flight need to do?
8 How big is the discount and on what?

3 a Read the Focus box then match the beginnings of public announcements 1–8 with their informal meaning a–h.

1 In the interests of customer security ...
2 Please be aware that ...
3 Please make your way to ...
4 We ask that you ...
5 Please move right down inside ...
6 The service has been delayed due to ...
7 Please exit via ...
8 Your attention please, ...

a Go to ...
b It's late because ...
c Please listen, ...
d Please (do what I am about to say) ...
e In order to keep you safe, ...
f Make room for other passengers ...
g Note that ...
h Leave by (this way) ...

b Work in pairs and check your answers.

4 ◖ 5.7 Listen to some public announcements where the sound quality is poor. Choose the correct summary for each (a or b). Sometimes <u>both</u> options are correct.

1 a Wait.
  b Get off the bus.
2 a Leave via the south side.
  b Don't leave via the south side.
3 a The train is delayed.
  b The journey may take longer.
4 a Someone is going to check your bus ticket.
  b Find your bus ticket now.
5 a Sit down now.
  b Turn off all electronic devices.
6 a This message is for customers only.
  b This message is for staff only.
7 a Leave as fast as you safely can.
  b Do nothing. This is just a practice.
8 a If this is your flight, go to gate 8.
  b This flight has just arrived at gate 8.
9 a Be careful.
  b Don't put your bags somewhere and walk away.
10 a If this is your car, move it.
   b If this is your car, it has been taken away.

5 Work in pairs and discuss the questions.

1 What public announcements do you often hear? Which annoy you?
2 Would you be a good public announcer? Why/Why not?
3 What could be done to make public announcements more attention-grabbing?

6B Develop your listening

> **Goal:** understand the main points of a complex presentation

> **Focus:** recognising nouns used as verbs

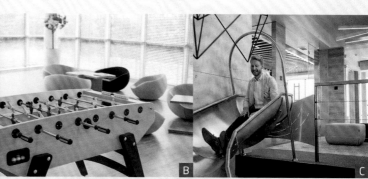

Recognising nouns used as verbs

Over time, many nouns in English become used as verbs. For example, the first text message was sent in the 1990s. *Text* quickly became a verb and now people often say 'I'll text you'.

Other nouns which are often used as verbs include:

battle   hand   task   staff   rumour   host

Recognising when a word sounds like a noun but is a verb can help your listening comprehension.

1 a Work in pairs and look at the photos. Where would you prefer to work? Why?

b Imagine you and your partner are the CEOs of a big technology company and you want to build a new headquarters (HQ) somewhere in your country.
   1 Where would you build it and why?
   2 How would your HQ attract employees?

2 🔊 6.8 Listen to the first part of a news report and complete the notes.
   1 Internet retail giant Zanzing wants to build a _____ .
   2 They will announce their decision in _____ .
   3 Their plans will cost more than _____ .
   4 They will create up to _____ jobs.
   5 Zanzing is looking for:
     • a well-educated and diverse _____ of over _____ .
     • a well-developed _____ with good international _____ .
   6 They will also require:
     • grants and _____ .
     • a city that is _____ .

3 Read the Focus box. Then complete the extracts from the news report using the verbs in blue in the Focus box. Use the correct form.
   1 Marisa Soler _____ the company's management with finding a new home for its headquarters.
   2 ... several cities have been _____ with each other to _____ the new HQ.
   3 It _____ that Zanzing will invest over five hundred million dollars to build their new headquarters.
   4 ... cities have been desperate to _____ Zanzing an attractive deal.
   5 ... a lively and exciting place where the people that _____ the company will be happy.

4 a 🔊 6.9 Listen to the second part of the news report and complete these details for Stanfield, Riverborough and New Haling.
   Name: _____
   Population: _____
   Main attraction of city for Zanzing: _____
   Other attractions: _____
   Main negative point: _____

b Work in pairs and compare your answers. Then listen again and check.

5 a Work in pairs. What do you think the words in the box mean when used as a verb?

   face   hammer   balloon   house   bag   highlight

b Complete extracts 1–6 from the news report with the correct form of the verbs in the box in Exercise 5a.
   Stanfield
   1 Stanfield, with a population that has recently _____ to 600,000 residents, is seen as ...
   2 ... and it already _____ several multinational digital companies
   Riverborough
   3 ... they genuinely believe that they are most likely to _____ the new HQ.
   4 It is undeniable that Riverborough has _____ a number of challenges over the last two decades.
   New Haling
   5 ... city leaders are _____ the thriving inner city
   6 ... an extra five thousand people ... would _____ the already strained infrastructure of the city.

6 Work in small groups and discuss the questions.
   1 Which city should Zanzing choose? Why?
   2 Which city in your country would make the best host?
   3 What should cities offer to attract new businesses?

7B Develop your listening

> **Goal:** understand a discussion or debate
> **Focus:** understanding hypothetical situations in an argument

1 **Work in pairs and discuss the questions.**
   1 What are the biggest stories in the news right now?
   2 Who, if anyone, do you discuss news stories with?

2 a 🔊 **7.5 Listen to five discussions about different news reports. Answer the questions for each discussion.**
   1 What is the news story about?
   2 What do the speakers disagree about?

   b **Check your answers in pairs.**

3 **Listen again and answer the questions.**
   Discussion 1
   1 How much rainfall has London had so far this year?
   2 How much water should the average person use in a day?

   Discussion 2
   3 How much are train fares going up on average?
   4 What will happen next year if they don't take action, according to one speaker?

   Discussion 3
   5 What stage of the competition is the team through to?
   6 Who will they play next?

   Discussion 4
   7 What does the report say that the Prime Minister did?
   8 Who do they think would replace the Prime Minister?

   Discussion 5
   9 How many people were injured when the plane landed?
   10 What was one reason that might have added to the problem?

4 a **Look at these questions and statements from the discussions. Which discussion does each one come from?**
   a But imagine if she does resign.
   b If that were true then nothing would ever change.
   c Yeah, but what if they did? Just imagine!
   d If that were the case, they would have cancelled all flights.
   e What if everyone did that?

   b **Read the Focus box and then match the sentences and questions in Exercise 4a with the uses of hypotheticals 1–3 in the box.**

Understanding hypothetical situations in an argument

When we are discussing or debating a point, we often use a hypothetical statement or question. We do this to:
1 suggest that someone is being selfish.
   What if *everyone behaved like you?*
   Imagine if *everyone did that.*
2 move a discussion forward.
   Yes but ***what if*** *it were true?*
   Just imagine! What if *they did win?*
3 explain why someone's point is not logical.
   If that were the case then *we'd all be in trouble.*
   If that were true then *everyone would do it.*

5 a 🔊 **7.6 Listen to three more discussions about news stories. Use the Focus box and decide what the speaker might say next. Check your ideas in pairs.**

   b 🔊 **7.7 Listen and complete what the speakers say.**
   1 A: I don't think the hurricane will strike here.
      B: Yeah, _____ ? _____ ?
   2 A: Nah ... I don't think so. I don't get involved in local politics.
      B: Oh come on. _____ ?
   3 A: They're wasting their time. You can't cure aging.
      B: If _____ .

6 **Work in pairs. Discuss the news stories you thought of in Exercise 1 and give your opinion. Use hypothetical statements and questions when possible.**
   A: *I don't really care about the floods in the south. I don't have any family there.*
   B: *That's a bit heartless, isn't it? What if everyone thought like you?*

92

8A ▶ Develop your listening

> **Goal:** follow extended unstructured speech

> **Focus:** identifying clarification language

A   B   C

1 a Look at the pictures and discuss the questions.
1 What is each interviewee doing wrong?
2 What else can go wrong in a job interview?
3 What can you do to make sure a job interview goes well?

b Work in pairs and discuss the questions.
1 Have you ever had a job interview? How did it go? What questions were you asked?
2 If you were to interview someone for a job, what questions would you ask them?

2 a Match things that people sometimes do in interviews a–e with example sentences 1–5.
a show ambition
b give specific examples of past achievements
c be boastful and egotistical
d blame someone else for problems and failures
e be clued up about the company

1 All my colleagues love working with me.
2 I know that you have offices in twelve different cities.
3 My colleagues made it hard for our project to succeed.
4 I'd like to take on more responsibility.
5 I introduced a new way of dealing with customer complaints.

b ◁» 8.4 Listen to four extracts from job interviews. Match them with four of the items a–e in Exercise 2a.

3 Listen again. Are the statements (T), false (F) or not mentioned (NM)?
Interview 1
1 Her colleague didn't have the right qualifications.
2 She knew how to do her colleague's job.
Interview 2
3 Her previous job involved collaboration and facilitation.
4 She believes other people find it hard to be as good as she expects them to be.
Interview 3
5 She is applying for the role of Marketing Director.
6 She hopes that it is the Marketing Assistant's job to go to trade shows.
Interview 4
7 He has a lot of experience in the hotel and restaurant sector.
8 He wants to be a manager.

4 a Read the Focus box and then match 1–4 with a–d below to complete the extracts from the interviews.

Identifying clarification language
When a fluent speaker is talking, they will often clarify what they have said by giving extra information, examples or an alternative explanation. Certain phrases are often used to introduce these clarifications.

*I have researched the company, **as in** what it does, where it operates, and so on.*

*He wasn't easy to work with, **in that** he lost his temper sometimes.*

*I enjoyed the work, **specifically** those tasks to do with online marketing.*

*I think I am right for this role. **By that I mean** I have the right skills.*

When you hear these phrases, you know that the speaker is clarifying what they have already said rather than adding new information.

1 I was responsible for everything digital,
2 I'm an excellent collaborator and facilitator.
3 High standards could be considered a weakness,
4 I'd like to manage a chain of hotels within a region,

a specifically an international region.
b By that I mean I'm able to work with all kinds of people.
c in that they can be hard for other people to live up to.
d as in the website, the database and so on.

b ◁» 8.5 Listen and check your answers.

5 Work in pairs and ask and answer these classic interview questions.
1 What would you say are your greatest strengths?
2 What would you say are your weaknesses?
3 Where do you see yourself in five years' time?
4 Why should we hire you?

6 Discuss what advice you would give someone who is about to have their first job interview.

1 **Work in small groups and discuss the questions.**

1 How many hours a week do you spend on social media?

2 Do you think social media is good or bad for your mental health? Explain why.

3 What are the symptoms of someone who is addicted to social media?

2 9.3 **Listen to the first half of a panel interview on people who have given up using social media. Match details 1–6 with Maha (M), Bahar (B) or Pablo (P).**

1 realised he/she was lonely

2 won some money

3 couldn't be alone or bored any more

4 had a difficult home life

5 received online abuse

6 cried when he/she realised how addicted he/she was

3 **Read the Focus box then listen again. Which strategy does each person use to avoid answering a question?**

Recognising when someone avoids answering a question

There are various strategies that people use to avoid answering a question.

1 Give a vague answer

A: *How many hours a week was it?*

B: **Let's just say** *it was more than it should be.*

2 Change the focus of the question

A: *Was it 20 hours a week?*

B: **I think what's important is** *that I realised it was too much.*

3 Say politely that you don't want to answer

A: *Why were you lonely?*

B: **I don't want to go into specifics,** *but …*

4 **Look at the short conversations. Which of the strategies in the Focus box does Speaker B use?**

1 A: How much did you spend?

   B: Well, not much, in the end. Less than I expected.

2 A: Was he eating too much?

   B: To be honest I think the key thing was that he wasn't exercising enough.

3 A: Was the job well paid? How much were you earning?

   B: Well, let's just say I didn't struggle.

4 A: Will you leave, then?

   B: I'm not prepared to say right now.

5 A: So, you guys didn't get on very well? What did you argue about?

   B: Well, I'd rather not go into details, really.

6 A: Don't you think it's OK, just for tonight?

   B: It's not about whether it's OK tonight, it's about whether it's OK at all.

5 a 9.4 **Listen to the second part of the panel interview and complete the sentences.**

1 Through giving up social media Bahar rediscovered …

2 According to Bahar, in order to feel fully satisfied, humans need to …

3 In order to avoid answering the host's questions, Tim …

b **Work in pairs and check your answers.**

6 **Listen again. Are the statements true (T), false (F) or not mentioned (NM)?**

1 Bahar won less than a million euros.

2 Bahar didn't know how to deal with the online abuse.

3 Bahar wasn't used to feeling bored.

4 Now, after rediscovering drawing, Bahar is never bored.

5 Tim Meadows has been the CEO of the social media company Gobby for five years.

6 Tim says he feels responsible for people who become addicted to social media services like Gobby.

7 **Work in pairs and discuss the questions.**

1 Do you think social media companies should do something to avoid people becoming addicted? If so, what do you think they should do?

2 What do you think about the statement: 'You've got to create as well as consume in order to be fully satisfied as a person'?

3 Do you have a positive or negative story to tell about social media?

> **Goal:** follow a conversation between two fluent speakers
> **Focus:** improving listening skills

1 **Look at the pictures above and discuss the questions.**

1 Why did the mother tell her son a lie?
2 Do you think it is OK for a parent to lie to their children like this? Explain why.
3 Did your parents or other adults tell you any lies like this when you were a child?

2 a **You're going to listen to a podcast about lies that parents tell their children. Work in pairs. Look at the pictures below and guess what each lie was.**

b 🔊 10.8 **Listen to the podcast and check your answers.**

3 a **Listen again and answer the questions.**
Interview 1

1 What did the speaker usually have for breakfast?
2 Why was her mother's lie effective?
3 Until what age did she believe the lie?

Interview 2

4 When does the speaker tell her son the lie?
5 What will happen when he finds out the truth?
6 How many children does the woman have?

Interview 3

7 Where did the speaker's father say the scar came from?
8 Who told the speaker that it was a lie?
9 Why did the speaker think he was stupid to believe the lie?

Interview 4

10 What question did the man's daughter ask?
11 What did the speaker say he learnt at Dad School?
12 Why is the lie a problem now for the speaker?

b **Work in pairs and check your answers.**

4 **Read the Focus box. Have you ever done this activity to improve your listening skills? What do you think about it?**

Improving listening skills

It can sometimes be hard to understand fast, natural speech between native speakers, so one way to practise is to find an audio recording of an extract of a conversation or a monologue and then listen to it multiple times. Try to make a transcript of the extract and then notice which parts of the extract are hard to hear. Listen to these parts again and again until you can match what you hear with the words on the page.
This kind of detailed listening activity can dramatically improve your listening skills in a short space of time.

5 a 🔊 10.9 **Listen to an extract from the podcast and underline the parts which you find difficult to understand. Compare with a partner and discuss why they were difficult.**

I haven't got the heart to tell her I was only joking and, like, when I take her to bed now I kiss her goodnight and then she says 'Are you going to Dad School now?' and I say 'Yeah, love, I'm off to Dad School.' So I've really dug myself a bit of a hole now and I'm not sure how to get out of it.

b **Listen at least two more times to the extract. Do those parts become easier to understand?**

6 **Work in pairs and discuss the questions.**

1 Which lie from the four speakers do you think is most and least serious? Why?
2 Do you think these kind of lies have a negative effect on children? If so, what?
3 Would you (or Do you) tell lies to a child to make life easier for yourself? Can you give an example?

1c ▶ Develop your reading

> **Goal:** understand newspaper and magazine articles

> **Focus:** recognising similarities and differences between opinions

A
B
C

1 a Look at the photos. Why might other people not like it if you ate these foods at your office desk or in a library?

b Work in pairs and discuss the questions.

1 If you had a desk job, would you eat lunch at your desk? Why/Why not?

2 What would you say to your colleague if he or she ate noisy or smelly food at their desk every day?

2 Read the article and then give one reason given to:

1 ban eating lunch at your desk at work.

2 not ban eating lunch at your desk at work.

3 ban snacking at your desk at work.

4 ban tea or coffee at work.

Eating al desko

With one Fortune 500 company recently banning the practice, is it ever OK to eat lunch at your desk? We asked a range of experts and office workers to give their opinion on what you can and can't eat at your desk.

1 Is it OK to eat lunch al desko?

'No way', says Jemma Spicer, CEO of management consultancy Frobisher White. 'It doesn't make anyone happy: not the worker, not their boss and certainly not the co-workers who have to put up with the smell of salad dressing or spicy noodles.' And Spicer **¹has a good point**, according to Professor Hadley Wakeham of the Fens School of Business Studies. He notes that all the research shows that workers are happier and more productive if they can take a proper break. That means getting away from their screens and desks and interacting with other people in an enjoyable manner. 'Anyone who eats at their desk is actively harming the organisation they are working for', says Wakeham.

So that's agreed then – eating al desko should be banned? **²Not so fast**, says Seldon Meier, founder of Software Links, a company with over 500 workers. He points out that research also shows that the more rules you introduce, the less happy people are, so a rule about where you can eat lunch is actually likely to do more harm than good. 'Although the theory is correct, the reality is that treating people like children rarely works.' **³Nevertheless**, many people remain in favour of a ban, including Felicity Cope from consultancy company The Happy Work Place. She remembers a boss who made everyone have a sit-down lunch with their fellow workers at 1 p.m. every day. 'At first we really fought it', she says, 'but after a while we came to appreciate the chance to socialise. If you only meet people in pointless meetings, you never build a bond with them.'

2 What about snacking al desko?

Again, the answer depends on who you talk to. 'If you're opening cans of fizzy drink and taking mouthfuls of crunchy crisps from a noisy packet every ten seconds, then the answer is a big no,' says Felicity Cope. 'But no one is going to complain if you eat an apple at your desk.' **⁴Or will they?** Kayleigh Milton's company recently banned workers from eating certain kinds of fruit at their desks, including apples. 'I actually think it was the right thing to do', says Milton. 'I had a colleague who ate apples all day and it was so distracting.' Jemma Spicer **⁵takes the opposite view**. She suggests that everyone has the right to a snack at their desk, as long as it's not too noisy or smelly. Professor Wakeham **⁶concurs**. 'Lunch is one thing, but snacking is quite another', he argues.

3 Tea or coffee, anyone?

On this issue there is substantial agreement. 'No one can have a go at you for drinking a cup of coffee while you work', says Seldon Meier. 'Actually many people find it hard to think about working without caffeine to get them going!' **⁷Similarly**, Felicity Cope says 'I've never worked in an office where drinking tea or coffee is an issue. It should never be a problem.' **⁸So everyone agrees then? Not quite.** According to Professor Wakeham, there are people who drink so much tea or coffee that they spend half their time by the kettle chatting to colleagues rather than working. 'It doesn't happen often', he says, 'but it does happen and in that situation it's up to the manager to have a quiet word with the coffee addict and suggest that they drink a bit less and work a bit more. After all', says Wakeham, 'no one is being paid to drink tea!'

3 Read the article again and answer the questions.

1 What makes workers work harder, according to Professor Wakeham?

2 What happens when you introduce more rules, according to Seldon Meier?

3 How did Felicity Cope feel about eating with her colleagues at first?

4 How will people feel about you eating an apple at your desk, according to Felicity Cope?

5 What snacks can't be consumed at your desk, according to Jemma Spicer?

6 What will your colleagues <u>not</u> do if you drink a coffee at your desk, according to Seldon Meier?

4 Read the Focus box. Decide if the phrases in bold 1–8 in the article introduce a similar or a different opinion.

Recognising similarities and differences between opinions

When a text presents a variety of opinions, it's important to know when someone is agreeing with the previous opinion and when they are disagreeing. There are various ways that a writer uses to show this apart from simply saying *agree* or *disagree*.

Language

Verbs and phrases like *concur* and *has a good point* indicate that someone has the same opinion.

Verbs and phrases like *take the opposite view* and *see it differently* indicate that someone has a different opinion to the previous person.

*Spicer **has a good point**, according to Professor Wakeham.*

*Jemma Spicer **takes the opposite view**.*

Linkers

Similarly shows that a similar view is going to be presented.

***Similarly**, Felicity Cope says …*

Linkers such as *however, on the other hand* and *nevertheless* show that a different opinion is going to be presented.

***Nevertheless**, Professor Wakeham remains in favour.*

Rhetorical questions and short responses

Rhetorical questions can indicate a change in opinion.

*But no one is going to complain if you eat an apple at your desk. **Or will they?***

Responses to rhetorical questions can do the same thing.

*So everyone agrees then? **Not quite**.*

5 Decide whether the sentences about the article are true (T) or false (F)?

Section 1

1 Professor Wakeham agrees with Jemma Spicer.

2 Seldon Meier agrees with Professor Wakeham.

3 Felicity Cope agrees with Seldon Meier.

Section 2

4 Kayleigh Milton agrees with Felicity Cope.

5 Jemma Spicer agrees with Kayleigh Milton.

6 Professor Wakeham agrees with Jemma Spicer.

Section 3

7 Felicity Cope agrees with Seldon Meier.

8 Professor Wakeham agrees with Felicity Cope.

6 Choose the correct alternatives to complete the extracts.

1 … which is why he believes that eating al desko is likely to damage your computer. Professor Ponting *concurs/ disagrees*, adding that getting crumbs in your keyboard is not the only problem.

2 … so plenty of people would be happy to see a ban. Georgina Rose *believes they have a good point/sees it differently*, arguing that a ban creates more problems than it solves.

3 … and she argues that companies should provide free fruit. *Similarly/Nevertheless*, Dr Kelmendi is in favour of companies encouraging workers to eat more healthily.

4 … he encourages companies to offer free gym membership to their workers. *Similarly/However*, many bosses say this is not practical.

5 … most people feel it is up to them what they eat at work. So everyone agrees then? *Not so fast/Yes they do*, says Paul Hammond. Sometimes you need rules about what you can eat at your desk.

7 Underline words or phrases in the article on page 96 which express the same ideas as the phrases below.

1 in a way that causes something to happen (paragraph 2)

2 have more negative effects than positive ones (paragraph 3)

3 continue to support (paragraph 3)

4 develop a friendship (paragraph 3)

5 absolutely not (paragraph 4)

6 attack someone (verbally) (paragraph 5)

7 give someone the energy/enthusiasm to do something (paragraph 5)

8 talk to someone privately about a sensitive issue (paragraph 5)

8 Work in pairs and decide on the rules for lunch, snacks and coffee that you would introduce in an office.

> **Goal:** understand intended meaning in a blog
>
> **Focus:** recognising positive and negative connotations of words

1 Work in pairs. Look at the photos and discuss the questions.

    1 How much exercise is too much for one week?

    2 Do you know anyone who over-exercises? How much do they do?

2 Quickly read the blog post below and complete the details about the blogger.

    1 Favourite sport as a teenager: _____

    2 University course: _____

    3 Favourite sport as an adult: _____

    4 Symptoms that drove her to hospital: _____

    5 Cause of symptoms: _____

    6 Time in hospital: _____

A

What happens when you do too much exercise?

My personal journey

From an early age I was into sports and fitness. As a child I often chose to run to school because I liked the exercise. My parents thought I was **hyperactive** and took me to a doctor to see if anything was wrong. She recommended that they encourage my passion, so from that point on they took me to all the sports clubs and training that I wanted.

Growing up, my favourite sport was probably hockey. As a teenager I was part of the national under-15 team and I trained several times a week. To be honest, there were other much more talented players on the team, but I was **confident** and **focused** and that was enough to get me a place.

Later at university I studied sports science and began coaching a school hockey team. I also got into triathlons and started competing regularly in those. At first I was doing half triathlons but then I started doing full ones: a 3.8 kilometre swim followed by a 180-kilometre bike ride and then a marathon to finish (42 kilometres). All that has to be completed in under seventeen hours. Every time I finished one I felt exhausted, but at the same time **ecstatic** and I wanted to start training for the next one.

Three years ago I entered a triathlon, but when the day of the race came I didn't feel so great. I thought about pulling out, but sometimes I'm a bit too **stubborn** so I started the race anyway. It was agony, but I pushed myself hard. Half-way through the bike ride, though, I had to stop. I had swollen joints and I wanted to vomit. I went straight back home to bed and didn't drink enough water.

The next day I couldn't get out of bed. I felt like I'd been hit by a bus and my body was swollen and sore. I was planning to drive over to my parents that day but I knew it would be too much so I just stayed in bed and let my flatmate look after me. People say we're like chalk and cheese. He's not into exercise at all and is very **laid-back**, but that day he was quite worried about me and suggested I call the doctor. I just thought I'd come down with a bug or something so I didn't, but the next day I felt even worse and I looked like I'd put on ten kilos. My whole body was swollen. That's when I decided to take it seriously.

My flatmate took me to A&E[1]. The doctors put me on an IV drip[2] and took blood samples. They asked me all sorts of questions about my exercise regime, my diet and stuff like that. I found them incredibly **nosy** but now I realise that they were trying to find out if I was using any performance-enhancing drugs. I wasn't of course, but they didn't know that.

They kept me in overnight but I wasn't getting any better, so eventually I was seen by a specialist in sports medicine and he diagnosed 'rhabdomyolysis' – a condition caused by extreme physical workouts, where your kidneys start to fail. That was why my body was swelling up – I was in full-blown kidney failure.

Fortunately rhabdomyolysis can be cured. I spent a week in hospital, but it took another three weeks before my body was back to its normal size. The whole experience had a big impact on me though. I took up yoga and meditation and started to be more **selective** about exercise. I still do quite a lot but I don't push myself as much as I used to and I try to respect my limits.

[1] A&E = accident and emergency department

[2] IV drip = intravenous drip (a small tube going directly into a vein so that fluids and medicines go directly into the bloodstream)

My name is Danielle Jackson. I'm a sports and nutrition fanatic and I blog about staying healthy (and not overdoing it!).

What to eat when training for a half triathlon

Training for a triathlon – everything you ever wanted to know

Recommended sports clothes

Correct swimming technique

3 Read the blog post again. Are the sentences true (T) or false (F)? Correct the false ones.

1 The doctor told Danielle's parents to prevent her doing too much exercise.
2 She was the top under-15 hockey player in the country.
3 After each triathlon she felt very happy.
4 She felt unwell before the triathlon race.
5 The next day she was in a traffic accident.
6 She realised that she had come down with a bug.
7 The doctors immediately diagnosed the problem.
8 Her illness was caused by her exercise regime.

4 Read the Focus box then complete the table with the words in bold from the text.

Positive connotation	Negative connotation
1 _____	lazy
2 strong willed	_____
3 curious	_____
4 _____	obsessed
5 energetic	_____
6 _____	manic
7 _____	egotistical
8 _____	fussy

Recognising positive and negative connotations of words

Words have meanings, but they also have connotations, too. The connotation of a word is the positive or negative feeling behind the word. Some words with a similar meaning have a very different connotation. For example, *laid-back* and *lazy* both mean that someone is not very physically active, however the connotation of *laid-back* is positive while the connotation of *lazy* is negative.

*He's not into exercise at all and is very **laid-back**.*

*He never does any exercise. He's so **lazy**.*

When you learn a new word, it is useful to make a note of the connotation.

5 Complete the sentences with the correct word from each pair in Exercise 4a. The words are used in the same order.

1 I like being around her. She's very *laid-back* .
2 I wish you weren't quite so _____ .
3 I knew we weren't going to get on. She's so _____ .
4 If you want to pass that exam you need to work hard and stay _____ .
5 She causes the teacher real problems in class because she's so _____ .
6 When I found out I'd passed I was _____ .
7 I didn't like her at first; I thought she was a bit _____ .
8 He always wants things to be perfect. He's so _____ .

6 a Read two different descriptions of a person. Which one is positive and which is negative?

My first flatmate was a young woman from Leeds and she was very peculiar. She was pushy but she was also immature and she often had a childish smirk. She bought a lot of toiletries and hoarded them in her room so the stench of cheap perfume was always present throughout the house.

My first flatmate was a young woman from Leeds and she was unique. She was assertive but she was also youthful and she often had a child-like smile. She bought a lot of toiletries and stored them in her room so the aroma of perfume was always present throughout the house.

b Work in pairs and compare your ideas. Which words helped you to decide?

7 Think of someone you know who could be described by some of the words in Exercise 4. Tell your partner about them.

My friend is obsessed with gaming. We try to get him to come out with us, but he's a bit lazy and he's also very stubborn.

⟩ **Goal:** understand magazine interviews

⟩ **Focus:** recognising lexical clues

1 a Work in pairs and discuss the questions.

1 Do you often read interviews with well-known people in newspapers, magazines or online?

2 What sort of people do you prefer to read about?

3 Does reading about well-known people usually give you a more positive or a less positive opinion about them? Why?

4 What kinds of things would you like to know about your favourite famous people?

5 How would you feel about being interviewed for a magazine? Why?

6 Who would you interview if you had the chance? Why?

b Read the introductory paragraph to each interview. Which subject would you rather study? Why?

2 a Before you read the full interviews, match terms 1–4 with definitions a–d.

1 technology evangelist

2 research fellow

3 mentor

4 field work

a a person who advises and helps you in your study or career

b a person who is passionate about all things digital and wants to share their passion

c research and data collection which happens outside the university

d a person who is paid by the university to research a particular subject

b Read both interviews and decide who these sentences describe: Sue, Emma, both or neither.

1 She knew from a young age that she wanted to work in her current field.

2 She didn't go to university until later in life.

3 She has had more than one mentor.

4 She sees herself as very physically fit.

5 She feels that ambition is more important than talent.

6 She loves buying gadgets.

7 She finds the greatest happiness in her work.

8 She Is ambitious to educate others.

3 a Read the two interviews again more carefully and then answer these questions.

1 Who is probably a good negotiator?

2 Who has the more physically demanding job?

3 Who is probably more family-oriented?

b Work in pairs. Compare your answers and explain your ideas.

Government adviser and social entrepreneur Sue Black, 56, is a professor of computer science and 'technology evangelist' at Durham University.

What was your childhood or earliest ambition?
To be a big red London bus driver. I've always loved vehicles and engineering-type stuff and I thought it must be the most exciting job in the world.

Private school or state school? University or straight into work?
Chelmsford Technical High School, as it was then. I left school at 16 because I left home and was working in a café to pay my rent. I had various jobs, got married and by 23 I had three children. Then my marriage broke down; I ended up living in a women's refuge and starting my life again. I decided to get back into education, went to Southwark College and ended up on a course called polymaths. The qualification gave me entrance to London South Bank University, where I did computing.

Who was or still is your mentor?
I am a great fan of mentors. I don't have just one, but my first was [computer scientist] Professor Dame Wendy Hall. She gave a talk in London about 20 years ago — I didn't know who she was, but I knew I wanted to be her. I asked her to be my mentor and she said she was too busy. I asked her for one hour a year and she said she didn't think she could refuse that. We are friends now.

How physically fit are you?
I love exercising but I don't do it enough.

Ambition or talent: which matters more to success?
One without the other, you're not going to get anywhere.

What would you like to own that you don't currently possess?
I can't think of anything! I'm not into ownership.

In what place are you happiest?
Sitting in my back garden with all my children, all my grandchildren, my husband, having a lovely family day, is perfection.

What ambitions do you still have?
I run a social enterprise called Tech Mums and I want to reach a million mums by 2020. I want to change our society by making mums more respected, teaching them technology skills, helping them see opportunities to improve their lives, their families' lives, their community.

Emma Liu, 29, is the Leverhulme research fellow in volcanology at Cambridge University's department for earth sciences.

What was your childhood or earliest ambition?

To study volcanoes, since I was six. I saw Mount St Helens on a family holiday and my parents couldn't drag me away. I wrote a primary school essay about what I wanted to be and everyone just smiled.

Private school or state school? University or straight into work?

The Sele School, a state school in Hertfordshire. I studied Earth sciences at Oxford, then did a PhD in Volcanology at Bristol University.

Who was or still is your mentor?

I have had many, and that has helped me get to where I am. Most have been women. Having inspiring female mentors has helped me navigate the sometimes challenging world of science for women. One of my very early mentors was Tamsin Mather *[professor of earth sciences at the University of Oxford and volcano specialist]*, a previous L'Oréal fellow as I am now.

How physically fit are you?

My physical fitness is something I'm extremely proud of. My field work is challenging and being in good shape allows me to collect data that otherwise wouldn't be possible. Outside work, I'm a fitness instructor.

Ambition or talent: which matters more to success?

A bit of both. To succeed in science, you need the raw material of intellectual curiosity and the ability to think creatively but logically. But you also need the desire to progress.

What would you like to own that you don't currently possess?

I always seem to need more socks.

In what place are you happiest?

Nothing can compare to watching a volcano erupt. It's such a raw display of power — particularly the sound, which I can never describe.

What ambitions do you still have?

Scientifically, there will always be questions to answer and every question will lead to 10 more and those will each lead to 10 more.

4 Read the Focus box and then say who uses more informal language in their interview, Sue or Emma.

Recognising lexical clues

The two interviewees use language very differently. Compare these two answers to the same question.

Q: Ambition or talent: which matters more to success?

A1: One without the other, you're not going to get anywhere.

A2: To succeed in science, you need the raw material of intellectual curiosity and the ability to think creatively but logically.

The first answer is more informal and the second more formal. This tells us how each interviewee uses language and it also allows us to predict how they will answer other questions in the interview.

5 a Read the answers to five more questions from the interview. Which person, Sue or Emma, do you think gave each answer?

1 If you had to rate your satisfaction with your life so far, out of 10, what would you score?

 a It varies. On average, a solid eight. But there have been times when it's been a 10 – and those are the moments I treasure.

 b Eleven.

2 What do you find most irritating in other people?

 a People who put other people down. I can't stand that.

 b Writing off slightly unusual ambitions or ideas without applying lateral thinking to see if you can make them happen. It's the way to find solutions.

3 Which object that you've lost do you wish you still had?

 a I'm not really bothered about things.

 b Spare time. It got mislaid along the way in the career trajectory.

4 If your 20-year-old self could see you now, what would she think?

 a I don't think she'd believe it was me. I've changed a lot. I'm more outgoing, more independent, more inquisitive.

 b She wouldn't believe it.

5 What is the greatest challenge of our time?

 a There are many. One close to my heart is getting children out and about in the outdoors from a young age. Losing our instinct to be comfortable with the natural environment is contributing to our environmental problems.

 b Solving global poverty. We have enough resources in the world to feed everyone but the disparity between rich and poor is ridiculous.

 b Which lexical clues gave you your answers? Work in pairs and compare your ideas.

6 Think of two more questions you would like to ask the interviewees about their academic lives.

7 Work in pairs. Ask and answer the questions from the interview and the ones you thought of in Exercise 6.

Develop your reading

> **Goal:** understand online responses to a question

> **Focus:** recognising repetition of ideas

A B C D E

1 Work in pairs and discuss the questions.

1 What can you tell about the people in photos A–E just by looking at them and/or what they are doing?

2 Would you describe yourself as a good judge of character? Why/Why not?

3 Have you ever misjudged someone's character completely? If so, what happened?

2 Read five responses to the question: *What one small thing can tell you the most about a person's true character?* Choose the best option (a or b) to complete the summary.

What tells you the most about someone is …

1 a how they treat people who serve them.

   b how they serve other people.

2 a what they do when they think they're alone.

   b what they do when they know they're being watched.

3 a how they write.

   b what they write.

4 a whether they apologise.

   b how they hold their umbrella.

5 a their friends.

   b how easy it is to be friends with them.

What one small thing can tell you the most about a person's true character?

1

Josh, Freelance coder

I say what I mean and mean what I say.

There are many small things that can tell you what a person is really like, but ᵃ**the one** which stands out for me is how someone treats people who work in the service industry: waiting staff, cab drivers, checkout workers, that kind of thing. This ¹<u>is a complete giveaway</u>. For obvious reasons people who are not nice will show no gratitude and treat service staff like second-class citizens. ᵇ**In doing so**, they're showing their true character. They're showing that they're only nice if they benefit from being nice. I work in the service industry and I meet people like this on a daily basis. The genuine people are the ones who treat me as an equal.

3.3k Votes ⬆Upvote ⬇downvote

2

Reyansh, Software engineer

All you need is love … and software.

The other day I was in a bakery and this guy came in to order some bread. He ²<u>helped himself to</u> a small piece of cake on the counter that the bakery had provided for customers to try for free. They ᶜ**did this** to encourage people to buy the cake but they assume you will only take one. So anyway, this guy took a piece and then, when he thought no one was looking, he took a big handful and stuffed them in his mouth. For me, ᵈ**this kind of behaviour** tells me everything I need to know about someone. What a person does when they think no one is looking is the key to understanding their character.

2.3k Votes ⬆Upvote ⬇downvote

3

Wang Wei, Student (of life)

Life is what you make it.

Look at their handwriting! That will tell you a lot about someone's true character. You might not think so and I was sceptical too, but a stranger looked at my handwriting once and they described me perfectly. ᵉ**That** had a really big impact on me and now I ³ <u>have complete faith in</u> it. For example, people whose handwriting slants to the right are more emotional and are ruled by their heart. People whose handwriting slants to the left are more logical and are ruled by their head. ᶠ**It's** true! Don't believe me? Look at a friend's handwriting and see – you'll be surprised!

115k Votes ⬆Upvote ⬇downvote

4

Jesse, Looking for work

If you can buy it, it can't be that valuable.

It sounds a bit strange but look at how someone holds their umbrella, particularly when they're walking along the street with another person. Do they keep it to themselves or do they share it? I once had a boyfriend who I was crazy about, but every time it rained, which is quite a lot here in Belem, I [4]couldn't help noticing how he kept the umbrella over his own head and let me get wet. When I said something about [g]**it**, he apologised, but after a while the umbrella would be back over his head again. [h]**That kind of thing** rubs off on you after a while and I became more selfish too. That was a relationship that didn't last.

4.9k Votes ⬆ Upvote ⬇ downvote

5

Ruth, Storyteller

My stories have a beginning, a middle and an end, but not necessarily in that order.

Somebody once said that you can judge a person by the friends they keep and I [i]**agree** [5]wholeheartedly. If you want to get to know someone, take a look at who they hang out with. If you don't like their friends, I think it's pointless to even try getting to know the person.

5.1k Votes ⬆ Upvote ⬇ downvote

3 a **Answer the following questions about responses 1–5 on the website.**

1 In what situation is an unpleasant person nice?

2 What unspoken rule did the man in the bakery break?

3 Why is the writer convinced that handwriting can tell you about a person's character?

4 Why did the writer become more selfish?

5 According to the writer, what should you do if you like a person but not their friends?

b **Work in pairs and compare your answers.**

4 **Choose the correct definition (a or b) for the underlined words or phrases 1–5 in the responses.**

1 a is free
  b shows a secret

2 a took without asking
  b asked and then took

3 a trust
  b don't trust at all

4 a noticed because I was looking for it
  b noticed although I wasn't looking for it

5 a completely
  b with my heart but not my head

5 **Read the Focus box. Then decide which idea is being repeated in words and phrases a–i in bold in the online responses.**

Recognising repetition of ideas

Writers usually try to avoid repeating a noun in the same sentence or the next sentence. They use pronouns or other phrases to avoid repetition.

… this guy came in to order some bread. **He** *helped himself to a small piece of cake*

In the same way, it's often necessary to repeat an idea in a text without using the same words. Notice these examples from the text.

1 *There are many things that can tell you what a person is really like but* **the one** *which stands out for me is …*

In this example, *the one* refers to 'things that can tell you what a person is really like'.

2 *… egotistical, self-obsessed people will show no gratitude.* **In doing so**, *they're showing their true character.*

In doing so refers to showing no gratitude.

3 *You simply can not trust this kind of person and if you* **do**, *you'll regret it!*

Here *do* refers to trusting a particular kind of person.

6 **Read another response on the website. Identify two parts of the text which avoid repetition. What do they avoid repeating?**

Constance, Barista

Treat others as you would have them treat you.

Some people seem really calm and happy but when they're behind the wheel of a car they change completely. Suddenly they're out of control. They drive like maniacs and don't obey the rules of the road. That causes a lot of accidents, but they're always convinced that it's everyone else's fault. I had a friend like this once and every time I got in the car with her I was very frightened. In fact, my opinion of her changed over time and we eventually lost touch. You simply cannot trust this kind of person and if you do, you'll regret it!

1.1k Votes ⬆ Upvote ⬇ downvote

7 **Work in small groups and discuss the questions.**

1 Which response do you agree with most?

2 What one small thing, in your opinion, tells you the most about a person's true character? Explain your answer.

Develop your reading

> **Goal:** understand an article

> **Focus:** when to check the meaning of words

1 a Answer the questions in the Consumerism quiz.

THE CONSUMERISM QUIZ

1. How many possessions are there in the average US home?
   a) 3,000   b) 30,000   c) 300,000

2. How many toys does the average British 10-year-old own?
   a) over 100   b) over 200   c) Over 300

3. What percentage of teenage girls in the US say that shopping is their favourite activity?
   a) over 50%   b) over 70%   c) over 90%

4. In today's money, how much would it have cost to buy a shirt in 1750?
   a) £200   b) £2,000   c) £20,000

5. How much more do we consume now compared to fifty years ago?
   a) twice as much   b) three times as much
   c) four times as much

b Work in pairs. Compare your answers and then check on page 174. Which fact surprised you most?

2 Read the article without a dictionary and match titles a–g with paragraphs 1–6. One title is not needed.

   a The facts and figures

   b The future of self-storage

   c What's on offer?

   d Working in a self-storage centre

   e A typical customer

   f Home from home

   g A new trend towards minimalism

3 Read the article again. Are the statements true (T), false (F) or not mentioned (NM)?

   1 Conrad shares his house with friends.

   2 Conrad doesn't feel able to throw anything away.

   3 There are two kinds of self-storage facilities.

   4 Some companies will put your stuff in boxes for you.

   5 The woman who uses self-storage as a wardrobe was living in a small apartment.

   6 People often use self-storage because they have no other choice.

   7 British people have more self-storage space on average than people in the US.

   8 Self-storage is growing less quickly than before.

The madness of SELF-STORAGE

1 Conrad Bailey has a quintessentially 21st-century problem; he has a lot of stuff but nowhere to put it. Conrad rents a room in a shared house. Working as a psychiatric nurse with a modest income, he can sometimes afford to buy things such as clothes, books or ornaments (he has a collection of china teacups), but the chance of him being able to afford a place of his own, at least in the medium term, is slim. What then, does he do with all his stuff? The answer is self-storage. Every month or so, Conrad goes to the Easy-Pack Self-Storage Centre about five kilometres from his home and either deposits things in his storage unit or tries to find things, usually unsuccessfully. 'It's ridiculous', he admits 'to pay to store all this clutter that I don't need, but somehow I can't bring myself to get rid of any of it.'

2 Conrad is not unique. Modern society has turned us all into hoarders and the self-storage industry has arisen to offer us a place to put our possessions. Facilities now come in a variety of flavours from the budget end of the market, where you have to give three days' notice if you want to [1]**retrieve** something, to luxury, air-conditioned, temperature-controlled units offering 24-hour access. Some companies will even come to your house, label everything, give it a barcode, box it up and then bring your items back to you as and when you want them. 'As easy as ordering a pizza', according to the marketing brochure. But all of this comes at a price and if you [2]**neglect** to pay your bill, the self-storage companies can sell your possessions to recover their costs.

3 Some self-storage facilities are so **³extravagantly** nice that customers have moved in. A YouTuber made a video that showed how he had managed to spend two-months living in a self-storage facility in the US. Unfortunately for him, he was caught, but his video still went viral. Another woman uses her self-storage unit as a kind of wardrobe. She keeps most of her clothes there and goes every morning to choose what to wear for the day.

4 Most people, however, are forced to use self-storage when they are affected by one of the three most stressful events in life: moving house, **⁴separation** or death of a loved one. Often the plan is only to use the self-storage for a couple of months, but as the saying goes, 'out of sight is out of mind' and more than a third of units are rented for three years or more. In the UK alone, there are well over 1100 self-storage sites with almost half a million customers between them taking up over four million square metres of storage space. This is still well behind the US where the average person has ten times as much self-storage space.

5 However, is a sea change to our materialistic attitudes on the way? There are many blogs and TV shows around these days which give you pointers on how to streamline your life, and the impetus for this change is coming from the younger generation. Jerson, a trainee nurse at Nottingham Hospital, has a strict rule that if an item in his house is not used within a year, it gets given away to charity. 'The psychological benefits of not being surrounded by clutter far outweigh the benefits of the actual things themselves', he says.

6 It's just possible, then, that as a society we are beginning to see the madness of paying to store things that we don't need and will never see. Compared to previous generations, millennials have less need of self-storage. With big student debts and with little hope of owning their own home, they focus on experiences rather than possessions. It's a lesson their **⁵materialistic** parents might do well to learn.

4 a Read the Focus box and decide which words 1–5 in the article are more important to know the meaning of.

When to check the meaning of words

When reading, stopping to check the <u>exact</u> meaning of every word can spoil our enjoyment. It's often better to continue reading. Look at this example from the article.

*Conrad Bailey has a **quintessentially** 21st-century problem.*

In this sentence, it is probably <u>not</u> necessary to check the meaning of the word *quintessentially*. The word doesn't give us any information that changes the meaning of the sentence.

*Modern society has turned us all into **hoarders**.*

In this sentence it probably <u>is</u> necessary to try to work out the meaning of the word *hoarders*. If we don't understand this word, we can't understand the sentence.

When deciding if a word is worth checking, consider these questions.

1 Is it an adverb?
2 Do you understand what the word means approximately?
3 Can you understand the sentence without understanding the word?

If the answer is yes to any of these questions, it is probably <u>not</u> worth stopping to check the exact meaning.

b Work in pairs. Compare your answers and explain your ideas.

5 a Read the two article extracts. Decide which words 1–6 it would be more useful to know the exact meaning of. Guess their meaning.

> The **¹paradox** is that we keep buying more and more stuff. Much of it we only use a few times and for a short while and then it is **²promptly** thrown away. Because much of it is also made of plastic, however, it will still exist hundreds of years after we are dead. Even the plastic bags that we carry it home in will probably **³outlast** us.
>
> This habit of buying more and more stuff that we **⁴patently** don't need has **⁵baffled** economists. What's more baffling still is that we pay to store it somewhere and never use it. Economists expect us to behave **⁶rationally** but there is nothing rational about this behaviour.

b Work in pairs and compare your ideas.

6 Work in groups and discuss the questions.

1 Have you ever used self-storage or do you know anyone who has? How was it?
2 Do you buy more than you need? If so, what in particular do you buy too much of?
3 What do you think should be done about the problem of people buying more and more stuff that they don't need and the damage it does to the environment?

Develop your reading

> **Goal:** understand a story

> **Focus:** inferring what will come next

1   Work in pairs. Look at the statements about finding success at work. Which ones do you agree with? Explain why.

  1   It's not what you know, it's who you know.

  2   Success has nothing to do with hard work and everything to do with luck.

  3   If you believe you will be successful, then you will be.

2   Read the novel extract. Which statement (1, 2 or 3) from Exercise 1 would Justin agree with? Explain your choice.

3 a   Read the extract again. Are the statements true (T) or false (F)? Underline evidence in the extract for your answer.

  1   Justin tries to be the first person into the office every morning and the last person to leave at night.

  2   He carries on working through his lunch break every day.

  3   He has made friends with some of his colleagues.

  4   He keeps a hard copy of all emails sent to him.

  5   He deals promptly with all the queries and questions in the emails he received.

  6   He tries to be a model for his colleagues.

  7   He stays positive and optimistic.

  b   Work in pairs and check your answers. Then decide whether each statement in Exercise 3a is good or bad practice in a new job. Explain why.

ALL WORK and NO PLAY

Jed Brabant

I pushed open the heavy glass doors and scanned my pass at the barriers. The sun was just coming up and the day felt full of potential, full of possibilities. Today is a day when anything could happen, I reminded myself. Unfortunately, my positive attitude wasn't shared by the security guard who was just finishing the night shift.

'A bit early, isn't it?' he said. 'You only left eight hours ago.'

'First in, last out', I replied with a big smile. 'That's my motto!'

'All work and no play makes Jack a dull boy', retorted the guard as he packed his bag to leave. 'That's mine.'

It was true, I had become rather work-obsessed since joining Hakeford Financial Management Services three weeks previously, and that hadn't helped me to integrate with my new colleagues. But I was still on my probation period and once I had a permanent position, I planned to take it a bit easier and maybe even take some time for lunch to chat to the people in my department. They seemed nice enough, although I'd only spoken to one or two since arriving. In the meantime it was important to show how committed I was and not lose focus by chatting to people.

At my desk on the third floor I spent the next hour and a half printing out all the emails I'd received the previous day and filing them according to sender. Do the uncommon things uncommonly well, I repeated to myself. The important emails I marked with a big red star and added them to the growing pile of urgent emails on my desk. Then I began replying to each email in turn with my standard but friendly response.

Thank you very much for making contact. Please rest assured that your email is very important to me and I intend to give it my full attention.

Kind regards,
Justin Blakeley
Junior Assistant (probationary)
Hakeford Financial Services (annual turnover $17 million)

It surprised me that my colleagues didn't reply to each other with the same kind of politeness and efficiency that I did but I felt sure that they could see the benefits of my approach and would all start to copy it in due course. As I reminded myself regularly, success isn't just what you achieve, it's also what you inspire others to do.

4 Read the exchange from the extract below. What does it tell us about what the colleague thinks of Justin? Read the Focus box and check your answer.

'… Nice to meet you.'

'Yeah, whatever, um, the boss wants to see you, pronto.'

Inferring what will come next

A text will often contain clues that, together, allow you to infer (work out) what is happening now and what is going to happen next. The clues might be small pieces of information which suddenly make sense when you know the outcome.

What can we infer from the following text?

Terry sighed, rubbed his eyes and lowered both elbows heavily onto his desk. When Jess arrived with her usual cheery hellos, his face was carefully buried in a magazine.

From this text we might infer that Terry is tired (*rubbed his eyes*), bored (he sighs, his body's movements are *heavy*) and that he isn't very interested in at least one of his colleagues (he starts to read a magazine to avoid greeting a colleague).

Around quarter to nine when most (although unbelievably not all) of the staff in my department were at their desks, someone who I didn't know came over to my desk.

'You're the new boy, Justin, right?'

'That's right. Nice to meet you.'

'Yeah, whatever, um, the boss wants to see you, pronto.'

'Me?'

'You're the one who sends all those emails, aren't you?'

'That's right. And prints and files the ones I receive', I said, beaming.

'Then it's definitely you she wants to see. I'd get up there ASAP if I were you.'

'Will do!' I said, then added 'ASAP' because it shows good communication skills to use the same language that the person you are talking to uses.

I was a little surprised, though very excited, to be invited to the boss's office so soon after joining Hakeford Financial Management Services, but I figured that maybe they'd decided to give me a permanent position already. Who knows, maybe a promotion even! *In order to succeed*, I reminded myself, *we have to have big dreams.* Certainly Ms Rashford would be aware of me by now as I copied her in to all my emails. *Today anything can happen*, I reminded myself again as I headed on up to Ms Rashford's office on the fourth floor.

from *All Work and No Play* by Jed Brabant

5 Read the novel extract again. Underline the sections which imply that Justin is not good at his job and may have a difficult relationship with his colleagues. Check your answers with a partner.

6 a Look at the short texts. Infer what might happen next.

1 Her husband changed the channel once, twice, finally settling on the tennis, which he didn't like. Her fingers began to drum on the coffee table, first softly, then with a more insistent beat and increasing volume. She cleared her throat once, twice. Then silence.

2 As she passed, he looked down immediately at his shoes, which were brown and unremarkable. He smiled. A smile that he hoped was smooth and attractive. He tried it again, looking at the distorted reflection of his thick glasses in the back of his coffee spoon.

3 Sheila hadn't arrived for work that morning. The last Bethan had heard of her was that she was going to the [1]bingo the night before, and she was putting on her lucky blue dress. Never been lucky for you yet, Bethan had sneered to herself.

4 There was water on the floor, and broken glass. I stepped carefully around it, and into the hall, where I was met by Caspian, the family cat, who was cleaning his paws with evident satisfaction.

[1] *bingo = a game in which players try to win money by matching numbers on their cards with numbers that are called out.*

b Work in pairs and compare your ideas.

7 a Work in pairs. What do you think will happen to Justin in the meeting with his boss?

b Read the rest of the extract on page 169 and check to see if you were correct.

c Work in pairs. Look at the extracts below and decide what we can infer from them.

1 [she] didn't even look up to acknowledge me.

2 She looked up at me but didn't take my hand.

3 'Do you know what we do here, Mr Alsop?' said Ms Rashford

4 'Printed out?' she almost shouted

5 … said a tearful goodbye to my colleagues, who managed not to cry

8 Work in small groups and answer the questions.

1 How do you feel about Justin? Why?

2 Which of the sayings or mottos he repeats to himself do you agree with?

3 What advice would you give to Justin?

Develop your reading

> **Goal:** understand an article

> **Focus:** understanding cause and effect in a complex text

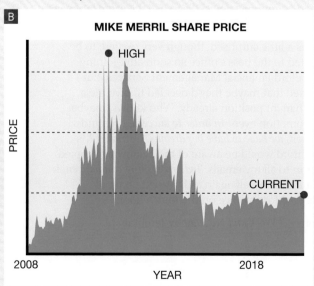

1 Work in pairs. Discuss the questions.

1 Do you follow financial news, for example about shares and share prices? Why/Why not?

2 What company do you wish you had bought shares in five years ago?

3 If you were starting a company, who would you ask to be an investor?

2 a Read the summary about Mike Merril and, in pairs, explain images A and B below.

At the age of 30, American Mike Merrill decided to try an experiment. He divided himself into 100,000 shares, just like a company, and sold those shares to investors for $1 each. If the shares went up in value, the investors could choose to cash out and make a profit. Unlike a company, however, investors in Mike had the right to vote on major decisions in his life, including his personal life and Mike promised to abide by the decisions.

Mike's partner was not keen on the idea, but she bought 19 shares anyway. Other investors bought a lot more. What could possibly go wrong?

b Work in pairs and answer the question at the end of the summary in Exercise 2. Then read the article on page 109 and check your answer.

3 Read the article again and choose the correct answer (a or b).

1 How is Mike different from David Bowie?
   a Mike is a celebrity who sold shares in himself.
   b Mike became famous by selling shares in himself.

2 What was Mike's response to some investors being upset?
   a He became vegetarian, didn't grow a moustache and joined a political party.
   b He decided to give them greater control over more aspects of his life.

3 Why did Mike tell his partner to buy more shares?
   a He saw it as a solution for her unhappiness and frustration.
   b He wanted her to have more control than other shareholders.

4 Why did the price of shares in Mike start to rise?
   a Someone started purchasing other people's shares.
   b Mike's brother sold his shares.

5 What happened in 2013?
   a Mike's story was covered in the press and he became known to many more people.
   b Mike sold a total of 1.2 million shares.

6 Why did the price of shares in Mike later fall?
   a The stranger sold his shares.
   b The press got bored of him.

7 What is the aim of polyphasic sleeping?
   a to improve a person's health by having extra short periods of sleep
   b to increase the amount of time that someone has in a day

8 Why did Mike and his partner break up?
   a She felt he didn't listen to her and was tired of her lack of influence over his life.
   b She was disappointed that he gave up the sleeping experiment.

A

REJECTED	Q: WINTER MOUSTACHE CLOSED [Yes: 45.91%	No: 54.09%] READ MORE
APPROVED	Q: ATTEMPT POLYPHASIC SLEEPING SCHEDULE CLOSED [Yes: 63.14%	No: 36.86%] READ MORE
APPROVED	Q: A VEGETARIAN DIET CLOSED [Yes: 61.13%	No: 38.87%] READ MORE
APPROVED	Q: REPUBLICAN REGISTRATION CLOSED [Yes: 84.31%	No: 15.69%] READ MORE

Most shares		Greatest total investment	
Rank	Shares	Rank	Dollars
1	662	1	3843.62
2	420	2	3472.44
3	416	3	2206.58
4	375	4	2182.51
5	365	5	1976.33
6	348	6	1917.22
7	323	7	1838.57
8	298	8	1740.22
9	250	9	1710.02
10	244	10	1327.80

B

MIKE MERRIL SHARE PRICE

HIGH

CURRENT

PRICE

2008   2018

YEAR

Meet Mike Merrill –
the man who sold his life

Treating yourself as a company and selling shares is not a new idea. Popstar David Bowie and various footballers have all sold shares in their future earnings but Mike Merrill from Oregon in the US took the idea to new extremes. He built a website that allowed shareholders to buy and sell shares in him. Shares entitled the owners to vote on the decisions he put before them and Mike always implemented their decisions.

Initially, Mike only asked investors to cast their votes on smaller issues such as what to do with any spare cash. Investors voted, for example, for Mike to invest $80 in a chicken farm (the farm went bankrupt). However, when Mike moved in with his partner, certain investors felt upset that they hadn't had a chance to vote on the decision. They accepted that it was very personal but even so they felt it had major implications for their investment. Mike realised that they had a point and started putting more and more decisions to a vote, including whether to have a moustache (shareholders voted no), whether to become vegetarian (yes) and whether to join a political party (yes, although it was not the party he voted for).

To Mike, this all felt like the right thing to do but it had a big impact on his private life. Shareholders' decisions inevitably affected his partner, too, but she felt that she had no say. When she talked to Mike about it, he simply said 'Buy more shares', leaving her feeling hurt and angry. She found herself questioning the whole relationship.

Eighteen months after Mike began selling shares in himself, someone Mike didn't know began buying up shares from other shareholders. This drove the price higher and several people, including Mike's brother, cashed out, effectively giving control of Mike to a total stranger. 'I didn't blame him', said Mike of his brother. 'He needed a dishwasher.' Later in 2013, when Mike's story was picked up by the media, many more people became interested and bought shares, driving the price up even higher and making Mike worth $1.2million. As the media lost interest, however, Mike's share price dropped and so did his value.

A crunch point for Mike's relationship came when Mike asked investors to vote on whether he should try polyphasic sleeping. The idea of polyphasic sleeping, which was first floated in the 1940s, is to reduce total daily sleep time to less than four hours by taking a series of short naps over each 24 hour period. Mike's partner thought it was an awful idea and voted against it, but she only had nineteen shares. Other shareholders were more keen and the idea was approved by a vote of 639 to 373. Mike accepted the decision and duly began his sleeping experiment.

It was a disaster. Mike began sleeping in short intervals throughout the day and night, causing him to feel constantly tired and irritable. His partner was also unhappy. Never knowing when he would be awake, she started to feel again that she was being ignored. After four weeks Mike gave up polyphasic sleeping, but the damage to their relationship had been done and after five years together, Mike and his partner split up.

4   Read the Focus box and find three more examples in the text of a participle clause showing how one thing affects another.

Understanding cause and effect in a complex text

Notice how we often use a participle clause beginning with an *-ing* verb to show how one thing affects another. The *-ing* clause is dependent on the main clause and has the same subject.

… he simply said 'Buy more shares', **leaving her feeling hurt and angry**.
Never knowing when he would be awake, *she started to feel …*

5   Combine the pairs of sentences using a participle clause.
   1   Mike moved in with his partner. This annoyed some shareholders.
   2   Mike turned himself into a company. This gave control of his life to his shareholders.
   3   Interest in Mike's experiment waned. This caused the share price to drop.
   4   Mike's brother wanted to buy a dishwasher. He cashed out for a profit.
   5   Mike's shareholders voted no to a moustache. This meant he wasn't allowed to grow one.
   6   Mike blogged about his experiment. It caught the attention of the national media.

6   Work in pairs. Discuss what you think Mike did after he split up with his partner? Then read the last part of the article on page 174 to check.

7   Work in pairs and discuss the questions.
   1   Do you admire Mike Merrill or not? Explain why.
   2   What do you think he did right or wrong?
   3   Would you buy shares in your friend if he/she did something similar? Say why.

8   Imagine you did the same as Mike Merrill. What decision about your life (real or imaginary) would you ask investors to vote on? Explain the situation to the class and ask them to vote.

> **Goal:** understand an online diary
> **Focus:** recognising topics that idioms refer to

1 a Work in pairs and match photos A–H with the words and phrases from the box.

> broccoli   cannoli   a chocolate waffle   lasagne
> nachos with cheese   muesli with yoghurt
> pancakes   tiramisu

b Discuss the questions.

1 Which of the things in Exercise 1a would you eat in a typical week?
2 Which of them do you like/not like? Why?
3 Do you associate any of the food in the photos with a particular country?
4 How does the food you eat affect your mood?
5 Do you ever regret eating a particular sort of food?

2 Read the online diary. Which is the only food in the photos that Greta doesn't eat over the weekend?

Food and mood – a weekend diary
Greta Kitching

Friday evening

I usually unwind on a Friday evening by going out with friends after work, but tonight I've got guests so I need to shop, cook and spruce myself up. It's been a tough week, but I'm feeling ready for the weekend. At the market I buy courgettes, spinach, basil, ricotta and mozzarella and get an iced coffee to go. Then I dash home, and cook the lasagne and tiramisu, shower, get dressed and do my make-up. It's all a bit manic, but I'm ready just before the guests arrive. Later I eat one helping of lasagne and two of dessert, which I instantly regret, but have a great evening anyway.

Saturday

I begin the day as always with two espressos. I used to have just one, but these days I need two to get me going. Then I wander down to the bakery with my flatmate, R, and we buy cannoli, which are Italian pastries filled with cream. We eat them under a tree in the park and chat about her love life, which is way more complicated than mine, although I always take her stories with a pinch of salt. By the time we get back, it's lunchtime and R says she **1could eat a horse**. I have a look in the fridge to see what we have. It's empty so we just have leftovers from the night before.

In the afternoon my best friend, S, picks me up and we drive to a river. I forget to bring my swimming stuff (on purpose), so I just sit at the side and enjoy the view. It's busy but not too packed. We get two skinny lattes from a coffee van and a chocolate waffle, which I **2wolf down**. I ask myself why I ordered a skinny latte when the waffle clearly wasn't. My good eating habits just go out of the window at weekends.

On the way back we stop at a bar to watch the sun go down. We order a drink and a bowl of nachos but I only **3pick at** the nachos because I'm still full from the chocolate waffle. We reminisce about the good old days when we were studying. I tell S that I don't want to work in an office anymore. I want to be a writer. S tells me that's a novel idea and we laugh until tears roll down our faces.

Sunday

I wake up feeling bad about the chocolate waffle and nachos from yesterday and decide it's time to do some sport. After a breakfast of muesli and yoghurt I call my sporty friend, L, and we arrange to meet at the tennis courts. We play three sets and L wins all of them. I've only played a few times and it's nowhere near as easy as it looks.

By lunchtime we've **4worked up an appetite** so we get a bagel and an espressino freddo from a café. An espressino freddo is a small iced coffee cream, which is **5to die for**. I want two, but I resist.

In the afternoon I go to the supermarket and buy lots of vegetables for the week to come. My good intentions usually last till Tuesday. For dinner I steam broccoli and eat it with roasted peppers, grated carrots and tofu. I tell R that it tastes like airline food and she agrees that it's a bit plain. We laugh for the last time before Sunday evening blues kick in and I decide it's high time I look for a new job that doesn't stress me out so much. In the evening I watch an old series of *Game of Thrones* with R and we drink chamomile tea. I go to bed early and try to read in bed, but I fall asleep after a couple of pages, as usual.

E   F

G   H

3 **Read the text again and answer the questions.**

1 What is different about this Friday compared to normal?

2 Why does Greta have two espressos every Saturday morning?

3 What does she eat for lunch on Saturday?

4 What does she do during the week that she doesn't do at weekends?

5 What do Greta and her best friend talk about in the bar?

6 Why does she decide to do sport on Sunday morning?

7 What usually happens every Tuesday?

8 How does she feel on Sunday evening and what decision does she make?

4 **Work in pairs and discuss the questions.**

1 Why does Greta laugh at two points in the diary?

2 What tense does the writer mostly use? Why?

3 How does the writer refer to her friends? Why?

5 **Read the Focus box and then match idioms 1–5 in the text with meanings a–e below.**

a eat only a little bit of something over a long period of time

b to become hungry through sport or exercise

c exceptionally tasty and delicious

d to be very hungry

e to eat very quickly

Recognising topics that idioms refer to

All the idioms in bold in the text are generally used to talk about food and eating.

*... which I **wolf down***

*we've **worked up an appetite***

Sometimes it is possible to guess the meaning of an idiom from the words, for example:

*I could **eat a horse**.*

This idiom means that I am hungry and I could eat a lot.

Often, however, it is not possible to guess the meaning from the words in the idiom. For example:

*I always **take** her stories **with a pinch of salt**.*

This idiom means that she exaggerates when she tells stories so I don't completely believe them.

Although the words *pinch of salt* suggest that the idiom refers to cooking or eating, it actually refers to how much we believe what someone tells us. When trying to understand the meaning of an idiom, it is important to look at the context and also to remember that the meaning may not be obvious.

6 **Work in pairs and discuss the questions.**

1 Do you normally pick at your food or wolf it down?

2 Does learning English help you work up an appetite?

3 When was the last time you felt you could eat a horse?

4 What food would you describe as to die for?

7 a **Underline the idioms in the online diary extracts. There are three in each extract. What does each idiom mean?**

1

I've been in pretty bad shape recently, so on Saturday I signed up for a 'boot camp' class. The trainer promised us all he would whip us back into shape but the class was so intense I nearly blacked out. I think I need to take things more slowly.

2

We discussed the fall in sales but without the figures for the previous year, it was hard to see the big picture. Jen promised to get us ballpark figures by the following week. Nobody, however, was talking about the elephant in the room: how much longer can we survive?

b **Work in pairs and compare your ideas. What topic is each diary extract talking about?**

8 **Match the pairs of idioms with similar meanings.**

1 I **flew off the handle** when I heard they'd crashed my car.

2 She **chickened out** when she saw how deep the water was.

3 I'm guessing he passed, because he was **grinning from ear to ear**.

4 Sorry, what did you say? **I'm really not on the ball** today.

a He **got cold feet** about the marriage after meeting his girlfriend's mother.

b Argh, I left it at home. Seriously, **I don't know whether I'm coming or going**, I really don't.

c He **saw red** when the guy insulted his family.

d You **look like the cat who got the cream** – did you get the pay rise you wanted?

9 **Work in pairs. Tell your partner what you ate and how you felt last weekend. You can invent the details if you like.**

111

9c Develop your reading

> **Goal:** compare a text and its summary
> **Focus:** critically evaluating a summary

1 a Work in pairs. Look at the ways of saying *thank you* or *thanks* in different languages. Do you know which language they come from?

b Do you know how to say *thank you* in any other languages?

c Work in pairs. Discuss what you think the benefits are of learning a language.

2 Read the article and the summary below. Note four things which are incorrect in the summary.

谢谢

obrigado

شكرا

merci

The problems and benefits of learning a language

1 Learning a second language is a complicated business. Not only do you have to know approximately 10,000 words in order to achieve 'fluency' in that language, you also need to know in which order they appear, how they morph grammatically, how they combine with other words to create new meaning as well as which combinations sound natural and which unnatural. The muscles in your mouth need to know how to make the right sounds to produce those words and all of this knowledge needs to be available to you in a split second so that you can engage in natural conversation.

2 No wonder then, that learning a language is like a mental workout for the brain and, just like a workout for the body, it has enormous benefits. Research in Canada has shown that learning a second language delays the onset of mental diseases such as dementia by five years, learning two foreign languages delays it by over six years and learning three or more foreign languages delays dementia by nine years. If ever there was a good reason to learn a language, this is it.

3 What then is the most difficult language to learn? The answer to that question naturally depends on which language you speak in the first place. Native Spanish speakers find Italian relatively easy to learn but like most other people, find Hungarian much harder. Native Finnish speakers, find Hungarian easier than Spanish speakers because of its similarities to their language.

4 The Foreign Service Institute (FSI), which is the organisation responsible for training US diplomats and other employees to speak foreign languages, rates languages from one to five in terms of how difficult they are for a native English speaker to learn. A category one language will typically take 24 weeks of full-time study for an FSI student to reach 'general professional proficiency', a category three language will take 36 weeks and a category five language 88 weeks. French, Spanish and Swedish, for example, are considered category one, German is category two, Indonesian category three, Hungarian, Polish, Russian and Thai are category four while Arabic, Chinese (Cantonese and Mandarin), Japanese and Korean are category five.

5 There are other languages which don't have an FSI category but which are possibly more complex than even a level five language. Take Tuyuca for example - a language spoken by fewer than a thousand people in parts of the Amazon rainforest. While languages such as Spanish and French have two classes of noun (for example, *el* and *la* in Spanish), Tuyuca has up to 140. Or take Xhosa, a language widely spoken in South Africa. One of the sounds of Xhosa is a click that you make by pressing your tongue against your upper side teeth and then pulling away. It's the sound that some people make when encouraging a horse to move. In fact the 'X' of Xhosa is that click sound, so the name of the language is pronounced with a click followed by 'hosa'. And if you think that Xhosa sounds difficult to learn, imagine learning the strangely named *!Xóõ* language, which has five ways of pronouncing the click!

6 Unfortunately, the very act of learning a foreign language is in danger. The number of languages spoken around the world has plunged in recent years and around half of the approximately six and a half thousand languages that are still in active use are already in danger of dying out. Some predictions estimate that 90 percent of all languages could die out by the end of the century as children stop learning the language of their parents and ancestors and instead learn the language which will allow them to participate in the modern economy. Every language that dies, however, represents a loss of knowledge, culture and history as well as a unique way of seeing the world.

Summary

Speaking a foreign language is the most difficult thing the human mind can do, however it has many benefits and it can actually cure dementia. The FSI, a US organisation, grades languages from one to five. Everyone will struggle to learn a category five language. Some languages, such as Tuyuca or Xhosa, are difficult because of their unusual grammar or sounds. Unfortunately, 90 percent of languages will die out by the end of the century.

danke
Спасибо
ありがとう
teşekkürler
dziękuję
grazie

3 Read the Focus box, then check your answers to Exercise 2.

4 Read the sentences below and say if they are accurate summaries of the paragraphs in the article. Change the sentences which are not accurate.

Paragraph 1

Learning a language is the most complicated thing that the human mind can do.

Paragraph 2

The more languages you learn, the more you delay the onset of dementia.

Paragraph 3

If a language is similar to the speaker's native language, they will find it easy to learn.

Paragraph 4

Each higher category of difficulty means twelve extra weeks of learning.

Paragraph 5

Tuyuca and Xhosa are difficult for native English speakers to learn.

Paragraph 6

Only 10% of the world's languages will survive to the end of the century.

5 Choose the correct answer (a, b or c) for the questions below.

1 Why is learning a language compared to a physical workout?
   a Because it is challenging but good for you.
   b Because it takes a long time to improve.
   c Because it is uses the muscles of your mouth.

2 Which language will a Finnish person find easier to learn.
   a Italian
   b Hungarian
   c It isn't known.

3 Who will usually find Arabic harder to learn than Thai?
   a Everyone apart from Arabic speakers.
   b Native English speakers.
   c Everyone.

4 Why are some languages dying out?
   a People are choosing to speak languages that are used globally.
   b People have forgotten how to speak them.
   c People see the world differently.

6 Underline words or phrases in the text that express the same idea as the phrases below.

1 a very short period of time (paragraph 1)
2 it's not surprising (paragraph 2)
3 beginning of (paragraph 2)
4 obviously (paragraph 3)
5 (which) many people speak (paragraph 5)
6 fallen dramatically (paragraph 6)
7 no longer exist (summary)

7 Work in groups and discuss the questions.

1 Should governments try to protect languages that are in danger of dying out? Why/Why not?
2 What can they do to protect those languages?

> **Goal:** understand linguistically complex texts

> **Focus:** recognising small details that change meaning

1 **Work in pairs and discuss the questions.**

1 How often do you visit a library?
2 How important do you think libraries are in a community?
3 What alternatives are there to libraries?

2 a **Read the title and introduction to the article. Work in pairs and discuss why someone might set up a library like this.**

b **Read the complete article and check your ideas. Then answer the questions.**

1 What does Guanlao feel about books?
2 What motivated Guanlao to start the library?
3 How have other people been inspired by the Reading Club 2000?

3 **Read the text again. Are the sentences true (T) or false (F)? Underline the information in the text that helped you decide.**

1 Guanlao lives in or near the centre of town.
2 Guanlao's real name is Nanie.
3 More books are taken than are donated.
4 The library was an instant success.
5 The library only offers a few different types of books.
6 Guanlao has helped to establish more libraries like his.
7 Mark has collected 90 books to help him pass his accountancy course.

4 a **Look at the article again. How do we know these sentences are incorrect?**

1 Guanlao is a tax accountant.
2 Guanlao's parents liked the library.
3 Guanlao has a brother and a sister.

THE LIBRARY WITH NO RULES

Manila's Reading Club 2000 is a library like no other: it lets anyone borrow and then bring back or keep any of its thousands of books.

Books, believes Hernando Guanlao, need to live. And they're only alive if they are being read. Thought, effort, time and money went into making them; they will never repay it lying idle in a cabinet or on a shelf. Books need to be set free. So walk by his home on Balagtas Street in Makati, downtown Manila, and books are pretty much all you'll see. Thousands of them, on shelves and in crates, outside on the pavement, piled high in the garage and on the stairs, each one free to anyone who wants it.

'People can borrow, take home, bring back or keep', says Guanlao, 60, a former tax accountant, ice-cream salesman and government employee known by all as Nanie. 'Or they can share and pass on to another. But basically they should just take, take!' Guanlao reckons books 'have lives, and have to lead them. They have work to do. And the act of giving a book … it makes you complete. It makes your life meaningful and abundant.'

Thankfully for Guanlao's faith in human nature, people also give – often people he has never previously met, or doesn't even see: they leave boxes of books outside his door. 'What's taken gets replaced many times over', he says. 'I don't keep an inventory. But there are a lot of books. They want to be read, so they come here.'

The Reading Club 2000, as it is called, began two decades ago as a tribute to Guanlao's late parents, both civil servants. 'They gave me my love of reading', he says. 'I wanted to honour them and to do some kind of community service. So I put my old books – and my brothers' and sisters', maybe 100 in all – outside, to see if anyone was interested.'

It took a while for people to work out that this was, as Guanlao puts it, a library 'open 24/7, and with no rules', but the scheme, offering everything from battered crime paperbacks to fashion magazines, technical manuals, arcane histories and school textbooks, is booming.

The success of the project is helped by the fact that despite a 1994 act pledging 'reading centres throughout the country', the Philippines, with a population of 92 million, has fewer than 700 public libraries, and buying books is a luxury many cannot afford.

Fortunately the Reading Club is spreading. Guanlao takes boxes of books into Manila's neighbourhoods himself, on a specially adapted book bike. He has also helped friends set up similar schemes at ten other sites around the country, and inspired student book drives.

Aurora Verayo, from a town several hours drive from Manila, says she came to see Guanlao to donate books, but he persuaded her to open her own centre. 'I'm going a step further and offering reading sessions for children', she says. 'This is the start of a movement.' Mark, a 16-year-old accountancy student at the Philippine Christian University in Manila, is organising a book drive with friends. 'We've collected 90 books so far, and we expect many more', he says. 'We're taking them to the barrios next month. Books open minds. A book can take you anywhere.'

b **Read the Focus box and check your answers to Exercise 4a.**

Recognising small details that change meaning

Sometimes small details in a text can change the meaning and it is important to be aware of what those small details are.

former and _late_ before a noun

Putting _former_ before a noun shows that the person no longer has that position.

... a **former** tax accountant (he's not a tax accountant now)

It can also be used for things and places.

the **former** prison is now a hotel

The word _late_ before a person means that the person is dead.

... Guanlao's **late** parents

When used in a historical context it means that the person was dead at that time.

It was built in honour of his **late** father.

's vs s'

Remember! _'s_ shows that the noun is singular. _s'_ shows that the noun is plural. Compare these examples:

my brother**'s** books
my brother**s'** books

5 **Read the two descriptions and add _former, late, 's_ or _s'_ to words 1–8 in the correct position.**

A

One of the most famous libraries of the classical period was the Library of Celsus in Ephesus in modern-day Turkey. The library was built by the son of a **1**Roman senator to honour his **2**father. The **3**building ruins were rediscovered in the early 20th century.

B

In the US it is usual for a **4**president to establish a library after leaving power. The **5**president libraries are usually established in their home states. Thus **6**president George W Bush had his library built in **7**Texas third largest city, Dallas. His **8**father, who was also a president, also had his library built in Texas.

6 **Work in groups and discuss the questions.**

1 What do you think Guanlao has achieved with his library?

2 In your opinion, is it important to encourage people to read?

3 Are you a member of a library? Why/Why not? When did you last go to a library?

4 Some people believe that libraries are no longer necessary. Why might they think this? What is your opinion?

> **Goal:** write a report

> **Focus:** changing the register of spoken information

1 Work in pairs and discuss the questions.

1 What would you change about your work–life balance (or study–life balance) if you could?

2 Do you think people work to live or live to work? Why?

3 What do you think of the idea of a four-day working week for everyone? Why?

2 a Look at the different kinds of source information A–G used in a written report. What arguments are made for and against a four-day working week?

b Work in pairs and compare your answers. What information did you find interesting or surprising?

A **Four-day working week leads to 29% increase in productivity for companies**

That's the result of a recent investigation into the effects of giving every member of staff Friday off as well as the weekend – and without any loss of pay or benefits!

B ❝I reckon it won't last. Productivity might go up at first, but it'll soon go back down again when all the excitement has gone away. Trust me on that!❞

C Recent research has shown that workers on shorter working weeks actually produce more than workers who do a full five-day week. The reason is thought to be that staff on shorter contracts get a longer break from work and hence have more energy and focus to tackle the tasks that they need to achieve.

D

	staff	management	customers
Total	12	4	15
In favour	11	1	10
Don't know	1	2	2
Against	0	1	3

E The thing our firm has found is that we spend much less time and money recruiting and training new members of staff. Before we introduced a four-day week we had a staff turnover rate of around 12% a year. Now it's more like 3%. Staff also take far fewer sick days which also saves us money.

F ❝The thing you have to remember is that it's not going to suit every company. If you serve customers, they expect to be able to contact you every day of the week and if there's no one there they might look for a different company.❞

G ❝I love the idea! I'd have time to do more outdoor pursuits and to switch off from work. It would really make me more motivated in my work.❞

3 Read a report by an employee at an insurance company. Is the report for or against the proposal for a four-day working week? How do you know?

Report on the proposal to introduce a four-day week at Evergreen Insurance

Introduction

The purpose of this report is to consider the advantages and potential problems of introducing a four-day working week for all Evergreen Insurance staff with no loss of pay or benefits. As preparation for writing this report, I have researched the topic and spoken to staff, management and customers.

Background

Recent research suggests that staff who work fewer than thirty-five hours a week [1]**are more productive than full-time staff**. Several companies have experimented with introducing a four-day week and the results have been positive.

Potential advantages for us

There are two main advantages for Evergreen Insurance:

• [2]**an increase in productivity of around 30%**

This stems from more motivated and focused sales staff.

• [3]**a decrease in costs**

This is related to recruitment, training and sickness pay. Evergreen can expect a healthier workforce who take fewer sick days and stay longer with the company. This will result in a decrease in recruitment and training costs.

Potential problems

Our customers expect to be able to call us five days a week and for this reason a four-day working week may have [4]**a negative impact on them**.

There is a risk that any gains in productivity from a four-day working week [5]**will not be permanent**.

Views of staff and customers

[6]**Staff were overwhelmingly in favour while management were more evenly split**. Some staff commented that the increase in free time would [7]**increase their desire to work**. Management were concerned about the impact on customers and that there would be no increase in productivity.

Conclusions and recommendations

Taking everything into account, I would recommend a limited trial of a four-day week for two months. Customers would need to be given plenty of notice and workers would need to be warned that this was an experiment which might not continue.

4 Tick the features that apply to the report.

- ☐ headings
- ☐ a clear statement of the purpose of the report
- ☐ lists
- ☐ an introduction and a conclusion
- ☐ informal language
- ☐ a summary of sources for the report
- ☐ a summary of statistics and/or opinions
- ☐ a recommendation at the beginning
- ☐ frequent use of *I* and *we*
- ☐ analysis of disadvantages as well as advantages
- ☐ contractions such as *won't* and *wouldn't*

5 a Match the parts of the report in bold 1–7 with source information A–G in Exercise 2.

  1C

b Work in pairs. Compare your answers and discuss how the source information has been changed in the report.

6 a Check your ideas in the Focus box. Find one more example of where the register of spoken information has been changed in the report.

Changing the register of spoken information

When taking information from various sources and putting it into a report or essay, it is important to express the information in the correct register. Spoken comments need to be expressed in a more formal register using reporting verbs such as *comment, suggest, be concerned, indicate* and *express doubt*.

Some people **commented/suggested** *that …*
A few people **were concerned** *that …*
Several people **indicated** *that …*
Certain people **expressed doubt** *that …*

For example:
"I reckon it won't last … Trust me on that!"
is expressed in the report as:
Management were **concerned** *… that there would be no increase in productivity.*

b Read statements 1–3, then complete the sentences in a way that is suitable for a report.

1 'A four-day week! That would be amazing! I could take up some new pastimes like keep-fit or martial arts. I'd get healthier and hopefully live longer.'
Some staff _____

2 It's never going to work. It's a ridiculous idea. How can you get more work from shorter hours?'
Some members of the management team
_____

3 'Sounds nice for you but what about us, your customers? What happens if I call you up on a Friday and no one's there?'
Certain customers _____

Prepare

7 You're going to write a report on the possibility of getting rid of all exams at a university. Read the information below and find arguments for and against the proposal.

A leading university is looking into the possibility of getting rid of exams. The director of the university has asked you to conduct research and write a short report about the topic. Your report should include details of the results of your research and a recommendation.

	students	lecturers	employers
In favour	72	5	2
Don't know	9	3	3
Against	31	20	2
Total	112	28	7

'If I can't give my students an exam, how can I know if they've understood what I've taught?'
Lecturer

'I'm a good student but I'm hopeless at exams. I get stressed and ill every time I take one. That's not fair on me.'
Student

Recent research has shown that university students are suffering from ever-increasing levels of stress related to exam pressure.
Academic research paper

'I don't care about what grade somebody got at university! If they finished the course, that's enough for me. The important thing is what kind of person they are.'
Employer

Write

8 a Write the first draft of your report using the information in Exercise 7 (you can also make up your own information). Use the checklist in Exercise 4 and the verbs in the Focus box to help you.

b When you have finished the first draft of your report, exchange with your partner and prepare feedback on good points and any suggestions for improvements.

9 Use your partner's feedback to write a second draft of your report.

2B Develop your writing

> **Goal:** write an email to build rapport
> **Focus:** building rapport with an email recipient

1 a Work in pairs. Have you ever taken part in a big organised charity event? Or have you ever given money to someone you know who has done one?

b Look at charity events a–d below and answer the questions.

1 How would each event raise money for charity?
2 Which one(s) would be the easiest to organise?
3 Which one(s) would probably be the most successful in raising money?
  a a fun run
  b a concert
  c an auction
  d an art exhibition

c Can you think of any other ways to raise money for charity? Have you or has anyone you know been involved in events like these?

2 a Read the three emails from charities to local business owners asking for support. Answer the questions.

1 What is the name of each charity?
2 What does each charity do?
3 What event has each charity decided to organise?
4 What help are they asking for from the business or individual?

b Circle the numbers to show which emails:

1 use the recipient's name. 1 2 3
2 explain the problem the charity is trying to tackle. 1 2 3
3 explain why the recipient's help is important. 1 2 3
4 explain what the charity event is. 1 2 3
5 explain what the charity is asking for. 1 2 3
6 suggest different ways for the recipient to help. 1 2 3
7 emphasise the importance of acting quickly. 1 2 3

1

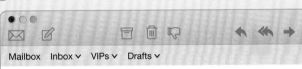

from: collette@fanfitforeveryone.net
to: Jolene_Khan@khansportsclothing.net

Dear Ms Khan,

As a successful local business owner in the sports sector, we know you understand the need to help everyone in the community stay fit and healthy.

Our organisation, Fantastic Fitness for Everyone, is actively trying to raise awareness and tackle the problem of the lazy lifestyle that many people these days have.

However, our efforts won't be successful without the backing of the community. That's why I'm writing to you.

We're holding a Fitness in the Park day and we need your support. Would you consider sponsoring our event?

The endorsement of a well-known sports brand such as yours would raise the profile of our event as well as help us to achieve our goal. It would also be a great opportunity for you to promote your business.

There are a number of sponsorship opportunities:
- be our main corporate sponsor and have your name prominently displayed at the event
- sponsor an individual race at the event and get your company logo in the programme and on our website
- provide gifts that can be used as prizes

If you are interested in helping us to get everyone fit, please get in touch with at me at collette@fanfitforeveryone.net or on 07438 612 99.

We're looking forward to hearing from you!

Kind regards,
Collette Edwards
Director, Fantastic Fitness for Everyone

P.S. There are only five weeks to go till the event so please get in touch as soon as possible!

2

from: janine@kidsgroup.net
to: ina_passard@ina_passard_catering.net

Dear Ina,

Like you, we are concerned about the fact that local disadvantaged children sometimes go to school hungry.

Here at Kids Group, our goal is to ensure that no local children ever have to go to school without a good healthy breakfast. We also provide support for those children with emotional and psychological needs.

An organisation like ours relies on the support of high-profile individuals like you.

Our tenth annual auction is coming soon and we badly need your help. Will you offer us and local children your support?

Last year we raised over €1,000 and this year we're hoping to do even better. It would mean a lot to us to receive donated items from respected members of our community like you. Would you be able to help us by donating an item for our auction?

We're specially looking for items which are:
- greater in value than €25
- new or hardly used
- unique or special in some way

Alternatively, if you don't have any suitable items to donate, perhaps you would be willing to provide an 'experience' that can be auctioned, for example, learn how to cook with famous local chef, Ina Passard.

If you are able to help us at Kids Group, please get in touch with me at janine@kidsgroup.net or 07384 713 23.

Thank you in advance for your generosity!

Kind regards,
Janine Govely,
Director of Kids Group

P.S. Please don't delay in contacting us. There are only six weeks to go till the auction!

3

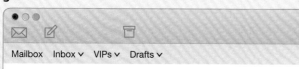

from: keith@localseniorsupport.net
to: info@niceandhealthysnacks.net

Dear Sir or Madam,

We are organising a charity event in order to raise money for Local Senior Support and we need your help.

Can your company support us?

The event will take place on Saturday 23rd July in Bigly Park. Last year over 200 people took part and we are expecting a similar number this year.

If you are able to help us, please get in touch with me as soon as possible.

Kind regards,
Keith Barra

Director of Local Senior Support
keith@localseniorsupport.net

3 a Work in pairs. How do emails 1 and 2 build a rapport (a closer connection) with the recipient?

   b Read the Focus box and check your ideas. Find examples of the ways of building rapport in email 2.

Building rapport with an email recipient

When you ask someone to do something for you by email (or letter), it is important to establish rapport by making the recipient feel important and valued. This makes them more likely to agree to your request. You can establish rapport by email in several ways.

1 Personalise your emails to each recipient by including their name.
   Dear Ms. Khan
2 Show that you believe the recipient shares your goals.
   we know you understand the need to …
3 Emphasise that the recipient's help is important.
   … our efforts won't be successful without the backing …
4 Compliment the recipient.
   The endorsement of a well-known sports brand such as yours …

4 Add the phrases in the box to the sentences below in order to build rapport with the recipient. Use at least one phrase in each sentence.

> as a local citizen   like you   of ours   respected
> successful   such as yours   well-known

1 We are worried about the lack of green spaces in this unique city.
   Like you, we are worried …
2 You will know that litter is a big problem.
3 Our charity relies on the support of local people.
4 Securing the sponsorship of a local company would really help.
5 Last year we received a lot of support from leaders of the community.

Prepare

5 a You're going to write an email to ask for sponsorship from a local business. Choose a goal from the list below and a name for your charity.
   • provide warm meals to homeless people
   • build more cycle lanes
   • help older people learn to use technology
   • promote a healthy lifestyle
   • your choice

   b Choose an event to organise from Exercise 1b. Plan what you will ask the local company to donate or do.

Write

6 a Write the first draft of your email to the company. Use the checklist in Exercise 2b to help you.

   b Work in pairs. Read your partner's email and check that it builds rapport with the recipient.

7 Exchange feedback with your partner, then write the second draft of your email.

3A Develop your writing

> **Goal:** write an effective leaflet

> **Focus:** writing effective paragraphs

1 Work in pairs. Look at the cover of the information leaflet. Do you think leaflets like this are effective? Why/Why not?

2 a Read the leaflet and answer the questions with a, b or c.

1 Who is the leaflet written for?

    a people who think that climate change is a problem

    b people who don't know if climate change is a problem

    c people who think that climate change isn't a problem

2 What does the leaflet aim to do?

    a convince the reader that climate change is real

    b explain why people don't want to talk about climate change

    c show the reader how to talk to others about climate change

3 The general message of the leaflet is:

    a stay positive and talk about the future.

    b inspire fear and talk about the present.

    c stay positive and talk about the present.

4 What do you need more of if you want to talk to people about climate change?

    a facts

    b scare stories

    c predictions about the future

b What do you think about the advice in the leaflet and the way it is presented?

3 a Tick the features below that you think make an information leaflet effective.

- [ ] a strong, attention-grabbing headline
- [ ] an introduction that encourages you to read more
- [ ] an academic tone
- [ ] a call-to-action that encourages you to do something
- [ ] an attractive design
- [ ] a balance of opinions
- [ ] short, direct sentences
- [ ] sends a powerful message to the reader

b Work in pairs and compare your ideas.

4 a Work in pairs and discuss the features of an effective paragraph in a leaflet.

b Read the Focus box and check your ideas.

Writing effective paragraphs

Leaflets need to be as easy to read as possible, so the information is broken up into short paragraphs in order to create as much impact as possible. They often include an attention-grabbing heading, sometimes written as a short question or instruction.

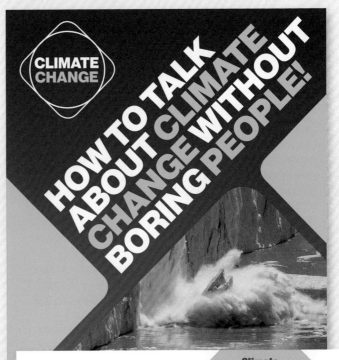

CLIMATE CHANGE

HOW TO TALK ABOUT CLIMATE CHANGE WITHOUT BORING PEOPLE!

Climate change is the single biggest issue of our time but do you find that some people look bored and start yawning when you talk about it? If so, there are a few simple rules that we should all follow when talking about climate change and trying to encourage people to take action.

1 Don't talk about cutting, talk about growing

Everyone assumes that cutting greenhouse gas emissions will be painful so they choose not to think about it. But some studies estimate that the green economy will create many millions of jobs.

That's not pain, that's growth!

So stop talking about cutting and start talking about growing the green economy and creating green jobs.

2 Don't talk about what people <u>will</u> do, talk about what people <u>are</u> doing today

We all find it hard to think about the future. It seems unreal and uncertain and we prefer to trust that things will be OK.

So instead when you talk about climate change, focus on the present and what people and governments are doing to control CO2 emissions right now.

It's much more inspiring than what they might do in the future.

3 Don't talk about future climate disasters, talk about present ones

It's not necessary to scare people with predictions of a cataclysmic future – there are enough climate change disasters happening in the present.

From wildfires in California to tropical storms in South America to flooding in Europe to drought in Australia, the effects of climate change are real and they're happening now.

120

CLIMATE CHANGE

HOW TO TALK ABOUT CLIMATE CHANGE WITHOUT BORING PEOPLE!

4 Don't repeat facts, tell stories

Facts don't change people's minds, stories do. Research shows that the more facts you show people, the more tightly they cling to their existing beliefs.

So make the facts into a story. Stories have the power to move people and to change emotions.

For example, instead of pointing out the facts about plastic pollution, tell the story of the boy who made friends with a seal, and was so sad to see the amount of plastic in his friend's ocean home that he recruited everyone from his village to clean it up.

5 Stop predicting the end of the world

Talk of doomsday simply encourages people to feel helpless and do nothing.

Instead present a positive message that change is possible.

6 Ignore climate change deniers

There have always been people who ignore science and there always will be. Arguing with them just gives them attention.

Focus on connecting with people who are willing to make a difference.

So now go out there and talk to people about climate change. It's the most important conversation ever!

For more information check out howtotalkaboutclimatechange.uk.net

---

5 a Divide the information below into sections for a leaflet. Write the sentence numbers to show which go into each section.

Introduction: *1, 2*

Section 1:

Section 2:

Section 3:

Section 4:

Call to action:

Phone-free day

[1]Do you ever feel our phones are in control of us rather than us in charge of them? [2]We do, and we think it's time to do something about it. [3]Research has recently revealed that the average person spends up to eight hours a day looking at their phones, whether it's messaging, watching videos or gaming. [4]That number is rising every year, as phones do more and more things for us. [5]Why is it a problem? [6]Have you ever seen a couple staring at their phones in a restaurant rather than talking to each other? [7]How about a boy trying to get the attention of his parents, who are ignoring him, lost in instant messaging? [8]People are getting more and more isolated from each other and it's becoming harmful for our relationships. [9]There are also medical considerations when it comes to phone use. [10]Excessive phone use been linked to health problems such as headaches and attention deficit. [11]Back problems are another concern as we are all bent over our phones for so much of the day. [12]We'd like to invite you to take part in a **phone-free day** on 12th June. [13]We're encouraging people to take a walk, chat with friends (face to face!), read a book or just do anything that doesn't involve being glued to their phones all day. [14]We think it might just help us reconnect. [15]So, remember the date, and don't forget to put that phone away!

b Now write a heading for each section.

Section 1: _____   Section 3: _____

Section 2: _____   Section 4: _____

Prepare

6 a You're going to write an information leaflet. Choose one of the topics below or use your own idea.
- what everyone should be doing to prevent climate change
- how to relax and stop worrying about things
- how to learn English
- how to deal with online bullying

b Make notes about what ideas to include for your leaflet.

c Make a plan for your leaflet. Decide on the content and think of a heading for each section.

Write

7 a Write the first draft of your information leaflet. Use the checklist in Exercise 3a to help you.

b Work in pairs. Exchange leaflets and check that your partner's includes effective paragraphs and is written in an appropriate style.

8 Give feedback to your partner, then write the second draft of your leaflet.

> **Goal:** write an academic essay
> **Focus:** developing an argument in an essay

A

B

1 Work in pairs. Look at the photos and discuss the questions.

1 Do all or most of the schools in your country have a school uniform?

2 What do you think is the reason many countries have a compulsory school uniform?

3 Are you for or against school uniforms for children from 4–16? Why?

2 a Read the notes and try to choose the correct alternatives.

> History of school uniforms in the UK
> 1 first school uniform was in 1222/1522/1822
> 2 became more popular in the 14th/16th/18th century
> 3 became associated with rich/poor people's schools
> 4 these days 30%/60%/90% of UK schools have uniform
> 5 often only black trousers and sweatshirt/tie/shoes
> 6 average uniform costs £200/£1000/£2000 per child per year

b Check your answers on page 166.

3 Read arguments 1–8 about school uniforms. Decide if each one is for or against.

1 Uniforms prevent inappropriate and offensive clothing.

2 Uniforms stop students expressing their own identity.

3 Uniforms allow all children to feel equal.

4 Strict rules of students' appearance create problems for the teacher.

5 Uniforms can teach children the importance of looking smart.

6 Uniforms allow the teacher to focus on teaching.

7 Uniforms are more expensive than normal clothes.

8 Schools with uniforms do no better academically than schools without.

4 a Read the essay below. Is it for or against school uniforms? Which arguments from Exercise 3 are mentioned?

b Tick the features that apply to this essay.

☐ Each paragraph deals with one main point only.

☐ The introduction states the side of the argument that the essay will take.

☐ Equal weight is given to both sides of the argument.

☐ The conclusion states which argument the speaker finds most important.

☐ Each main point is supported with facts or examples.

☐ Each main point is developed within the paragraph.

☐ The writer frequently uses *I* and *We*.

Do school uniforms benefit the students?

School uniforms are a requirement in several countries around the world and they have been gaining in popularity in others. This is, perhaps, as a result of the increasing competition within education and the need for schools to 'brand' themselves. However it is now time to stop and consider whether they really offer a benefit for the people who matter most in schools, the students.

In principle, school uniforms enable students to feel equal, but in practice children see school uniforms as taking away their right to choose, at an age when they want a chance to express their individual identity. If an adult can choose to wear a dyed T-shirt or a stripy top, why not a teenager? In addition, the existence of a school uniform does not mean that children automatically see each other as equal. Children with an old uniform or a uniform made of cheaper material will feel different to those who have a new, high-quality one.

With regard to cost, uniforms tend to be more expensive than normal clothes because they are specially made for a school. In fact, a school in Tokyo recently introduced an expensive uniform branded with the logo of a well-known global fashion

5 Read the Focus box then underline examples of this way of developing an argument in the essay.

Developing an argument in an essay

In an essay you can build your own argument by undermining an opposing argument. You do this by saying that the opposing argument is just a theory or an idea but the truth is different.

These are common phrases to undermine an opposing argument and present your own one:
In principle, ... but in practice ...
Theoretically, ... but in reality ...
While some people argue that ... the truth is ...
Instead of ... (the teacher) is forced to ....

6 Combine the two arguments below with one of the phrases from the Focus box.
1 Fashion allows us to show our individuality.
  Fashion simply encourages us to follow the crowd.
2 Clothes don't matter.
  We judge people by their appearance.
3 Everything becomes more expensive over time.
  Clothes have become cheaper over recent years.
4 Top models have glamorous lives.
  Top models have to work very hard to stay in shape.

7 Join the sentence halves.
1 In principle, the idea of casual Friday is good,
2 Theoretically, everyone should wear a bike helmet,
3 Instead of wearing jeans,
4 While some people look good in that colour,
5 Theoretically, that outfit should work,

a but in reality very few people do.
b the truth is that many people don't.
c but in practice, people use it as an excuse to dress badly all the time.
d but actually the skirt doesn't go with the blouse.
e they are choosing to dress more formally.

Prepare

8 a You're going to write an essay arguing for or against a topic. Choose a statement below to write about or use your own idea.
• No fashion brand should use animal fur.
• Companies should allow their staff to wear what they want to work.
• Underweight models should not be used in adverts for clothes.

b Make a list of arguments for and against the statement.

c Decide whether you are going to argue for or against the statement. Plan your essay.
• Remember to include the correct features of an essay in Exercise 4b.
• Try to add a striking or interesting point in the introduction.

Write

9 a Write the first draft of your essay.

b Work in pairs. Check that your partner's essay has effective arguments and is written in an appropriate style.

c Give feedback to each other, then write the second draft of your essay.

company, apparently because they felt that it fitted the image of the school. Such policies and, indeed, school uniforms in general, discriminate against families with less money. They make education less accessible and less fair. It is no surprise that some clothing companies spend a lot of money lobbying governments to introduce a school uniform.

A further reason to get rid of uniforms and, in fact, all strict rules that apply to a child's appearance at school, is that they create multiple problems for the teacher. Instead of educating the students, the teacher is forced to waste time checking that the uniform that each child is wearing meets the regulations. The length of skirts has to be measured, ties have to be done up correctly and sometimes even haircuts have to be inspected to ensure that they meet the regulations – neither too short or too long. This is a ridiculous waste of time and it is no wonder if children think that the school cares more about what they look like than who they are.

Overall, it is clear that it is time for schools to get rid of the school uniform, as its disadvantages far outweigh its advantages. In my view the most persuasive argument is the unnecessary problems uniforms create for the teacher, but this is by no means the only argument against them. It has been 800 years since the first one was worn and it's now high time that they were left to history.

5B Develop your writing

> **Goal:** write a narrative

> **Focus:** using evocative and descriptive language

1 a Label the parts of a volcano A–F with the words in the box.

ascent   crater   core   descent   fumes   lava

b Look at the photos of volcanos below. What words or phrases can you think of to describe them? Make a list, then compare as a class.

2 a Read the text and answer the questions.

1 How many nights did the team wait at the top of the volcano?

2 Why did they have to turn back on their first attempt?

3 What was the purpose of their mission?

b Work in pairs and check your answers. Would you like to be a part of a mission like this? Why/Why not?

JOURNEY TO THE BOTTOM OF A VOLCANO

Sleeping on a ridge above a volcano is not for the **¹nervous**. You have to wear a gas mask to protect yourself from the toxic fumes and at night you only snooze, constantly aware that if you roll too far in your sleep you will fall off the narrow ridge and into the **²hot** core below. Having spent three nights there, we were ready to make our descent.

Using ropes to rappel down in stages we made good progress but after half an hour **³heavy rain** forced us to turn back. The volcanic gas turned the rain water to acid and the acid threatened to eat through our ropes and send us **⁴falling** into the lava below. We spent a fourth sleepless night at the top of the crater, waiting for morning.

When morning came, the rain had cleared so we decided to try again. Supplies were **⁵almost gone** and we knew that if this attempt failed we would have to **⁶give up** and return home. Fortunately, the rain held off and we made good progress. As we got closer to the core we put on shiny aluminium suits to protect ourselves from the **⁷very strong** heat. We felt like astronauts but ones who were travelling in the wrong direction. The ground shook and trembled and the volcano felt like a bomb that might explode at any moment. The descent from the rim of the crater to the bottom took seven hours.

Reaching the bottom we looked out across a lake of lava as big as a football field. The earth beneath our feet trembled and the noise was **⁸very loud**. It was without doubt the most **⁹amazing** experience of my life. We unpacked the delicate equipment that we had brought with us and began the series of experiments which were the purpose of our journey. Then, experiments done, we packed up, took selfies and began the long journey back – a **¹⁰hard** climb which took almost twice as long as the journey down.

3 a With your partner think of more descriptive alternatives for the words and phrases in bold in the narrative.

   1 nervous *easily scared*

 b Now look at the original narrative on page 167 and find the actual words or phrases that the author used.

4 a What effect does the original choice of words for 1–10 have?

 b Read the Focus box and check your ideas.

Using evocative and descriptive language

When writing a narrative, our aim is to engage the reader's imagination. We use imaginative and descriptive language to achieve this aim. Here are three techniques:

1 Replace standard adjectives and verbs with more descriptive and evocative ones.
very hot - fiery   fall - tumble

2 Compare a thing to something else entirely using *as* + adj + *as* + noun.
as tall as a skyscraper
as hot as a furnace

3 Compare an experience to something else entirely using (*feel*) *like* + clause.
It's like you are walking on jelly.
It felt like returning home after a long journey.

---

5 Find examples for points 2 and 3 in the Focus box in the description in Exercise 2a.

6 Work in pairs. Choose the more engaging sentence (a or b). Explain what makes it more engaging.

  1 a She called his name just as he jumped on the train.
    b She cried out his name just as he leapt for the train.

  2 a My fingers were as cold as icicles.
    b My fingers were cold.

  3 a It felt like coming home to a place you'd never been before.
    b The place was strange, yet familiar.

  4 a I wandered the melancholy streets with the soft rain caressing my face.
    b I walked through the sad streets, with the soft rain falling on my face.

  5 a My head really hurt.
    b I felt like a million tiny hammers were tapping on my skull.

  6 a My mind was empty.
    b My mind was as empty as an abandoned house.

---

7 a Rewrite these short descriptions to make them more engaging. Decide which words or phrases to change and use the techniques in the Focus box.

  1 The most vivid memory from my childhood is of me standing under a tree in the middle of a storm. I was very wet.

  2 I feel most relaxed when I'm lying on a beach, the sand under me and the sea in front of me.

  3 I'm very scared of dogs. When I meet a big one my mouth goes dry and legs start to shake. I want to run away fast.

  4 On my first day at school, the school felt very big and I was surrounded by a lot of other children.

 b Take the beginning of each sentence in Exercise 7a and complete it to make it true for you. Then compare with your partner.

Prepare

8 a Think of an important event from your past that you would like to describe or use the ideas in Exercise 7a to imagine an event. Make notes on:
- what you saw, smelt and heard.
- what you or other people said.
- your feelings and thoughts at the time.

 b Organise your notes into a clear order. Check they focus on *what* to describe as well as *how* to describe the event.

Write

9 Write your description. Remember to use language that is engaging for readers.

10 a Reread your description and check for use of evocative and descriptive language. Make any necessary changes.

  b Exchange descriptions with a partner and read about their important event. Give feedback on your partner's use of evocative and descriptive language.

Develop your writing

> **Goal:** write a review
> **Focus:** checking and correcting spelling

A

B

1 a Work in pairs. Look at the photos of concerts and tell your partner which one you would rather go to. Explain why.

b Discuss the questions with your partner.

1 Do you ever go to concerts? Why/Why not?

2 What was the last concert you went to?

3 Who would you most like to see in concert?

2 a Read the review and answer the questions.

1 What did the reviewer think of the show?

2 How long did the show last?

3 Would you like to go to this show? Why/Why not?

b Read the review again. Are the statements T (true) or F (false)?

1 The singer put on an unforgettable show.

2 Joellen usually performs in bigger places.

3 She mostly sings sweet love songs.

4 The reviewer found the performance moving.

5 Joellen ran out of energy half-way through.

3 a Match sentences 1–4 with descriptions a–d below.

1 I promised myself, however, that I would see her next show. You should, too.

2 But the real highlight for me came ninety minutes in.

3 Watching Joellen O's sell-out show at the Roundhouse last night, I was literally breathless.

4 She maintained that extraordinary energy throughout the performance.

a Favourite moment

b The details of who, where and when

c An overall impression

d A recommendation to see it or not see it

b Put sentences 1–4 in Exercise 3a in the correct place in the review a–d.

The high-energy magic of Joellen O

by Nancy Williams

(a) Her energetic performance will stay in my memory for a long time. 'I can do anything' she sang at one point and like everyone else in the hall, we found it easy to [1]**believe** her.

Compared to the venues Joellen O usually plays, this was a small gig but that made it all the more special. The show began with 'No Way!' – the song for which she [2]**received** a GRAMMY award last year and like most of her songs it was [3]**fierce** and passionate. **(b)** Even the quieter, sadder songs that came later in the evening were intense and when she sang 'Don't [4]**Die**' alone on stage, I'm pretty sure that many people in the audience, like me, were crying.

At one point in the evening Joellen O [5]**seized** a rope from one of the acrobatic dancers and climbed to the [6]**ceiling** where she continued singing. It was an extraordinary moment. **(c)** The music faded and Joellen O lay on the floor as though she had run out of steam. She was [7]**deceiving** us. Suddenly the backing band started up with [8]**their** familiar high-energy beat and she was up and bouncing around again just like before. In fact, she performed for another hour and a half.

The only disappointing thing about the evening was that it had to end. I certainly wanted her to carry on and as we left the venue [9]**neither** I nor the people I was with could find words to describe it. **(d)**

4 Read the Focus box then look at the words in bold in the review. Do they follow the spelling rule or are they exceptions?

Checking and correcting spelling

English spelling can be challenging, particularly when there are lots of exceptions to the rules. For example, it is often difficult in English to know whether a word should be spelt with *ie* or *ei*. There is a rule which says '*i* before *e* except after *c*':

friend, receipt

However there are a lot of exceptions to the rule:

science, neighbour

The rule is more often true when the sound is a long '*e*' /i:/ as in sh<u>ee</u>p:

piece, believe

For many people, however, the best solution is to keep a good vocabulary notebook with the correct spelling and to look at it often.

5 Try to choose the correct spelling to complete each sentence from a review.

1 It was a great performance but *weirdly/ wierdly* my friend didn't enjoy it.

2 Despite the fact he is only eighteen, his songs sound *anceint/ ancient* and wise.

3 Going to concerts is usually my favourite *leisure/ liesure* activity, but not when it's as bad as this.

4 Fortunately, I still had my *reciept/ receipt* so I could demand my money back.

5 The band used to be called *The Science/ Sceince of Art* but recently they changed their name to simply *Art*.

6 He sang with such passion and energy that I could see the *viens/ veins* in his forehead pumping.

7 Whoever *concieved/ conceived* of the idea should be congratulated.

8 She seemed to *weigh/ wiegh* nothing as she floated across the stage.

6 Look at these commonly misspelled words. Tick the ones with correct spellings. Correct the words with incorrect spellings.

1 definately _____

2 separate _____

3 occurred _____

4 aceptable _____

5 spectacular _____

6 particulaly _____

7 achieve _____

Prepare

7 a Think of a music performance that you have seen or use the photos in Exercise 1 to imagine one. Decide how positive or negative your review will be.

b Make notes about the performance under the headings a–d in Exercise 3a.

c Think of a title for your review.

Write

8 a Write the first draft of your review. When you have finished, exchange with a partner.

b Read your partner's review and prepare feedback. Has your partner:

1 included a title and the basic details of the performance?

2 included an overall impression and a highlight?

3 included a recommendation?

4 spelt everything correctly?

5 written a review that you enjoyed reading?

c Give your feedback to your partner and then use the feedback on your review to help you write a second draft.

▸ **Goal:** write notes, cards and messages for important events

▸ **Focus:** expressing the personal significance of an event

1 **Work in pairs and discuss the questions.**

1 When was the last time you handwrote a card or message to someone?

2 In what situations do people often or sometimes send handwritten messages in your country?

3 What is the difference between receiving a handwritten message and a digital message?

2 **Read situations 1–9 below. What would you usually do in each situation, particularly if you were not able to talk to the person soon?**

- send a card with a handwritten message in it
- send an email
- write a letter
- write a short message in a group card
- send a message by text or social media
- nothing

Situations

1 One of your colleagues is leaving to start a new job in a different company.

2 A friend gave you a thoughtful birthday present that you liked very much.

3 The relative of a friend has died.

4 A niece or nephew has got a place at university to study medicine.

5 You attended an old school friend's wedding recently and had a great time.

6 A colleague has got a promotion and you are happy for him/her.

7 A cousin has had a new baby.

8 Your friend is about to emigrate to another country.

9 A colleague at your company has just lost their job.

3 **Read messages A–I and match them with the situations in Exercise 2.**

A
> I can't thank you enough for the book and voucher. It was so kind of you! You're a great friend and I'm lucky to have you in my life.

B
> Congrats on your promotion! You really deserve it ☺
>
> Thanks! Really excited (and nervous) ☺

C
> Dear Morris,
> Congratulations on the latest addition to your family! It's great news and you must be so proud. Wishing you and your new family member all the very best.
> Lots of love,
> Ade

D
> Really sorry to hear the news. I know how much work you put in and how good you were. I know you'll find another position soon. Let me know if you want to meet up and talk.

E
> I start my new job next week! Excited but also sad to leave my wonderful colleagues behind.
>
>
>
> Wishing you all the best in your new job. We'll miss you!

F

Dear Liam,

Congratulations on getting a place - we're really thrilled for you.

You're going to have the time of your life and we can't wait to hear all about it!

Lots of love,
Pat and Felix

G

Dear Nikola,
With deepest condolences to you and your family on your loss.
You are in our thoughts.
Noah and Aysel

H

Dear Yasmine,

I wanted to write and tell you how much I enjoyed myself last week. It was a fabulous event and we all had such a great time. I particularly enjoyed the speeches and thought your father's was hysterical.

You and Li Jing are going to have a wonderful life together and it was really special to be there to celebrate it.

Lots of love, Mia

I

Dear Jovana,

Really sorry to hear you're leaving, but at the same time excited for you. It's a new adventure and I'm sure you will have a wonderful time. Send us a postcard!

Warmest wishes,
Laura

4 a Read the Focus box then underline examples of similar language in the cards, notes and messages in Exercise 3.

Expressing the personal significance of an event

Notes, emails, cards and so on which mark a significant event often break the custom of subject + verb + object. They often leave out the subject or begin with a noun as below.

Happy events

Congratulations on …
Congrats on … (informal)
So glad to hear that …
Wishing you every happiness.

Sad events

So sorry to hear that …
Really sorry that …

Death

With deepest sympathy/condolences on your loss.
Wishing you strength in the coming weeks.

b Rewrite these messages to make them more natural. Use the Focus box to help you.

1 I congratulate you on passing your exams.
2 I am sad to hear that you have lost your job.
3 I am sorry that your aunt has died.
4 I am happy that you have found a new house.
5 I hope you feel strong in the coming days.

Prepare

5 Choose two of the situations below and complete the missing information with your own ideas.

- I'm moving house next week. It's my dream home because _____ . I can't wait!
- Yesterday my aunt was in a car accident. Now she is in hospital with a minor injury: _____ .
- We are colleagues and today is the last day in my job. Next week I'm going to emigrate to _____ .
- My boyfriend/girlfriend and I got engaged last week in _____ .
- We are colleagues and today our boss told me that I am going to _____ .

Write

6 a Work in pairs. Exchange the completed situations in Exercise 5 with your partner. Write an appropriate message to your partner.

b Find two more partners and repeat the activity.

c Read the messages that you have and decide which one you like best and why. Can you help the writers to improve their messages?

> **Goal:** write a response to an article
> **Focus:** challenging evidence used in an article

A   B   C   D

1 a Match pictures A–D with the name of each generation in the box.

> baby boomers   Generation Z   millennials
> Generation X

b Check your answers on page 174.

c Work in pairs and discuss the questions.
1. What character traits do you associate with each generation? Make a list.
   Generation Z = short attention span
2. What do you think are some of the advantages or disadvantages for other generations?
3. Do you think that your life is easier or harder than your parents' lives? Explain why.

2 a Columnists are people paid to write about their opinions in newspapers. They often have very strong opinions. Read the article by a columnist and answer the questions.
1. How much sleep do Generation Z'ers get, according to the columnist?
2. Where does this information come from?
3. How long is the attention span of Generation Z'ers, according to the columnist?
4. Where does this information come from?

b Work in pairs. Do you agree with the columnist? Explain why.

My opinion: Generation Z are lazy and easily distracted

Bernard Waller

Tue 14 May, 8:00 BST

What is it with the younger generation these days? All they do is sleep and stare at their phones. It's not just me saying that, research proves it too. A recent report from the Kew Research Centre concluded that Generation Z, as they are apparently called, is the laziest generation ever. They sleep up to ten hours a day. Ten hours! I only need six. I'm an early riser and I'm usually wide awake by 6.30 a.m. It's pure laziness to spend ten hours in bed. Not only that but research by Stephen Baker from the University of Eastleigh also shows that Generation Z has an attention span of, on average, just eight seconds. EIGHT seconds! It's shorter than most goldfish. How do they ever read a book or even a newspaper article? Youth is wasted on the young – that's my opinion.

3 Now read a comment from a reader. What is the truth about sleep and attention span in Generation Z, according to the comment?

Comments 132 `Comment`

Aisha, Milan, 38 minutes ago

This article makes some generalisations about Generation Z (Gen Z) which are simply false. Firstly, it claims that research proves that Generation Z are the laziest generation ever and it cites a Kew Research study to prove it. However, the Kew study does not support the arguments in the article at all. The study actually shows that teenagers in general are <u>not</u> getting enough sleep. In fact, they need between eight and ten hours of sleep but they are often only getting around seven hours. This can have a serious impact on their health and happiness. The teenage brain requires much more sleep than, for example, that of a 50-year-old man, because it works much harder.

Secondly, the article asserts that Generation Z have an attention span of just eight seconds on average. It points to research by Stephen Baker of the University of Eastleigh as proof of the claim. Unfortunately, the article completely misrepresents the study's findings. What the study found was that Generation Z in fact has only a slightly shorter attention span than other generations. This is probably because they are better at multi-tasking than other generations and if something doesn't grab their attention, they shift quickly to a different task or topic.

In short, I found the article misleading and just plain wrong and I think that much more care should be taken to check facts before publication.

REPLY   ⬆ UPVOTE 54   ⬇ DOWNVOTE 0

4 Read the Focus box and then find one more statement in the comment in Exercise 3 to match each of the steps 1–4.

Challenging evidence used in an article

To challenge the evidence used in an article, we often follow these steps.

1 Summarise the false claims
  It claims that ...

2 Give the source of the false claim
  It cites ... to prove it.

3 Reject the false claim
  However, the Kew study does not support ...

4 Summarise the truth
  The study actually shows that ...

Note that effective comments refer to the article or the study rather than the person who wrote it.

Prepare

5 a You're going to write a comment on an article and challenge its claims. Read the article and the summaries of the research below. In what way does the article misrepresent the research?

Millennials are the laziest generation

I've always been of the opinion that millennials are not as hard-working as us baby boomers and now a global study of thousands of people proves it. According to a report by the Hein Foundation, millennials are much more likely to complain that they don't get enough time off than other generations. This doesn't surprise me. All the millennials that I know spend their time complaining about everything possible. Not only that but an even larger study by the Strauss Research Centre proved that almost half of millennials regularly got ill which resulted in them taking time off work. Baby boomers are made of harder stuff. Around a fifth of them said the same thing. Good for you, fellow Baby boomers!

Hein Foundation
Work habits of millennials
Executive summary
This report presents the results of a detailed survey into the work habits of millennials. Comprising interviews with almost 500 millennials in five countries, the research shows that millennials are much more likely than previous generations to criticise their colleagues for taking time off.

Strauss Research Centre
Work and illness habits across the generations
Executive summary
The study into the work and illness habits of different generations shows that 43% of millennials said that they regularly came to work when feeling ill while only 23% of baby boomers said the same.

b Think about what response you would write in the comments section to the article. Use the Focus box to help you.

Write

6 a Write the first draft of your comment. Make sure that you talk about the article and the study rather than the authors.

b Exchange your comment with a partner and prepare feedback. Suggest revisions to the wording or ways to improve your partner's comment.

7 Use the feedback on your first draft to help you write a second draft.

Develop your writing

> **Goal:** write a narrative
> **Focus:** linking two actions together

1 **Work in pairs and discuss the questions.**

　1 Can you think of events in life that might change people for the better?

　2 Have you experienced any of these events? If so, what happened and how did you change?

2 a **Read the first paragraph only of the short story. Work in pairs and discuss why you think Robyn did what she did.**

　b **Read the whole short story and check your answers to Exercise 2a. Then answer the questions below.**

　　1 How did Robyn see herself before the incident?

　　2 How did her colleagues react afterwards?

　　3 When did the man steal Robyn's phone?

　　4 How did Robyn find him?

3 a **Put the sentences below into the correct place (1–4) in the story.**

　　a Robyn realised that she would never think of herself as shy again.

　　b It was a moment she would never forget.

　　c Robyn could feel her blood begin to boil.

　　d This had never happened to Robyn before and it made her angry, very angry.

　b **Sentences a–d in Exercise 3a all focus on feelings. What is the effect of adding this kind of information to the story?**

4 **Read the Focus box and find two more examples in the narrative of the -ing form used to join two clauses.**

Linking two actions together

The simplest way to join two clauses is with *and*. Sometimes the two clauses can also be joined by starting the sentence with the first verb in the -*ing* form.

She apologised profusely and helped him to his feet.
> ***Apologising** profusely, she helped him to his feet.*
She took her mother's phone and opened up the app.
> ***Taking** her mother's phone, she opened up the app.*

This form is common in narratives but it is only possible when the subject is the same in both clauses and the first action explains what was happening just before or during the second action.

This type of linking can focus on the relationship between two actions in terms of when they happened.

Crossing the road, she saw the singer from the night before.

It can also explain why something happened.

Being an expert on the subject, he knew the answer to the question.

In The Spotlight

Robyn, a 22-year-old architecture student, always thought of herself as a quiet and shy person right up until the moment she used a microphone to scream at a man in a shopping mall. **1**_____

It was a busy Saturday and Robyn and her mother were out shopping. The mall was full of eager shoppers hunting for the perfect sunglasses and the latest gadgets at bargain prices. Completely by accident, Robyn bumped into a man in a green jumper and sent him crashing to the ground. Apologising profusely, she helped him to his feet. 'I really have no idea how that happened', she said. 'No worries', said the man and quickly walked away.

'That was a bit weird', said Robyn's mother and Robyn had to agree, but it wasn't until she checked her back pocket that she realised what had happened. The man must have stolen her phone from her pocket while she was helping him up. **2**_____

Taking her mother's phone she opened up the 'Find my phone' app and logged into her account. By following the GPS location of her phone she could see exactly where the man was. Robyn told her mother to wait and headed after the man. She caught sight of him on the second floor of the mall near the north entrance and followed him into a shoe shop. Robyn watched as the thief sat down on a chair and casually started checking out the phone he had just stolen. He seemed not to feel any guilt at all at what he had just done. **3**_____

Moving slowly and calmly, Robyn picked up the store microphone on the cashier's desk, pressed the broadcast button and screamed at the top of her voice 'THAT MAN STOLE MY PHONE!' The noise shocked all the busy shoppers into silence and everyone turned to stare at Robyn. All of a sudden Robyn knew what to do. Picking up the nearest shoe she could find, Robyn threw it at the man. Then she threw another, and another, all the while shouting at the top of her voice 'GIVE ME MY PHONE, THIEF!'.

Needless to say, Robyn got her phone back and when she told the story at work the next day, all of her colleagues were surprised and amazed at what she had done. **4**_____

5 a Look at the sentences. Does the linking tell you the time (T) an activity happened, or the reason (R) why it happened?

1 Being a poor athlete, I was always the last one picked for the team.
2 Entering the room, she fixed me with a long cool stare.
3 Looking out of the window, he thought of the life he'd left behind.
4 Not having a key, I was forced to climb in through the kitchen window.
5 Being the youngest of three, I was picked on mercilessly by my siblings.
6 Sitting on the porch, I noticed the birds in the garden had fallen silent.
7 Arriving at your door, I felt my heart begin to race.
8 Knowing his temper, she tried to avoid him whenever possible.

b Rewrite the sentences in Exercise 5a using the words *when/while* or *because*.

6 Rewrite these sentences using the *-ing* form.

1 He looked out of his window and saw someone creeping around in the darkness.
Looking out of the window, he saw someone creeping around in the darkness.
2 She realised she was late and she started to run.
3 He was a smooth talker and he loved the chance to meet new people.
4 They were demanding parents and they didn't like it when their son failed one of his exams.
5 I was listening to his story and I began to feel that something was wrong.
6 She didn't know what to do and she decided to call her friend who lived next door.

7 Put the lines of the story in the correct order (1–8).

A ___1___ Opening his eyes on another working weekday,
B _____ what time it was, but guessing
C _____ who liked routine, waking up late was distressing to Charles. He liked the comfort of taking that same 8.07 train every day. Throwing on his clothes, he
D _____ Charles was met with a bunch of blurry shapes which only
E _____ it must be quite late due to the bright sun streaming in through the window, Charles
F _____ resolved themselves into clearer ones, (namely the furniture of his modest bedroom), when he had found his glasses. Not knowing
G _____ thought back to the day he'd started working for Peterson's, twenty years ago, and the strange way that his endless commuter days had begun.
H _____ jumped out of bed with a low groan of pain. Being the sort of man

Prepare

8 a You're going to write a story that begins with a brief outline of the climax. Choose one of the options below to begin your story or use your own ideas.

Peter was a very intense man and his friends were always telling him to lighten up and have fun, until the day that they saw him on the TV show 'You've got talent!'. That was a show they would never forget.

Sofiya was a cynical and unpleasant woman until the day that a stranger saved her from being eaten alive by a crocodile. It was a day at the zoo that she would never forget.

b Make notes on what happened before and after the climax and think about how the person changed.

Write

9 a Write the first draft of your story. Use the checklist below to help you.

☐ Begin with the climax of the story.
☐ Describe the events leading up to the climax.
☐ Describe the climax in more detail.
☐ Describe the events after the climax.
☐ Describe how the main character felt.
☐ Describe how the main character's personality changed.

b When you have finished the first draft of your story, exchange with a partner and prepare feedback to help improve your partner's story.

10 Use your partner's feedback to write a second draft of your story.

10A Develop your writing

> **Goal:** write a biography
> **Focus:** using a range of idiomatic phrases

You had nine olives while I only had seven and...

A

B

1 a Look at the cartoons and describe what's happening. Do you think the people are being careful with money or mean with money (misers)?

b Work in pairs and discuss the questions.

1 What other things does a miser do that normal people don't?

2 Do you think trying to save money is always a good idea? Why/Why not?

2 a Read the biography of Hetty Green and match descriptions 1–6 with paragraphs A–F.

1 The positives
2 Conclusion
3 Her career
4 The negatives
5 Her early life
6 General information

b Work in pairs. Discuss your opinions of Hetty Green. Was she more the Queen of Wall Street or the Witch of Wall Street? Explain why.

The world's greatest miser?
The life of Hetty Green

A In the world of misers, one name stands tall: Hetty Green. Hetty was born in 1834 into a Massachusetts family that had already made millions in shipping. By the time she died, however, Hetty had turned those millions into billions and earned a reputation as a cut-throat business woman. She was also, according to reports, incredibly mean with money. But was this the truth or has she been misrepresented by people jealous of her success?

B From a young age Hetty Green **¹was good with** numbers and she opened a bank account at the age of eight. In terms of business, she **²learnt how everything worked** from her grandfather to whom she read the financial newspapers every evening. By the age of thirteen Hetty had become the accountant for the family business and when, at the age of twenty, Hetty's father bought her a selection of dresses in order to attract a husband, Hetty promptly sold the dresses and used the money to buy government bonds.

C Later, when Hetty was **³in control** of the family business, she invested in industries like railroads and real estate. She became so rich that more than once the City of New York asked her for an emergency loan. She agreed, but **⁴demanded a good deal**. Running a successful business, to Hetty, was simple: buy low and sell high. By the time of her death in 1916 she had amassed a fortune worth over two billion dollars in today's money.

D Where, then, does Hetty's reputation for miserliness come from? It is undoubtedly true that Hetty tried to do everything **⁵as cheaply as possible**. She wore the same worn-out black dress every day and rarely washed it in order to save on soap. When her son broke his leg she tried to get him treated for free at a clinic reserved for the poor. Her son's leg later had to be amputated. When Hetty herself had a hernia, she simply tied a stick to her stomach in order to push the hernia back in.

E In order to really understand Hetty, however, you have to **⁶look at all aspects of the situation**. Just like her investing, Hetty hated being **⁷the centre of attention** and preferred to help people quietly in the background. She rescued her husband from debt and sued an insurance company to protect its customers. She donated money to a medical school on condition that they admit women and believed, contrary to the ethos of the time, that all women should learn about finance.

F In an age when business was dominated by men, Hetty made a lot of jealous enemies and, in short, she probably deserved her reputations as both 'The Queen of Wall Street' and 'The Witch of Wall Street'.

134

3 a Read the Focus box then choose the correct form of the idiom (a or b) to replace each phrase 1–7 in the text.

1 a had an eye for
   b had eyes for

2 a learnt about ropes
   b learnt the ropes

3 a in the driving chair
   b in the driving seat

4 a drove a bargain hard
   b drove a hard bargain

5 a on a shoelace
   b on a shoestring

6 a see the big picture
   b see the biggest picture

7 a in the limelight
   b in the light

Using a range of idiomatic phrases

When using idiomatic phrases, it's important to use the right words in the right order. If they are changed at all, the sentence can sound very wrong.

~~In the world of misers, one name stands high.~~

In the world of misers, one name stands tall. ✓

~~A throat-cut business woman.~~

A cut-throat business woman. ✓

It's also important to remember the small words that go into the idioms as well as the nouns and verbs.

~~We lived in a shoestring.~~

We lived on a shoestring. ✓

b Complete these biography extracts with the correct form of the idioms in Exercise 3a.

On taking over the company from his mother, however, Ryland soon found that he was not a natural businessman. He enjoyed being **1**_____ and often appeared in the newspaper gossip pages, but while his mother had lived **2**_____ , he spent lavishly on parties and jet planes.

Constanza showed early promise as a fashion designer and **3**_____ colour and pattern. She **4**_____ from Yves Gauguin, one of the top designers at the time and later, when Constanza was **5**_____ of the Lupin fashion house, she credited Yves for her success.

One of the reasons Chiara was such a successful politician was that she found it easy to **6**_____ and didn't get distracted by small details. When there was a deal to be made, she always **7**_____ and as a result, she progressed quickly up the hierarchy of the party.

4 a Complete the expressions in the text below with the words in the box.

a (x2)   at   in   of   my   no   the   to

Sometimes disaster can be **a blessing** **1**_____ **disguise**. My place on a Microbiology degree at Cambridge was cancelled **2**_____ **short notice** due to oversubscription, and I suddenly found myself **at 3**_____ **loose end** in my parents' home. In the following days I found myself **twiddling 4**_____ **thumbs**, until one day I flicked on the TV to see heart-breaking images of the destruction of the Amazon rainforest. It really affected me. I discovered that a charity called Green Wings was doing everything it could to **put a halt 5**_____ the destruction. **In 6**_____ **time at all** I was on the phone to the charity, and asking how I could **be 7**_____ **service**. A year later on, and reapplying to Cambridge is **out of 8**_____ **question** – I'm loving what I do for the charity, and I feel I'm finally **making 9**_____ **difference**.

b Match the expressions in bold in Exercise 4a with meanings a–g.

a help _____

b changing something in a good way _____

c a good thing which appears at first to be a bad thing _____

d stop _____

e very quickly _____ / _____

f not worth considering _____

g having nothing to do _____ / _____

Prepare

5 a You're going to write a biography of a famous person or someone you admire and know well. Make a list of possible people to write about.

b Choose one person for your biography and make notes on their life. Organise your notes into paragraphs.

Write

6 a Write the first draft of your biography. Use the checklist below to help you.

☐ Begin with general information about the person.

☐ Use time expressions to describe their early life and/or career.

☐ Describe the positives and/or the negatives about the person.

☐ Use a range of idiomatic phrases.

☐ Write a conclusion giving a fair summary of the person.

b When you have finished the first draft of your biography, exchange with a partner and prepare feedback to help improve their story.

7 Use the feedback from your partner to write a second draft of your story.

Language bank

1A Cleft sentences

Cleft sentences are complex sentences that have one main clause and one dependent clause. We can use them to focus on a particular part of the sentence and to emphasise what we want to say. We often introduce these sentences using words such as *What* or *The thing*.

They can be used to talk about general feelings or opinions and they can be used to talk about specific things in the past. Look at these common patterns.

Gardening's very relaxing. That's why I love it.
The thing I really love about gardening is *that it's relaxing.*
The thing I really love about gardening is *how relaxing it is.*
The teacher's very encouraging, which is great.
What's great about the class is *(the fact) that the teacher is very encouraging.*
What's great about the class is *how encouraging the teacher is.*

The idea of getting covered in mud has always put me off playing rugby.
One thing that's always put me off playing rugby is *the idea of getting covered in mud.*
One thing that's always put me off playing rugby is *how muddy you'd get.*
The class was great. It really helped me let off steam.
What I liked most about the class was *(the fact) that it helped me let off steam.*
What was great about the class was *(the fact) that it helped me let off steam*

When we want to emphasise how things make us feel, we often use cleft sentences with verbs like *annoy, scare, worry, love,* and *bother.*

What annoys me most is *the cost.*
What annoys me most is *how expensive it is these days.*
What I love most about it is *the fact that it's easy to do.*
What I love most about it is *how easy it is to do.*

1B Narrative tenses

We use different tenses in narratives to show how different actions relate to each other in terms of time and duration.

• past simple
Use this form to talk about past habits or list single completed actions in chronological order.
*This couple **pulled** over, **got** out of their car and **offered** to help.*

• past continuous
Use this form to talk about actions that were in progress around the time another action happened. The past simple is used for the completed action.
*I **was working** for a rival company when we first met.*
*He **was sprinting** for the bus and he ran into me and knocked me over.*
We use two past continuous forms to talk about two actions in progress at the same time.
*While I **was waiting**, I **was doing** a crossword.*

• past perfect
Use this form to talk about single, completed actions that happened before another action/event in the past.
*I got talking to this woman on the plane and it turned out we**'d been** to the same school!*

• past perfect continuous
Use this form to talk about actions that were in progress before or that continued up to another action/event in the past. The emphasis is on the duration or the reason for the action.
*Gina recommended a place to stay, which was good because I**'d been looking** for somewhere for ages without success.*

The past perfect isn't necessary when we use words like *after* and *before*, as the order of events is already clear.
After I had spoken/I spoke to him I felt a lot calmer.
Before we spoke I had been having/was having some doubts about it.

• present tenses
Use these to make a story more immediate. This is common in spoken English.
*Then at the next stop this couple **get** on and the man**'s lying** there and they**'re** shocked. They **start** asking questions, 'Is he all right? Has anyone told the driver?' And no one **knows**.*

Note that in a narrative we often report what was said. The same rules as above apply with reference to the moment the speech took place.
*He said he **worked** for a bank.*
*She said she**'d been waiting** for ages.*

1C Exaggeration

We sometimes exaggerate to make stories more interesting and to encourage a reaction from listeners. Here are four common ways we can exaggerate:
• making times, cost, distance, amount, etc. sound worse or bigger than they really are
*I spend **half my life** trying to fix this machine!*
*It cost her **a small fortune**, that bag.*

• repetition of key words, linked with *and*
*He just kept going **on and on and on** about it.*
*I've waited **years and years** for this moment.*
• comparisons
*It's **like** the North Pole in that back room today.*
*He looked **like/as if/as though** he hadn't slept for weeks.*
• death metaphors
*I'm **dying** for a coffee.*
*It's **murder** trying to find a place to park round there.*

1A

1 Complete the sentences with one word.

1 _____ I've always fancied doing is going hiking in Alaska. I think it'd be amazing.

2 The one _____ I really hate about my yoga class is the background music they play!

3 The thing _____ worries me about online gaming is how addicted some people get.

4 What I like most about judo is the _____ that it's not just about how strong you are.

5 The thing I particularly liked about the course was _____ friendly everyone was.

6 I used to play football, but what put me off in the end _____ all the injuries.

7 I find it boring and the _____ thing I don't like about it is how messy you get doing it.

8 What's great _____ that movie is the fact it's still relevant, even after thirty years.

2 Complete the sentences with the pairs of words in the box.

amazes/amount	like/way
fancy/going	love/fact
find/variety	understand/why

1 What I _____ most about boxing is that it's a great _____ of getting rid of stress after work.

2 The thing that I _____ fascinating about gaming is the _____ of different people who do it.

3 One thing I'll never _____ is _____ people choose to go out running in the rain.

4 What _____ me is the _____ of money some people spend on camping equipment.

5 To be honest, the last thing I usually _____ doing after work is _____ to the gym.

6 What I _____ about going fishing is the _____ I can just switch off and forget about work!

1B

1 Complete the story with the verbs in brackets in the correct past tense.

I had a funny dream last night. I was a child again and I ¹_____ (stand) on a street corner on my own. I ²_____ (shop) with my mum, but we'd got separated. It was busy and crowds of people ³_____ (walk) past in both directions and I was in floods of tears. Every now and then someone ⁴_____ (glance) down at me and at one point I asked a woman if she ⁵_____ (see) my mummy. The woman just ⁶_____ (stare) at me blankly and ⁷_____ (hurry) on. A terrible fear ⁸_____ (begin) to grow inside me. By this point, I ⁹_____ (scream) my head off … and the next moment I ¹⁰_____ (wake up) all sweating and confused.

2 Decide which sentence endings are grammatically correct. Change the ones that are incorrect.

1 There was an old man begging outside the station …

  a and everyone was just ignoring him.

  b who told me he didn't eat for days before.

  c so I was giving him some money.

2 He was struggling to get up the stairs …

  a as he broke his leg.

  b so I helped him carry the baby's buggy.

  c and he panted.

3 She was complaining …

  a before we'd even started.

  b because we don't finish any of the work we promised.

  c so I agreed to do my best to make things better.

4 The main road was closed …

  a because it was snowing for days.

  b because they were doing repairs.

  c because they'd found a suspicious package.

1C

1 Match the sentence halves to make comparisons.

1 Everything was perfect. The whole thing worked like

2 He just doesn't know how to let things go. He's like

3 Don't tell him you're vegan. It's like

4 I had quite a lonely childhood. Sometimes I felt as if

5 It was so cold my hands felt as though

6 Seriously! She looked as if

a they were going to fall off.

b she wanted the ground to open and swallow her up.

c a red rag to a bull.

d a dog with a bone.

e a dream.

f my pet dog was my only friend.

2 Choose the correct alternatives.

1 Thank goodness we're nearly home. I'm *dying/murderous* for a cup of tea.

2 Oh, you really should've been there. We nearly *killed/died* laughing!

3 I really need to sit down. My feet are *murdering/killing* me.

4 It's *death/murder* trying to get to the airport at this time of day.

5 I'd *die/death* for a chance to go there, but I can't really see it happening.

6 I used to be really into electronic music, but now I'm sick to *murder/death* of it.

Want more practice? Go to your Workbook or app.

2A The future in the past

We can talk about the future in different ways (*will, be going to,* present continuous, *be due to,* etc.). Most of these have past forms, which we use to talk about an action or event that was in the future at a particular time in the past. We often do this when what we planned or predicted didn't actually happen.

• past plans or intentions

Was due to shows a plan based on a timetable or arranged time.

*The work **was due to** be completed by the end of the month, but we knew it wouldn't be.*

Was (just) about to refers to an action someone was intending to do immediately.

*I **was just about to** suggest calling an electrician when the lights came back on.*

Past continuous can be used to describe someone else's past plans.

*He couldn't come because he **was working** that day.*

Was going to can show general plans and intentions. It could replace any of the above.

*I **was going to** go for a walk but the weather forecast wasn't very good.*

• past predictions

When used without an adverb (e.g. *probably*), *would/was going to/was bound to* show certainty.

*I knew it **wouldn't work**.*

*It **was bound to** be difficult.*

We use *might, wasn't sure,* or adverbs like *possibly* to show uncertainty.

*I had a feeling it **might** be difficult.*

*I **wasn't sure** he would make it.*

• reporting

We often report what was previously said or thought about the future.

*He asked me what I **was going to** do.*

*I asked Tom to help but he said he **was about to** go out.*

2B Double comparatives

We use double comparatives to show how one action/ situation can have an effect on another. The first half of the sentence shows a possible cause, the second half shows one or more possible consequences.

• With countable nouns, use *the more* and *the fewer*:

***The more** volunteers we have, **the fewer problems** we will have later.*

• With uncountable nouns, use *the more* and *the less*:

***The less information** people have about the condition, **the more** medication they take.*

• With adjectives, use these patterns:

*The more sustainable a business is, **the faster** it grows and **the more profitable** it is.*

***The longer** we wait, **the worse** the situation will get.*

• We often have one pattern in one half of a sentence, and a different one in the other.

***The more** money we have, **the easier** life often seems.*

***The less** stress we experience, **the lower** the probability of heart attacks is.*

• Notice that we often leave out the nouns or verbs when we think they're obvious from the context.

The more (people) there are, the easier it is.

The bigger the problem (is), the more expensive the solution (is).

• There are several common fixed phrases that use this pattern:

The sooner, the better./The bigger, the better.

The faster, the better./The more, the merrier.

2C Negative questions

We form these by adding *not* to *be* (*is, were*) or an auxiliary verb (*do, did, has, had*, etc.) at the start of a question.

We can use negative questions:

• to ask for confirmation of things we think are true.

***Didn't** you go there last year?*

(= I think you went you there, but want to check.)

***Don't** you live somewhere near the centre?*

(= I think you do, but maybe I'm wrong.)

• to make suggestions.

***Wouldn't** it be better to demolish it and build something else on the land?* (= I think it'd be better to)

***Don't** you think they should restore it?*

(= That's what I think. Surely you agree!)

• to show we're surprised.

***Aren't** you hungry after all that travelling?*

(= I can't believe you're not hungry! I would be.)

***Won't** you be cold if you go out in that?*

(= I'm surprised that's all you're wearing. I'd be cold in that.)

We can use *Wh-* questions about things that surprise us.

***Why didn't** you tell me before?*

(= I'm surprised that you didn't tell me before.)

***Who doesn't** like travelling?*

(= It would surprise me if someone didn't like travelling.)

We can use negative questions to ask about something we believe is true/correct. We expect the answer *Yes*.

A: Didn't you go there last year?

B: Yeah, I did. I had a work trip there in the summer.

A: Weren't you working in Budapest when they closed that place down, Stefan?

B: Yeah, I was. It was a sad day. I can still remember it.

We can also use negative questions to ask about something we believe is <u>not</u> true/correct. We expect the answer *No*.

A: Aren't you hungry after all that travelling?

B: No, I'm fine. Honestly. I ate on the plane.

A: Don't you like it there?

B: No, not really. It's just not my kind of place.

PRACTICE

2A

1 Choose the correct alternatives to complete the paragraph. Sometimes <u>both</u> options are correct.

My mum loves telling the story of my birth. She was on a bus one day when she was heavily pregnant as she ¹*was meeting/would meet* a friend of hers in town. She had just stood up as the bus ²*was going to/was about to* arrive at her stop when the bus stopped suddenly and she was knocked over. Anyway, people asked if they should call an ambulance but she said she ³*was about to/would* be fine and got off the bus. But then, before she got to the end of the street she felt a sharp pain. She still didn't think there ⁴*was going to/would* be a problem because she had over a month to go before I ⁵*was due/would* to be born, but by the time she met her friend, she could hardly walk because of the pain. Her friend said she looked as if she ⁶*was about to/might* pass out any moment, so she called an ambulance, but they told her it ⁷*will/might* take a while. Basically, everything happened so quickly that by the time the ambulance arrived, I ⁸*was due/was just about* to come out and the paramedics said they ⁹*might not/wouldn't* be able to get back to the hospital in time so it was better to stay there. Nobody thought I ¹⁰*would end up/was ending up* being born in the middle of a shopping centre!

2 Replace *was/were going to* in the conversations 1–6 with the correct form in the box.

be about to	be bound to	be due to	might
past continuous	would		

1 A: When I saw the car after the crash, I didn't think anyone was going to survive.
   B: I know. They were incredibly lucky.
2 A: Why wasn't Petra there tonight?
   B: She told me she was going to visit her granddad in hospital.
3 A: I can't believe he announced he'd been having an affair like that.
   B: Ah, the press were always going to find out sooner or later.
4 A: Well, he was going to have the operation next week, but they've cancelled it.
   B: Really? Isn't that going to be a problem?
5 A: Can I speak to you now?
   B: Actually, I was just going to have a break.
6 A: They weren't sure if it was going to get worse so they decided to operate.
   B: Well, better safe than sorry, I guess.

2B

1 Complete the sentences with the pairs of words in the box.

bigger/fewer	more/better	more/happier
more/harder	more/less	more/sweeter

1 The _____ you practise, the _____ your performance.
2 The _____ difficult the challenge, the _____ the taste of success.
3 The _____ time you spend helping others, the _____ you become.
4 The _____ the global population becomes, the _____ natural resources we'll have.
5 The _____ expertise you have, the _____ it can be to explain things in simple terms.
6 The _____ you learn, the _____ you know.

2 Complete the sentences with one word in each gap.

1 _____ richer the neighbourhood, _____ more homes are likely to be empty.
2 The _____ awareness we raise, the _____ lives can be saved.
3 The longer we ignore the problem, the _____ things will become.
4 Things are better in the south. The further north you go, the _____ the levels of deprivation _____ .
5 Please invite your friends: the _____ the _____ !
6 The _____ all of this is over, the _____ . It's been absolutely horrible!
7 The _____ complicated your password is, the _____ , but, of course, the _____ it is to forget, as well!
8 The _____ we get aid to those in need, the _____ .

2C

1 Complete the negative questions using the ideas in brackets.

1 Why _____ me last night? I was waiting for you. (you / call)
2 _____ very well? Maybe you should go home. (you / feeling)
3 _____ what you're doing tomorrow and help me instead? (can / you / change)
4 _____ come tomorrow? You should. It'll be good. (you / be going to)
5 _____ it's in an amazing location, though? (you / think)
6 _____ get a visa if you want to go there? (you / have to)

2 Write negative questions for answers 1–6.

1 No, I wouldn't like to see it demolished. I think they could just repair and improve it.
2 No, I don't think so. At least I don't recognise you.
3 Yes, that's right. I went to Japan last year.
4 Not really. I find these kinds of historical films quite boring.
5 No, I don't. I've actually found it very helpful.
6 Yes, she was. They were married for ten years before they split up last June.

Want more practice? Go to your Workbook or app.

3A Ways of expressing the future

These are some ways we can talk about the future:

- *be supposed to + -ing*

We often use *be supposed to + -ing* to talk about arrangements we have made in the future that we now think might change. Compare these two sentences.

I'm meeting a friend of mine tonight, I'm afraid.

Well, I'm supposed to be meeting someone later, but I guess I could call them and cancel.

We also use *be supposed to + -ing* to report predictions other people have made.

I heard it's supposed to be snowing this weekend.

Note we can also use *be supposed to + infinitive*.

I heard it's supposed to snow this weekend.

- present passive structures

In more formal speech or writing, we use structures like *be set to, be expected to* and *be predicted to* when we make predictions about the future.

The cold weather is set to/ looks set to continue.

The snow is expected to continue for another two days.

- present continuous

We use the present continuous form of verbs such as *consider, hope, think of,* and *plan* to talk about plans we already have.

We're thinking of renting a boat for a week.

He's planning to go travelling for a year.

- *should*

We use *should + verb* to make predictions about pleasant things we think we will happen. We can use *shouldn't + verb* to make predictions about unpleasant things we don't think will happen, based on experience.

The party tomorrow night should be fun!

It shouldn't be that expensive.

- future continuous

The future continuous form is *will be + -ing*. We use it to talk about something that will already be in progress at a point in the future. We use *may* to show less certainty.

Knowing my luck, it'll be raining when I get there.

I'll try and meet you, but I may be working that day.

3B Verb patterns and reporting

We use lots of different verbs to report what people say. These verbs are followed by a range of different patterns. Below are some examples, but remember that many reporting verbs can be followed by more than one pattern:

- verb + object, e.g. *admit, cite, confirm, criticise, demand, defend, dismiss, praise, reject*

The judge cited the case of Apple versus Samsung when he gave his ruling.

- verb + infinitive with *to*, e.g. *beg, demand, guarantee, promise, refuse, threaten, vow*

He vowed to appeal the verdict.

- verb + object + infinitive with *to*, e.g. *advise, beg, encourage, order, persuade, remind, urge, warn*

The judge urged the jury to avoid any media during the trial.

- verb + *-ing*, e.g. *admit, advise, consider, defend, deny, discuss, recommend, suggest*

The driver denied causing the fatal crash...

Note that we often use *express* with different emotions such as concern, joy, regret, relief, or sadness.

The defendant expressed no regret for his actions.

- verb + (*that*) clause, e.g. *admit, announce, argue, boast, claim, confess, confirm, deny, insist, promise, vow*

He claimed that he didn't know the victim.

- verb + object + (*that*) clause, e.g. *assure, convince, persuade, promise, remind, tell, warn*

My lawyer assured me that we would win the case.

- verb (+ object) + preposition, e.g. *accuse of, apologise for, blame on/for, criticise for/over, forgive for, insist on*

Our neighbours accused us of damaging their pot plants.

I know they blame me for the accident.

With reporting verbs, we often summarise the general content rather than report the exact words. Compare:

He said, 'It came to me as a complete surprise when the police turned up. I had no idea what was going on.'

He denied knowing anything about it.

3C *even* and *hardly*

Even is often used to emphasise that something is surprising, unusual, unexpected or extreme. It usually comes *before* the thing that we want to emphasise:

- verbs

I tried so hard to stop smoking. I even went to a hypnotist.

- subject nouns and pronouns

Even Ed found it difficult and you know how good he is.

- adjectives, adverbs and comparatives

They broke the world record in the semi-final, but then they went even faster in the final.

I won the race and I'm not even (that) fast.

- *though, if, when,* etc.

I watched the match, even though it was raining.

Even if I could run that far, I wouldn't do a marathon.

Hardly is used to emphasise that something is almost not true or almost doesn't happen at all. It goes with words like *any* and *ever* or before a verb:

- *any, ever, anyone*

I hardly ever do any exercise.

Hardly anyone offered to help.

- verbs

Hardly comes before the main verb and after a modal or an auxiliary verb.

I can hardly see anything.

We hardly spent any time there.

As *hardly* is a negative word (= almost not), we do not usually use it with other negative words.

I hardly spoke to no-one anyone.

3A

1 Complete the sentences with one word. Negative contractions count as one word.

1 I'm supposed to be _____ today, but I'm going to call my boss and say I'm ill.

2 Most of the country _____ set to get cooler next week.

3 I'm thinking _____ going for a run in the morning. Do you want to come?

4 We're _____ renting out our flat for the summer and going travelling.

5 It _____ be too cold, but bring a coat just in case.

6 You're best visiting in May. The weather _____ be OK by then.

7 It's already very cold there, so it may _____ snowing by the time we arrive.

8 They said it's _____ to rain later, but it doesn't look likely, does it?

2 Complete the second sentence so that it means the same as the first. Use the word in brackets.

1 I was planning to revise tonight, but I guess that could wait.
I _____ tonight, but I guess that could wait. (supposed)

2 They're saying there are going to be gales this week.
Strong gales _____ hit the area this week. (expected)

3 I don't think it will be that difficult to get a visa.
_____ hard to get a visa. (shouldn't)

4 Don't ring between 8 and 8.30. My favourite TV show is on then.
Don't ring between 8 and 8.30 as I _____ my favourite TV show then. (will)

5 They think it's going to be a lot hotter in the city by the end of the century.
The city _____ a much hotter place by the end of the century. (predicted)

6 Where do you want to go for your holidays?
Where _____ for your holidays? (thinking)

3B

1 Complete the second sentence with the word in brackets plus two to four additional words.

1 Listen, it's your fault we were late.
I couldn't believe it – he _____ late. (blamed)

2 Honestly, everything is fine - there's no need to worry.
She _____ fine and I didn't need to worry. (assured)

3 Listen, please go away or we'll call the police.
We threatened _____ they didn't go away. (if)

4 Honestly, that's the last time I will ever do that, I swear.
He _____ it again and I believed him. (vowed)

5 I can't put into words how sad we are that it ever happened.
They _____ the incident. (sadness)

6 Please, please come. They'll be so disappointed if you don't.
They absolutely _____ so I could hardly say no. (me)

7 I thought I might need to steal, I was so desperate.
He _____ because he was so desperate. (considering)

2 Find the mistakes in the underlined sections and correct them. Which sentence is correct?

1 At the trial, his wife insisted to know nothing about his criminal activity.

2 The victim's family praised the police for their investigation.

3 My friend encouraged I take the company to court for sacking me.

4 He denied to use the company profits to build an extension to his own house.

5 His lawyer managed to successfully convince that the gun had gone off by accident.

6 The police advised the young woman getting a new lawyer.

3C

1 Complete each sentence with *hardly* or *even* in the correct position. In some sentences you need both. In each sentence, there's one gap you don't need.

1 It was so noisy I _____ could _____ hear myself think, which is why we left.

2 It was so cold, _____ the local people were _____ complaining a lot and they're used to it.

3 I _____ could _____ stay awake, _____ though it was an exciting race.

4 I was so busy I _____ had time to _____ speak to anyone, which was a shame.

5 He was so rude, he _____ managed to annoy Juana, who's _____ one of the calmest people I know.

6 I offered to pay for the tickets, but _____ then _____ anyone _____ wanted to come with me to watch the game.

7 There are a lot of women joining our club and we _____ hope to attract _____ more in the future.

8 _____ I can't watch a whole game of snooker and there's _____ any sport that I wouldn't _____ watch.

Want more practice? Go to your Workbook or app.

4A Defining and non-defining relative clauses

Relative clauses refer back to nouns in the previous clause. Sometimes they add essential information that defines the noun, sometimes they add non-essential information.

• defining relative clauses

When a relative clause defines a noun or noun phrase, it is not preceded by a comma.

The relative pronoun *that* can refer to things or people.

*There are too many old people **who/that** have no-one to care for them.*

*It's a scheme **which/that** brings together old and young.*

*Many people live away from their home town in cities **where/in which** they have very few friends or family*

*The reason **why** we can't changes things is difficult to say.*

*There are several charities in the country **whose** main aim is to help young people.)*

We often don't use a relative pronoun if the pronoun refers to the object of the clause.

*The woman **I spoke to on the front desk** told me to come here. (I spoke to the woman)*

*What was **the place you went to** for your birthday? (You went to the place for your birthday)*

• non-defining relative clauses

Where a relative clause adds non-essential information, it is preceded , and sometimes followed, by a comma.

We don't use *that* in non-defining relative clauses.

*We stayed with my grandmother, **who** is still sharp.*

*The scheme, **whose** aim is simple, began last year.*

• of *which*/*whom*

We can talk about part of a group or thing using *of which* or *of whom*. *Of which* refers to things and *of whom* to people.

*He's got special educational needs, **the most serious of which** is his dyslexia.*

*The choir has 30 kids, **all of whom** are talented.*

Words/phrases that can precede *of which*/*of whom*:

some, a few, most, the vast majority, a small minority, the most famous, the most serious, the easiest, the newest

• times and periods of time

We can also add a non-defining relative clause using:

at which time/point, by which time/point, during which time, in which time

*They lived there until 2014, **by which time** their kids had a left home, and then they moved to a smaller place.*

4B Noun phrases

We can add information to nouns **before the main noun**:

• adding descriptive adjectives

Adjectives usually come before nouns and we rarely use more than three adjectives together. Generally, we put opinion adjectives before factual adjectives.

*a **lovely, old, gold** bracelet*

• adding purpose, material, etc.

We often add a noun immediately before the main noun to show what the noun is for, what it's made of, etc.

*a **baseball** cap*

We can also add information **after the main noun:**

• adding an explanation after a name

*Iman, **the Somali model, actress and entrepreneur***

• adding a phrase that starts with a preposition to highlight a particular feature**.**

*a winter jacket **with deep pockets and a high collar***

• adding a relative clause

*a fashion company **that could help save the planet***

• adding a relative clause starting with an -*ed* verb form

*her hair, **dyed bright pink and styled in a very unusual manner***

• adding a relative clause starting with an -*ing* verb form

*a new clothes shop **offering one**-off designs in a wide range of styles***

Note that these ways of adding extra information to basic nouns are more common in written English than spoken.

4C Prepositions 1

Prepositions show the relationship between words in a sentence and are used with verbs, adjectives and nouns.

• Some verbs are often followed by particular prepositions.

• Some adjectives often go with particular prepositions.

• Some nouns often go with particular prepositions in particular contexts.

• Lots of short phrases start with prepositions.

Here is a selection of common words and phrases used with different prepositions:

about: *crazy about, have a good/bad feeling about, worry about*

against: *against someone's advice/wishes, against the law*

at: *at the age of, stare at, be mad at, at (the) most*
by: *by accident, be surrounded by*

for: *for one thing, for some reason, a preference for, for the most part, for obvious reasons, an excuse for*

from: *from what I remember/know/heard, benefit from, free from (fat)*

in: *in my 20s, in particular, high in (fat), in(to) the habit of, in the long/short run, in terms of, in trouble, an interest in, play a role in, participate in, faith in, succeed in*

of: *approve of, dispose of, glad of, proud of, terrified of, tired of, of average height, of interest*

on: *on average, on a daily/weekly basis, on purpose, keen on, rely on*

to: *a credit to, appeal to, be attached to, draw attention to, (get) used to, the key to, lead to, relate to*

with: *with a view to, to begin with, fed up with, lose touch with, (un)familiar with,*

other: *out of interest/pity, out of control, over the limit, under control, under pressure, without doubt/question*

PRACTICE

4A

1 Put relative clauses a–h in the correct position to complete sentences 1–8 below. Add commas to the non-defining relative clauses.

a during which time there was an economic crisis

b at which time it was difficult to find jobs back home

c in which every employee gets a 5% bonus

d most of whom are a fairly similar age to me

e most of which was a bonus for good performance

f which is in the centre of the coffee-growing region

g that produces furniture

h we're staying in

1 His parents have a company, so he might be able to get us some cheap deals when we move house.

2 The town of Salento offers lots for tourists.

3 The student residence is fairly basic, but it is clean.

4 I have ten cousins, but I don't socialise with them.

5 Their boss received a 253% salary increase, while the rest of the staff only got a pay rise of 2.6%.

6 The company has a pay scheme and they also provide free health insurance.

7 When I was at school in the 1990s, we often had no heating, so we had to wear coats in class.

8 I graduated in 2009, so I came here to study for a Master's and I've never been back.

2 Read the text and choose the correct alternatives. Sometimes both options are correct.

Maria Montessori was an Italian doctor [1]*who/that* founded the Montessori method in education.

She wanted to study medicine, but her parents, [2]*who/that* were both well-educated, wanted her to become a teacher. However, in 1890, [3]*during/ by which time* she had already been rejected once, Maria became the first female medical student in Italy.

After she qualified, Montessori started working with young people with learning problems, most [4]*of which/of whom* were from poorer backgrounds. She argued that their problems were caused by the lack of support these children received, ideas [5]*who/which* were controversial at the time.

Her method focuses on creating a supportive environment, [6]*where/which* students learn for themselves with some guidance from the teachers. It's an unusual approach [7]*why/in which* older kids help teach younger ones in mixed age-group classes.

There are now over 20,000 Montessori schools worldwide, the majority [8]*of which/of whom* provide primary and nursery education.

4B

1 Underline the core subject and object in the sentences. The first one is done for you.

1 The Nehru <u>jacket</u> is a formal hip-length <u>coat</u> for men or women, with a short collar and no lapels.

2 It was named after the ex-Indian prime minister Jawaharlal Nehru, who wore a similar kind of jacket called an *ackhan*.

3 The jacket was popularised in the 1960s by the British band The Beatles, who mixed its simple style with other Eastern influences.

4 Several villains in the early James Bond movies like *Dr. No* wore Nehru jackets.

5 Though only a short-lived fashion on both sides of the Atlantic, the Nehru jacket has become something of a classic in those sectors of global society with significant Indian communities.

2 Add the words and phrases in the box below to the subject and object in the sentence to make one long sentence.

Audrey Hepburn popularised the black dress.

little
loved for her roles in such classic films as 1953's *Roman Holiday*
The British model, dancer and film star
to international praise.
wearing the outfit for the first time in *Breakfast at Tiffany's*
which was released in 1961
with elbow-length black gloves and a pearl necklace

4C

1 Complete the text with the correct prepositions.

[1]_____ doubt, becoming a father has played a huge role [2]_____ making me who I am now. I was only 19 when I had my first daughter. I got married to Lana when we were just 18. Getting married [3]_____ such an early age went [4]_____ my parents' wishes as they thought I was too immature. I had been [5]_____ trouble quite a lot at school and I suppose they had a bad feeling [6]_____ what might happen. My friends also thought our marriage would last a year [7]_____ most. From the first moment I held my daughter, I felt different though. I could just stare [8]_____ her for ages. Don't get me wrong, it was really hard to begin [9]_____ . You have to learn something new [10]_____ a daily basis and the lack of sleep takes a lot of getting used [11]_____ , but [12]_____ some reason I felt really calm. My parents are now really proud [13]_____ me and love babysitting and being surrounded [14]_____ all their grandchildren. I lost touch [15]_____ most of my school friends, as being with babies didn't really appeal [16]_____ them. I'm studying at the moment with a view [17]_____ getting a job as a social worker. I'd like to work with kids who are having problems at school as I feel I could relate [18]_____ them.

Want more practice? Go to your Workbook or app.

5A Continuous forms

We use continuous forms to show that an action is, was or will be temporary and/or unfinished at a particular point in time. Continuous forms can also emphasise repeated actions over a period of time.

• present continuous

Use this form to talk about temporary, unfinished actions.

The traffic's flowing freely out there now.

Note the passive form:

The whole area is being evacuated.

Use the present continuous to talk about things in the future that have already been arranged with other people.

A: How're you getting there?

B: We're taking the train.

• present perfect continuous

Use this form to talk about actions that started in the past and are still continuing now. It emphasises that these things happened regularly or continuously.

Be careful on those roads. It's been raining for hours!

They've been promising to visit for ages!

• past continuous

Use this form to show an action started, but was unfinished when another action happened. We often link clauses using *when* or *while*.

I was eating lunch when my friend rang.

While we were driving home, we saw a bad accident.

Note the passive form:

I dropped my phone while we were being evacuated.

• past perfect continuous

Use this form to talk about actions that started before a particular point in the past and continued up to it. It emphasises that these things happened regularly or continuously.

We'd been driving for hours and really needed a break.

It'd been snowing all day and the roads were quite icy.

• future continuous

Use this form to talk about future arrangements or plans when we want to say that an action will happen during this time, or will happen as a result of the arrangement or plan.

I'm going to be visiting Munich next week, so maybe we could sort out a meeting.

We'll be talking to her on the show tomorrow, so do let us know if you have any questions.

• modals with continuous forms

These repairs must be costing a fortune. (= I'm fairly sure, but not 100 percent)

He should be arriving around nine, I think. (= I think he will be)

I wouldn't be asking if I didn't really need your help.

Note that we don't usually use passive forms with the perfect continuous forms.

5B Participle clauses

We sometimes add a clause starting with a participle (*-ing* or *-ed* form). It is most common in writing, especially in stories or advertising. The participle clause can have the same meaning as one starting with *when, while, because* or *as*. It can also replace the conjunction *so*.

The subject of the participle clause is the same as the subject in the main clause of the sentence.

As I looked over the valley, I suddenly felt small and insignificant.

⟶ *Looking out over the valley, I suddenly felt small and insignificant.*

Because I am a man, my wife thinks I should do repairs in the house.

⟶ *Being a man, my wife thinks I should do the repairs in the house. X*

Participle clauses with a **present participle** (the *-ing* form of the verb) have an active meaning.

She runs every day so she's incredibly fit.

⟶ *Running every day, she's incredibly fit.*

Participle clauses with a **past participle** (*-ed* form) have a passive meaning.

As it is located deep in the countryside, our hotel is the perfect place to escape.

⟶ *Located deep in the countryside, our hotel is the perfect place to escape.*

Perfect participles (*having* + past participle) emphasise that one action happened before another They may replace a clause starting with *after* or *once*. Perfect participles can also be active or passive.

As we had visited the place before, we didn't really want to go again.

⟶ *Having visited the place before, we didn't really want to go again.* (active)

After it was damaged by the oil spill, the coast took years to recover.

⟶ *Having been damaged by the oil spill, the coast took years to recover.* (passive)

5C Translation and collocation

Go to practice exercise.

5A

1 Complete the pairs of sentences with the verbs in brackets. Use the same time for each pair, with a continuous form in one sentence and a simple form in the other.

1 (talk)

a Don't worry, I _____ to him tomorrow.

b Next week, we _____ about your commuting disasters.

2 (drive)

a Sorry I didn't answer your call earlier. I _____ .

b Last year, my dad _____ all the way to Rome.

3 (clear)

a They _____ the snow off the streets all night.

b The earlier hold-up on the M5 motorway _____ and traffic is now flowing freely again.

4 (commute)

a This week I _____ in and out of town for a course.

b I _____ by train for about two hours a day.

5 (not / have)

a I don't know how you manage it. I _____ the patience!

b If you'd done what I asked, we _____ this conversation!

2 Find the five sentences with a mistake and correct them.

1 The train had been crawling along for about an hour before it finally just stopped dead.

2 He should be here by now. I guess he must be running late.

3 The other car went much too fast when the accident happened.

4 We've just heard that the central station is evacuated at the moment.

5 I'll drive into town tomorrow so I can give you a lift if you want.

6 I'm taking this train for years, but nothing like this has ever happened.

7 You can't be planning to cycle to work in this weather.

8 The main road into town is closed at the moment. It's repairing.

5B

1 Read part of an advert for a luxury hotel. Change the underlined clauses to the correct participles. Two clauses cannot be changed.

¹As we are located in the heart of the Swiss Alps, we offer the best in luxury holidays. ²Because we cater for both active holiday makers and those just wishing to relax, we offer a huge range of activities. ³As you eat your breakfast, you can contemplate the morning ahead. Perhaps you want to have a workout in the hotel grounds ⁴while you look out over the crystal clear alpine lake. And then ⁵once you have exercised your body, why not take a treatment in our award-winning spa. And ⁶while you relax in our volcanic mud baths, you can look forward to the five-start dinner our world-class chefs will be making for you.

I came here ⁷because I had been told it was the best. And they were right! *Aaron, Canada*

⁸When we arrived late at the hotel, the staff sorted out an amazing meal and everything was just perfect from then on! *Himmat, India*

2 Choose the correct alternatives. Sometimes both options are correct.

1 *Stretched / As I stretched* to hit the ball back, I pulled a muscle.

2 *After I pulled / Having pulled* a muscle, I couldn't play for several weeks.

3 *Following / Followed* the path along a short ridge, we finally reached the top and saw the view.

4 *Being very rocky / Because the route was very rocky*, we took a long time to get there.

5 *As I am not keen / Not being keen* on walking, I stayed in the hotel while the rest went out.

6 *When we reached / Reaching* the top of the pass, we found a small café where we stopped for some lunch.

7 *Having burnt / Having been burnt* once, I didn't want to try it again.

8 I had to go to the hospital, *cutting / having cut* my hand really badly.

5C

1 Choose the correct alternatives.

1 We've got a lot to do today, so shall we *make / do* a start?

2 If we want to make sure we get a table, we'd better *make / do* a reservation.

3 You can go out once you've *made / done* your homework.

4 Thanks. It's been nice *making / doing* business with you.

5 It's hard to *make / do* predictions about how the housing market will change in the coming months.

6 I always *make / do* a point of checking I've locked the doors before going to bed.

7 Are you *making / doing* anything special to celebrate?

8 The new policy didn't help. In the end, I think it *did / made* more harm than good.

9 I wanted to stay with friends, but they're away so I've had to *make / do* other arrangements.

10 I'm almost ready. I just want to *make / do* my hair and my make-up.

Want more practice? Go to your Workbook or app.

6A Adverbs and adverbial phrases

We use single-word adverbs and longer adverbial phrases to add information about actions or situations. Different kinds of adverbs most commonly appear in particular positions.

Adverbs and adverbial phrases that explain **when** usually come at the beginning or end of a clause.

Over the last few years, *many businesses have closed.*
*They've been having money problems **recently**.*

Adverbs and adverbial phrases that explain **where** usually come at the end of a clause.

*We export **all over the region**.*

Note that in sentences that have both 'when' and 'where' adverbials, the 'where' adverb usually comes first.

*The firm was founded **in Munich in Germany** in 1888.*

Adverbs that describe **how often** usually go before the main verb.

*We **regularly** assess the threats we face.*

However, longer adverbial phrases describing how often usually go at the end of a clause or at the beginning.

*We meet face to face **maybe once or twice a month**.*
***From time to time**, we rethink our business plan.*

Adverbs and adverbial phrases that explain the **strength** or **speed** of an action usually go after the main verb. They can also sometimes go before the main verb.

*Prices rose **dramatically**.*
*Inflation has been **steadily** rising over recent months.*

Adverbs and adverbial phrases that explain **how** an action is done usually go just before the main verb. When there are two auxiliary verbs, they can go between them or after them.

*Someone had **secretly** been stealing money.*
*Someone had been **secretly** stealing money.*

Adverbs and adverbial phrases that show our **opinion** about a situation usually go at the beginning of a sentence, where they are followed by a comma. They can also go at the end of a clause.

***Apparently**, they made a £30 million profit last year.*
*It's a huge waste of money, **basically**.*

When adverbs **modify** adjectives and other adverbs, they come immediately before them.

***painfully** expensive/**incredibly** quickly*

6B Further passive constructions

Use passives to focus on who or what an action affects rather than the doer (who might be unknown or unimportant). Most tenses can be made passive by using the appropriate form of **be + a past participle.**

*The palace was closed while it **was being restored**.*

Passives also appear:
• after modal verbs.
Use with *be* + a past participle.
*Profits **can be ploughed** back into cultural projects.*
• as *-ing* forms.
Use after prepositions or as the subject of a sentence.
*The city collapsed after **being invaded**.*
***Being rejected** for a job can hit your confidence badly.*
• in reporting.
Use with reporting verbs.
*He **was accused** of lying.*
We can also use with + *to* infinitive, especially in writing.
*The city **is thought to date back** to the 10th century BC.*

Use the passive form of a reporting verb + perfect infinitive to emphasise something happened before.

*The city **is said to have spent** millions on its bid to host the event* (= perfect infinitive).
*The mayor **is said to have been involved** in corruption.* (= perfect infinitive passive)

Passives can also be formed without the verb be.

Use the past participle only, without a pronoun or *be*:
• as a reduced relative clause after a noun
*Aki Osaki, the city's mayor, **elected** last year, has launched a campaign against gangs.*
• in an *if* clause
*We are ready to answer your calls, **if required**.*
• in a participle clause (see Lesson 5B)
***Seen as a centre for crime**, the city attracted very few tourists.*
Sometimes we use two passive constructions together.
*He **was seen being taken away** by police.*

6C Word grammar and patterns (*expect, surprised*)

The grammatical patterns that go with particular words can cause confusion even with well-known words.
Here are some common patterns with the verb *expect*.

a   comparative + *than/as + I expected/was expecting*, etc
They were much better than I'd been expecting.
b   *expect* + noun/pronoun + infinitive with *to* + comparative
I expected the tickets to be cheaper.
c   expect *something* + comparative
I was expecting something a bit less violent.
d   *not + expect* + noun/pronoun + infinitive with *to + so* + adjective/adverb
I wasn't expecting it to happen so quickly.

e   *not + expect* + noun/pronoun + infinitive with *to + such* + noun
I didn't expect it to become such a popular show.
f   *(not) + expect* + infinitive with *to*
I honestly wasn't expecting to hear from her again.

The adjective *surprised* often goes with a clause beginning with *how*.

a   *surprised + how* + adjective/adverb
I was surprised how easy it was to find.
b   *surprised* can also be followed by infinitive with *to*
I was surprised to find out he was older than me.

6A

1 Add the adverbs and adverbial phrases in brackets in the most common position.

1 Prices have doubled in this country over recent months, yet they talk about it on the news. (hardly ever)

2 Considering it's only our third year, I think we've done well. (fairly)

3 The whole industry has had a difficult year so far. (terribly)

4 I'll be visiting several factories in the coming months. (in the area)

5 I copied in the whole of the office when I sent that email. (accidentally)

6 They managed to survive the year, despite having debts of almost £100 million. (amazingly)

7 Inflation rose, but we had quite a lot of money saved up. (dramatically, luckily).

8 The big department store in town is going to be closing. (sadly, soon)

2 Use a verb from box A and an adverb from box B to complete sentences 1–6 below. Change the verb form if necessary.

A

| deny | meet | react | rise | sell | understand |

B

| badly | dramatically | perfectly | regularly |
| strongly | well | | |

1 We're quite a close team and we _____ _____ to review how we're doing.

2 There's no need to explain. I _____ _____ what the situation is.

3 After the election, prices _____ quite _____ .

4 I find the boss quite difficult to talk to. He always _____ _____ to any kind of criticism.

5 We only launched the new range last month, but it's already _____ very _____ .

6 When the media started asking questions, the board _____ _____ any wrongdoing.

6B

1 Complete the text by putting the verbs in brackets in the correct active or passive form.

The European Capital of Culture programme ¹_____ (initiate) by the Greek culture minister, Melina Mercouri, and ²_____ (hold) each year since 1985. Her idea was that people could ³_____ (bring) together by an event ⁴_____ (put on) in a different country each year and that it would both ⁵_____ (highlight) the diversity and richness of Europe's cultures as well as their shared history and values. Generally, the programme ⁶_____ (think) to have been a great success, ⁷_____ (bring) both economic and social benefits to the host region. Perhaps ⁸_____ (wish) to follow this success, in 2014, the Culture City of East Asia program ⁹_____ (create) based on an agreement ¹⁰_____ (reach) at a meeting of ministers of culture from Japan, China, and the Republic of Korea. Every year one city in each country ¹¹_____ (select) with the aim to develop their ties through culture and the arts. ¹²_____ (choose) as a Culture City of East Asia not only encourages stronger links with other cities in the project, it can be used as a great opportunity for further development.

2 Decide which five of the underlined sections contain a mistake. Correct the mistakes.

1 Sarejevo had hoped to award The European Capital of Culture in 2014, but to everyone's disappointment, it wasn't.

2 If selected, Sarejevo had planned to combine it with events commemorating the centenary of the First World War.

3 The First World War began after Archduke Franz Ferdinand assassinated in the city in 1914, a hundred years previously.

4 Hull's year as the UK's City of Culture was a great success despite the doubts that had been raised.

5 Culturally, Hull was believed having little to offer as one of the poorest cities in the country.

6 The year's events, including one with thousands of people were photographed naked, boosted Hull's profile.

7 Having selected as Japan's East Asia city of Culture in 2019, Toshima planned events to promote the art forms of *manga* and *anime*.

6C

1 Find the five mistakes and correct them.

1 It was much more expensive than I was expecting, I can tell you.

2 I was quite surprised how big was the city.

3 I wasn't expecting it to be so a big event.

4 It's not fair to expect me do everything for you.

5 I wasn't that surprised to hear the show was losing money.

6 I bet you weren't expecting to see me here, were you?

7 It really wasn't as good I was expecting.

8 I hadn't expected it to be so bad as it was.

Want more practice? Go to your Workbook or app.

7A Adding comments using *must* and *can't*

We can use *must* and *can't* to comment on what we hear.

A: Our neighbours are always playing music late at night.
*B: That **must be** a bit annoying.*
A: I did my degree while still working full time.
*B: Wow, that **can't have been** easy,*

To comment on the present, we use *must/can't* + infinitive without *to*.

A: My boss says he's considering me for a promotion.
*B: That **must be** good.*

To comment on the past, we use *must/can't* + *have* + past participle.

A: Is that a sushi place? I don't think I've ever eaten sushi.
*B: Come on, you **must have tried** it before!*

We use *can't* to show we think our idea in the comment is unlikely and *must* to show it's very likely.

We generally respond to comments with *must* and *can't* as if they were questions.

We don't usually repeat the modal verb. We say something about the real situation.

A: Our neighbours are always playing music late at night.
*B: That **must be** a bit annoying.*
A: It is! / Yes, very. / Actually I don't mind it that much – they're really good.

A: I got my degree while still working full time.
*B: Wow, that **can't have been** easy,*
A: It wasn't, no. / It could be difficult at times / It was actually fine – I loved doing it.

Remember we also use *must* and *can't* to show we are making guesses about what is or was happening and the causes of different situations:

*I can't find my pen. Someone **must've taken** it.*
*I found it! You **can't have looked** very hard – it was on the floor by your desk.*

7B Second, third and mixed conditionals

We use **second conditionals** to talk about imaginary situations now or in the future. When the second conditional refers to the future, the event in the *if*-clause is possible, but not very likely.

The sentences have two parts, an *if*-clause and a result clause (the main clause).

• In the *if*-clause, use *If* + the past simple/continuous.

*If they **stopped** running stories like this, …*
*If I **wasn't enjoying** it here, …*

• In the result clause, use *would/might/could* (*not*) + infinitive without *to* / + *be* + *-ing*.

*… people **might become** less obsessed with gossip!*
*… I **wouldn't** stay.*

We use **third conditionals** to talk about imaginary situations in the past.

• In the *if*-clause, use *If* + the past perfect simple/continuous.

*If they**'d done** their research …*
*If I **hadn't been enjoying** it here …*

• In the result clause, use *would/might/could* (*not*) + *have* + past participle.

*… they **could've come up with** a very different story!*
*… I **would've left**.*

We use **mixed conditionals** when we want to talk about both the past and the present.

To talk about an imaginary past condition with an imaginary present result, use a third conditional *If*-clause with a second conditional result clause:

If I hadn't read it about online (= in the past), I wouldn't be talking about it. (= now)

To talk about an imaginary present condition with an imaginary past result, use a second conditional *If*-clause with a third conditional result clause.

If I didn't like that kind of thing (= now/always), I wouldn't have gone there. (= in the past)

Remember that the *if*-clause can also come after the result clause. When we put the result clause first, we don't use a comma.

I wouldn't have gone there if I didn't like that kind of thing.

7C Phrases to show the relationship between ideas

In spoken English, we use different words and phrases to relate what we are going to say to what has just been said. Here are some common contexts:

1 referring to a previous condition
Some phrases are used to refer to a previously mentioned condition or fact about something.

Bearing (all) that in mind   Considering (all) that
Taking (all) that into account Given (all) that

2 contradicting
Some phrases introduce a statement that partially contradicts what has just been said.

Despite / In spite of (all) that   (But) Then again
(But) All the same   And yet
Having said that (though)   (But) Even so

3 adding
We sometimes use these phrases to add to what was said.

(Yeah, and) What's more …
(Yeah, and) On top of (all) that

4 exemplifying
You can use *for example* in spoken language, but this is perhaps more common:

(Yeah) I mean …

PRACTICE

7A

1 Match statements 1–6 with responses a–f.

1 She was born eight weeks premature.
2 My daughter's doing a doctorate.
3 Her company's relocating their head office and told her she either has to move or lose her job.
4 She decided to make a clean break and she went back to her native Mexico.
5 John and I have finally decided to tie the knot. The big day is going to be in November.
6 It was their golden anniversary this year and we had a big get-together to celebrate.

a That must've been great!
b That's great! You must be excited.
c Really? That must have been quite worrying. Is she OK now?
d Wow, she must be very clever.
e That can't have been an easy decision given how long she'd lived here.
f Really? That can't be easy to decide given how long she's lived here.

2 Complete the conversations with the words in the box.

> can get   can't have been
> can't have taken   did   is   must be
> must find   must've enjoyed
> shouldn't have   was

1 A: I look after five kids under the age of 4.
   B: That _____ exhausting.
   A: It _____ , but it's also great fun.
2 A: Where have you been? I've been waiting ages.
   B: Sorry, I had to go to the bank to get a form.
   A: Really? That _____ that long.
   B: It _____ , but there was a massive queue.
3 A: For my birthday, she bought me a day out driving a racing car.
   B: Wow, that _____ cheap.
   A: I know I _____ a bit worried to be honest.
   B: Right. Anyway, you _____ it.
   A: Yeah, I _____ . It was fantastic.
4 A: You _____ it fun travelling for work.
   B: Actually, it _____ me down sometimes.

7B

1 Complete the sentences with the correct form of the verbs in brackets to make third or mixed conditionals.

1 The news could easily _____ (trigger) violence if they _____ (make) it public, so I understand why they didn't do it.
2 We would _____ (be) in tomorrow's final if our goalkeeper _____ (not / break) his leg.
3 The economy would _____ (not / do) as badly as it is if the last government _____ (impose) more tariffs on imports.
4 If the government _____ (not / withdraw) from that treaty last year, we might _____ (not / be) in the mess we're in now.
5 If I _____ (not / care) about you, I would _____ (not / send) you the invitation to my graduation party.

2 Which alternative (a, b or c) is not correct?

1 If she hadn't made such an offensive comment,
   a it wouldn't have caused such controversy in the media.
   b she might still be in a job.
   c she wouldn't lose her job.
2 If we didn't have 24-hour news channels,
   a we'd all be a lot less stressed!
   b this problem wouldn't have happened.
   c this story had been reported in a more serious manner.
3 If they hadn't exposed the cover-up when they did,
   a all the illegal payments would still be going on.
   b we might never know how corrupt the system is.
   c it wouldn't have led to all those resignations.
4 He wouldn't be resigning
   a if the story wasn't revealed on the news last night.
   b if he thought he didn't have to.
   c if the stories about him hadn't come out in the press.

7C

1 Choose the correct alternatives.

1 A: Politicians don't have as much authority now because the turnout in elections is so small.
   B: *Having said that/On top of that*, it doesn't seem to stop them from doing what they want.
2 A: Politicians don't have as much authority now because the turnout in elections is so small.
   B: *What's more/And yet* they have even less authority because business is so powerful.
3 A: Politicians don't have as much authority now because the turnout in elections is so small.
   B: Yeah, well *considering that/then again* maybe we should try get more people voting.
4 A: Politicians don't have as much authority now because the turnout in elections is so small.
   B: *Given that/Yeah I mean* I think in the last election only 52% of those who could voted.

Want more practice? Go to your Workbook or app.

8A Complex questions

We sometimes ask more complex versions of basic questions to:

- add emphasis to the question word and to the information we want to check.
- focus on the opinion of the person we are asking.

We add emphasis to the question word using this pattern: question word + *be* + *it* + *that* clause.

It's similar to a cleft sentence (see Lesson 1A). We often use it to show we are surprised, confused or frustrated.

What do you want?

⟶ **What** (exactly) **is it** *that you want?*

When did this happen?

⟶ **When was it** *that this happened?*

We sometimes insert the phrase 'on earth' to a normal question for a similar purpose:

*What **on earth** does that involve?*

We focus on the opinion of the person using the pattern: question word + *do you* + *think/suggest/recommend*, etc. + *that* clause.

What is she doing?

⟶ *What do you suppose (that) she is doing?*

How did he get the job?

⟶ *How do you think (that) he got the job?*

How on earth did that happen?

⟶ *How on earth do you think (that) that happened?*

Sometimes the pronoun *that* follows the *that* beginning a clause. This is perfectly correct!

*What is it exactly **that that** is supposed to mean?*

*When do you think **that that** happened?*

8B Auxiliary verbs

The most common auxiliary verbs are *be, have* and *do*.

The verb *be* can be used to form continuous tenses and the passive.

We're all suffering from terrible jet lag.

*Our flight **has been** delayed.*

The verb *have* is used in perfect tenses.

*I **haven't** slept for almost 36 hours!*

The verb *do* can be used to make questions and negatives and to add emphasis in affirmative sentences.

*I **do** like him, but he **does** annoy me sometimes!*

Modal verbs like *should, must, would, might* and *will* are auxiliaries, too.

Auxiliaries are used in short answers and in extra comments to avoid too much repetition.

*A: **Did** you sleep well?   B: Yeah, I **did**, thanks.*

When we respond to comments that don't have auxiliary verbs in them, we use *do/does/did* to avoid repetition.

A: I love this hotel.

B: So do I.

A: I enjoyed it. I thought it was fun.

B: Really? I didn't, I have to say.

We often respond with other auxiliaries to show a wide range of different meanings.

A: You really should talk to someone about that.

B: I have (= already spoken to someone about it).

A: Shouldn't you be working?

B: I am. Kind of. (= I am working at the moment.)

A: Can you give me a lift to the airport tomorrow?

B: I would if I could. Honestly.

8C Complex comparatives

There are two main ways to make comparatives, which can be modified by various words and phrases to show the degree of difference between the things being compared.

1 more/-er/less ... than

- a small difference

a tiny bit/a little bit/a bit (more complicated)

(just) a touch (nicer)

a tiny bit/a little bit/a bit/a touch (less complex/less nice than ...)

- a big difference

quite a lot (better)

much (more complex)

miles (more expensive)

way (easier)

ten/fifty/a hundred times (better)

In the same way you can use these words to modify an adverb *too*.

*It has **a tiny bit too** much salt.*

*It's **way too** spicy for my liking.*

2 (not) as ... as

- a small difference:

not quite as (complicated/easy) as ...

- a big difference

not nearly as (easy) as ...

nowhere near as (difficult/simple) as ...

nothing like as (tasty/filling) as ...

much/a lot/miles/way (less expensive) than ...

ten/fifty/a hundred times (less greasy) than ...

We sometimes use *not ... anywhere near as/... anything like as.*

*It **wasn't anywhere near as** good as our previous place.*

*We **didn't have anything like** as much time as I thought we had.*

In the same way you can use *not quite/not nearly/ nowhere near/nothing like* to modify the adverb *enough*.

*The coffee's **not quite** strong enough for me.*

*There's **not nearly** enough food for everyone.*

PRACTICE

8A

1 Decide which six questions are incorrect. Correct them.

1 What is exactly that you do here?
2 How do you suppose he get that job here?
3 Why on earth Jennifer want to do that job?
4 What was it do they ask you at the interview?
5 What was it that that woman you were talking to wanted?
6 Who do you reckon should we ask?
7 Why on earth do you think he tried to do that?
8 When is it that you started working here?

2 Complete 1–5 in the conversation with a complex question using the word in brackets.

A: Apparently he describes himself as a Thought Leader.
B: Really? So what exactly **1**_____ does? (that)
A: Basically, he writes articles and goes on talk shows.
B: OK. But what **2**_____ (writes)?
A: Usually something to do with business or parenting.
B: And how **3**_____ into that? (earth)
A: Well, I'm not sure about the business, but I do know he brought up five kids on his own.
B: But lots of people are single parents. What **4**_____ special about him? (think)
A: Well, he's written a lot about it – and he's a man!
B: Exactly! So how much **5**_____ from being a Thought Leader? (suppose)
A: I don't know. But he seems to be doing well.

8B

1 Find the four sentences with mistakes and correct them.

1 I had three coffees last night, but I wish I didn't. It took me ages to get to sleep.
2 I never get jet lag and neither do my wife.
3 You really do look tired. Are you sure you're OK?
4 My car's in the garage at the moment. If it isn't, I'd give you a lift. Honestly.
5 A: I was exhausted by the time I got there.
   B: You must've been, yeah.
6 A: Have you been to see the doctor about it?
   B: No, but if things don't change, I would.
7 A: You should've tried drinking chamomile tea!
   B: I did, but it didn't seem to help much.

2 Match questions and comments 1–6 with the best responses a–f.

1 You must've been furious.
2 You should've complained about it.
3 Are you coming tonight?
4 Did you use those ear plugs I got you?
5 Can't you have a lie-in at the weekends?
6 Have you read that research paper yet?

a I guess I might do, yeah.
b I usually do, but it's not enough to catch up.
c Yeah. I really was.
d I haven't yet, but I will when I have time.
e I did. But they didn't do anything!
f I would've, but I lost them.

8C

1 Complete the sentences using the words in brackets.

1 The last cooker I had was OK, but *the new one is miles more efficient* . (new one / miles / efficient)
2 The curry was really great – just _____ . (not / quite / tasty / the one I do)
3 It's nice but it _____ . (needs / touch / salt)
4 I'm not eating that. It _____ . (way / many calories)
5 I tried making it, but it _____ . (miles / complicated / I had expected)
6 I prefer the cakes at the new café. They're _____ . (nowhere / near / sweet)
7 I can't afford to eat out here. It's _____ . (ten / expensive / it is at home)

2 Complete the paragraphs with one word in each gap.

Our family moved to the city when I was ten. For me, it was a terrible time, much more **1**_____ I think my parents thought it would be. I'm **2**_____ a lot older than my brother and sister so they don't remember **3**_____ much about our previous house and so their experience of the move was a lot **4**_____ traumatic. Not only had the house been **5**_____ bigger, but it had been surrounded by fields. In the city, there was a hundred **6**_____ more traffic and as a result, I didn't have **7**_____ like as much freedom to play outside **8**_____ I'd had before.
We moved because my parents felt that there weren't nearly **9**_____ opportunities for us kids in terms of education, so we would be much **10**_____ off in the city. However, I hated my new school because teachers were way **11**_____ strict. After a while, I liked living there, although I didn't tell my parents that until a **12**_____ later in life!

Want more practice? Go to your Workbook or app.

9A *not only* and *no sooner/as soon as*

not only

We often use *not only* to link two things that happened. Both actions/feelings are surprising, but especially the second one. *Not only* goes before the first action/feeling. The second action/feeling is often introduced with *but* and often includes the words *actually* or *even*.

*We **not only** hit our target **but** we **even** broke the company record.*

We can add extra emphasis by starting a sentence with *not only*. When we do this, we invert the subject and the auxiliary verb, i.e. we put the auxiliary verb before the subject.

***Not only** had I not recognised the sound of my own phone, but I'd actually worked myself up into a temper.*

(= I hadn't recognised my own phone and I'd also worked myself up into a temper.)

When there is no auxiliary verb or main verb *be*, we use *do, does,* or *did*.

***Not only** did we raise enough money for my son, we had enough to establish a foundation.*

no sooner/as soon as

We use *as soon as* to link an action with an immediate reaction or consequence.

*There was a rush **as soon as** they opened the doors.*

We can add extra emphasis, especially when the reaction is surprising, by starting with *no sooner*. When we do this, we invert the subject and the auxiliary verb.

*No sooner **had I** pressed send than it was re-tweeted.*

(= As soon as I had pressed send, it was re-tweeted)

We often start sentences with *not only* and *no sooner* when we want to make stories more exciting.

9B *will* and *would* for habits; *I wish + would*

We can use *will/won't* to talk about **repeated actions or habits in the present.**

*I don't do much sport, but I**'ll** go swimming now and again.*
*We get on well generally, but I **won't** talk about politics with him, because it tends to end up in an argument.*

In both sentences above, we can use the present simple instead with no real change of meaning.

We use *would/wouldn't* (or *would never*) in a similar way to talk about **repeated past actions or habits.**

*When he was a kid, he**'d** often snore loudly. We**'d** shut his bedroom door but you could still hear him!*

*At work, she**'d never/she wouldn't** (ever) go out for lunch with us. She**'d** just eat at her desk.*

In both sentences above, we can also use the past simple or *used to* + verb without any real change of meaning.

We use *I wish you/he/she/it*, etc. + *would/wouldn't* to talk about **annoying habits that we would like to change**.

*I **wish they'd** clean up after they finished. It's not much to ask.*

*I **wish they wouldn't** keep chatting to each other at the back of the class. It's very distracting!*

While we use *will* and *would* for repeated actions and habits, we don't use them to describe states or situations which are ongoing over a period of time. For these we use the present or past simple or *used to*.

My hair ~~would be~~ was blonder when I was younger.
I ~~would belong~~ used to belong to a rugby club when I was a kid.
I wish he ~~would have~~ had a job or I wish he would get one.
She ~~will own~~ owns / does own a car. It's a Mercedes.

9C Making new words

Here are some more examples of words that have been created using the six main ways of word formation.

1 Derivation

The most common way of making a new word is to add a prefix or a suffix to words that already exist.

*It's a brilliant novel - completely **unputdownable**.*
*They provide **microcredit** for people living in poverty.*
*He's a real **foodie**.*
*I try to be **mindful** in my everyday actions.*

2 Conversion

Taking a word from one word class and using it in another, so a noun may start being used as an adjective or a verb.

*They've **upped** their initial offer.*
*The company is **transitioning** to an online model.*
You may also add affixes to these new words.
*I **unfriended** him from all my social media.*

3 Abbreviations

A short form of a longer word or phrase.
*When I read social media I get **FOMO**.*
*Sorry, I can't eat the beef. I'm **veggie.***
*I didn't win but I got a **PB**, which I was very happy with.*

4 Loanwords

Words taken from one language and used in another.
*The basic job of a trendspotter is to capture the **zeitgeist**.*
*I made some **tzatziki** as a starter.*
*I had a feeling of **schadenfreude** when they went bankrupt. They were horrible to me when I worked there.*

5 Compounding

Words formed by putting two complete words together.
*They **crowdsourced** $100,000 for their **startup**.*
*I created a special **playlist** for the party.*
*It was a **tickbox exercise**. It didn't mean anything.*
Notice how compounds may also often convert nouns to verbs.
*We need to **upskill** our staff if we are going to survive.*

6 Portmanteau words

Words formed by combining two other words where at least one part is missing.
*The children's **edutainment** market is growing fast.*
*It's a **fanzine** for people who are into electronic music.*
*I guess I'd describe myself as a **flexitarian**.*

9A

1 Match the sentence halves.

1 People started to push and shove
2 Almost as soon as I'd posted the video,
3 No sooner had he got the news
4 He not only completely lost it,
5 Not only is he hilarious,
6 After a few days, not only did I not miss social media,

a but he's a fascinating character as well.
b as soon as the doors were opened.
c it started to go viral.
d but I started feeling healthier and happier as well.
e than he literally started jumping for joy.
f but he even threw a punch at me.

2 Rewrite each sentence with more emphasis using *no sooner* or *not only*.

1 She sent me a message as soon as she heard the news.
2 As soon as she complained about the company on social media, they contacted her.
3 When people write posts like that, they not only feel powerful but they feel very clever, too.
4 I could not only feel myself hitting a wall, but I was starting to get really ill as well.
5 As soon as I heard myself saying it, I knew I'd regret it.
6 She seemed not only lost for words, but also didn't know what to do next.

9B

1 Tick the sentences which refer to a habit or repeated action.

1 I'll call you when I hear some more news.
2 He's a strange boy – he won't eat any vegetable that isn't green.
3 We loved it there, we'd go there most summers – even if it was just one or two days.
4 I wish he'd told me.
5 What would you do faced with something like that?
6 I will try but I'm not promising anything.
7 I go into her room and she'll just be sitting there glued to her phone.
8 I wouldn't do anything for the time being.
9 I wish I didn't have to go, but I really should.
10 I wish he'd tell me instead of bottling it up.
11 We had a great time in the summer, I'd go there again.
12 I will try to talk to him about it from time to time, but I haven't ever got very far.
13 I'm paying - I won't take no for answer.
14 He's one of those people who won't take no for answer.
15 I would insist but I can see you're not going to change your mind.

2 Choose the correct alternatives. Sometimes <u>both</u> options are correct.

My friend Pete ¹*used to/would* be really quite a miserable cynical person – he ²*was always/ would always be* moaning about things when you met him and you ³*would usually end up/ usually ended up* saying to yourself – honestly I wish you ⁴*will/would* lighten up! We actually fell out for a while as a result. Anyway, at some point he really ⁵*would get/got* into electronic music and somehow it changed his outlook. I bumped into him one day and he just ⁶*seemed/ would seem* a lot more positive – more content with himself and life. Maybe it was all the dancing and exercise he was doing! Anyway, since then we've become good friends again. ⁷*We see/We'll* see each other every two or three of weeks. ⁸*We have/we'll have* a drink together or, now that ⁹*he has/he'll have* a baby, I go round to his house. He can still be quite dry and cynical, but I find it funnier, now. He's just a lot better to be around. The only thing now is I wish he ¹⁰*won't/wouldn't* play electronic music whenever I'm at his place!

9C

1 Find the words in the language reference on page 152 that mean:

1 a new business
2 very small loans
3 a kind of magazine
4 being happy when something goes wrong for someone else
5 going through a change
6 someone who's mainly vegetarian, but occasionally will eat other things.
7 increased
8 a Greek dip
9 improve knowledge and ability
10 the best time or score you have personally done
11 pay close attention to what you are doing
12 something you do simply to show you have done it

Want more practice? Go to your Workbook or app.

10A Prepositions 2

Prepositions are always followed by a noun, pronoun or -ing form of a verb.

*I worry **about climate change**.*

*We believe **in** work**ing** together to achieve common goals.*

Some prepositions (see Lesson 4C) combine with specific verbs, adjectives or nouns or are part of a fixed phrase:

apologise for, fight against, opposed to, reason for, response to, scared of, in the short term, out of practice

In spoken and informal written English, a preposition connected to a question word or relative pronoun goes at the end of the clause.

*Who are you going there **with**?* rather than *With whom are you going there?*

In more formal English, we find examples of prepositions used at the front of clauses.

***In** which journal was the research first published?*

Both prepositions and adverbs can combine with verbs to form phrasal verbs. When a verb is followed by an adverb, the object of the verb can come between them.

*Can you help me **fill** this form **out**?*

However, when a verb is followed by a preposition, the object of the verb never goes between the two. There's no rule for knowing whether a verb is separable or inseparable – we have to learn them in context.

Here are some common phrasal verbs:

catch up, check in, come across, come up with, get on with, get over, get out of, get rid of, keep up (with), look after, pass out, put up with, run out (of), take after

Some prepositions/prepositional phrases can join two parts of a sentence.

*I didn't understand, **despite watching** it again.*

***As well as winning** an award, he also won some money.*

10B Linking words and phrases

Linking words and phrases can be used to show contrasts, conditions, time and order, etc. We show these relationships in two ways:

1 Joining two parts of the same sentence

We can join two clauses in the same sentence with a conjunction. We can usually put either clause first:

*I did finish it **even though** I found it a bit boring.*

***Even though** I found it a bit boring, I did finish it.*

Or we can use prepositions to link ideas in the same sentence:

*People believe there is a crisis in reading **despite** evidence that kids are reading more.*

Sometimes the noun phrase is replaced by *that/this* to refer back to a previous idea.

*There is evidence that kids are reading more these days. Despite **that**, many people still believe there is a crisis in reading.*

2 Referring back to a previous sentence

*People believe there is a crisis in reading. **On the other hand**, there is evidence that kids are reading more.*

Note the comma after the linking phrase. We can also add a conjunction such as *and* or *but* to join the ideas into one sentence.

*People believe there is a crisis in reading, **but on the other hand**, there is evidence to suggest that kids are reading more.*

Some of these words and phrases are more common in formal, written language (F).

	1	2
contrasts	despite (the fact that) in spite of (the fact that), even though, although, whereas, while	on the other hand, however, all the same, nevertheless (F), nonetheless (F)
conditions	provided, so long as, as long as, in case, whether, even if, unless, if … not	otherwise
time/order	during, once, as soon as, after, before, following	afterwards, meanwhile, then, subsequently
addition	as well as, not only … but also, not to mention	what's more, on top of that, also, as well, moreover (F), furthermore (F), additionally (F)
cause	because because of, due to, owing to, thanks to, on account of, as a result of, be down to	
result/ purpose	so, so as + infinitive with *to*, in order + infinitive with *to*	As a result, therefore, as a consequence (F), thus (F), as such (F), consequently (F)

10C Puns

There are many words in English that have the same spelling, but a different meaning. We call these words **homographs**: *address, excuse, park, train*.

As nouns or adjectives, the stress is often on the first syllable, as verbs, on the second: *contract, import, perfect*.

Words that are spelled differently, but which sound the same are called **homophones**: *brake/break, dear/deer, higher/hire, meat/meet, son/sun*.

We use both homographs and homophones a lot in jokes.

Did you hear about the blind man who picked up a hammer … and saw?

One other way we make puns it to use common idiomatic expressions in a more literal way.

*People who bite their own toenails really do **put their foot in their mouth**.*

PRACTICE

10A

1 Complete the sentences with the prepositions in the box.

except	for	from	in	of	out	to

1 The desire to search _____ answers to our questions is in our genes.
2 STEM careers consist _____ jobs in Science, Technology, Engineering and Mathematics.
3 Researchers from all over the world have been involved _____ the project.
4 Her contribution _____ the field has been huge.
5 Who did you hear that _____ ?
6 I haven't done this for ages, so I'm a bit _____ of practice.
7 If you ask me, this benefits no one _____ the big drug companies.

2 Complete the sentences with the correct form of the phrasal verbs in the box.

come across	come up with	get over
keep up with	look after	pass out	run out of
take after		

1 We still don't really understand why some people _____ when they see blood.
2 We're trying to find out why it takes some people longer to _____ colds than others.
3 I _____ a really interesting article about that the other day.
4 She's very creative. She often _____ interesting ideas for experiments.
5 In the near future, many children may well end up being _____ by robots.
6 There's so much new research coming out that I can't _____ it all.
7 I'd like to know if the human mind could ever _____ memory.
8 I don't really _____ my mum. We're different in many ways.

10B

1 Choose the correct alternatives. Sometimes both options are correct.

1 Some people are concerned that kids are reading less ᵃ*so as to/due to* their increased use of the internet. ᵇ*However,/Whereas* a lot of people have to do more reading these days as part of their jobs. ᶜ*Furthermore,/Nevertheless,* many people read a great deal because they stay in education longer.
2 The film *Schindler's List* was based on an award-winning book by Thomas Keneally. ᵃ*Subsequently,/Following* the success of the film the book has perhaps been forgotten. ᵇ*Even though/Despite* you might have seen the film, I would still recommend reading the book.
3 I don't think it's a suitable play for kids. They said children were allowed ᵃ*provided/as long as* they were accompanied by an adult, but many kids were obviously bored ᵇ*because/down to* they kept whispering. ᶜ*On top of that,/Moreover*, it's three hours long.

2 Rewrite the sentences using the words in brackets.

1 At the end of the book, he dies because he wants to protect his children. (so as to)
At the end of the book, he dies _____ .
2 She was a really funny woman. What's more, she was incredibly brave. (as well as)
_____ she was incredibly brave.
3 After he told me he was married, I found out he had been lying. (subsequently)
He told me _____ but _____ .
4 You can take my keys unless you are coming back after me. (so long as)
You can take _____ .
5 Despite telling him countless times to lock the door, he left it wide open. (all the same)
I told him countless times _____ .

10C

1 Match questions 1–6 with the best answers a–f to make puns.

1 What often falls but never gets hurt?
2 What goes all over the world but always stays in a corner?
3 What gets wetter the more it dries?
4 What has one head, one foot and four legs?
5 What has keys, but can't open locks?
6 What can you break without touching?

a a towel
b a bed
c a piano
d rain
e a promise
f a stamp

2 Find the homophones in the jokes below. How would you have to change the spelling to explain the jokes?

1 A: Did you hear about the kidnapping at school?
B: It's OK. He woke up.
2 A: Why will you never starve in the desert?
B: Because of all the sandwiches there.
3 A man just attacked me with milk, cream and butter. I mean, how dairy!
4 A: Why was the mortgage sad?
B: Because it was a loan.
5 A: Why didn't the lion enjoy the cooked vegetables?
B: He prefers them roar.

Want more practice? Go to your Workbook or app.

Vocabulary bank

1B Help and encouragement

1 Read the text and match words and phrases 1–10 in bold with meanings a–j below.

> When I started my degree, it was the first time I'd lived away from home and it was quite a big thing for me as I am registered blind. Fortunately, new students got a lot of support from the university. Firstly, there was a mentoring **¹scheme** so I had a couple of older students who **²took** me **under their wing** – showed me around the campus, introduced me to different people and generally **³put** me **at ease**. One of my mentors became a good friend and she gave me a lot of **⁴moral support** when I was feeling down. She would tell me she'd had similar feelings, and always found the words to **⁵reassure** me. Apart from this, I also received **⁶a grant** to pay for some of my additional needs like help with writing up my essays and buying books.
>
> When it came to studying, I found the lecturers **⁷made allowances** for different people by, for example, providing recordings of lectures and giving copies of notes in advance. They also **⁸went easy on** us in the first term as we were settling in. They gradually demanded more, but they always gave us lots of help and **⁹encouragement**.
>
> Actually, most of this support was available for any student, not just ones with disabilities, and most of us were **¹⁰in the same boat**, away from our families for the first time.

a   money to help

b   a programme

c   make (someone) feel that things will be fine

d   were gentle to and didn't demand too much of

e   made fair decisions that considered someone's needs or disadvantage

f   looked after (someone younger or with less experience) with kindness

g   words to give (someone) confidence and courage

h   helped to feel comfortable and happy

i   experiencing a similar situation

j   words or behaviour to help someone do better

2 a Complete the questions with one word from Exercise 1. Use the correct form.

   1   Do you think mentoring _____ are a good idea?

   2   When have you needed moral _____?

   3   Have you ever taken someone under your _____?

   4   Have you ever had to _____ allowances for someone?

   5   Who has _____ you the most encouragement in life?

   6   What situations have you been in where you weren't _____ ease? Did anyone help you?

b Work in pairs. Ask and answer four of the questions in Exercise 2a. Alternatively, work alone and write your answers.

1C Word building: negatives

1 Match the negative prefixes and suffixes with each group of words.

dis-	im-	in-	ir-	-less	un-

   1   point, hope, worth, care, meaning

   2   organised, respectful, honest

   3   realistic, reasonable, clear, equal, suitable, tidy, aware

   4   relevant, rational, regular, responsible

   5   mature, patient, moral, proper, perfect

   6   secure, experienced, adequate, sufficient, consistent, competent

2 Complete the sentences using a negative form of a word from Exercise 1.

   1   It annoys me that there's still _____ pay between men and women. We should get paid the same.

   2   Our boss is too demanding. A lot of the targets we're set are simply _____.

   3   It drives me mad when people use _____ jargon at work. They should just use language that everyone can understand.

   4   I'm absolutely _____ at all sport. I hate doing it!

   5   In my opinion, a lot of what you learn at school is _____ to everyday life.

   6   I know my fear of flying is _____ and that statistics show it's very safe, but I still hate it.

   7   The thing that concerns me is how _____ young people are to older people these days.

   8   Too many jobs are _____ these days. You just don't know how long they will last.

   9   It's basically _____ to avoid paying taxes.

   10 I find it annoying when people beep their horn as soon as the traffic light goes green. They are so _____.

3 Choose five words with a negative suffix from Exercise 1. Write sentences about your experiences.

2B Word building: noun formation

1 Complete the sentences using the noun forms of the words in brackets.

   1 There's a growing _____ of the impact that climate change is having on the world. (aware)

   2 The bigger the project, the lower the _____ of it actually being completed on time. (probable)

   3 These new laws represent a very real threat to _____ of expression on the internet. (free)

   4 They offer free exercise classes for older people and those with restricted _____ . (mobile)

   5 We need to do more to attract foreign _____ . (invest)

   6 We're opposed to the _____ of the airport. It'll be bad for the local environment. (expand)

   7 In the end, they came to the _____ that he wasn't the right person for the job. (conclude)

   8 We do most of our work in areas that suffer from economic and social _____ . (deprive)

   9 We've received a very generous _____ from a well-known local celebrity. (donate)

  10 He presents himself as an outsider fighting the political _____ . (establish)

2 a Form nouns from each group of words (1–6) with the suffixes in the box. Make any other changes necessary to the spelling.

-dom	-ity	-ment	-ness	-sion	-tion

   1 homeless, conscious, effective

   2 supervise, comprehend, persuade

   3 astonish, embarrass, amuse

   4 capable, authentic, secure

   5 star, bore, wise

   6 oppose, recognise, concentrate

  b Check your answers with a partner. Do you agree on the spelling and pronunciation of each noun?

3 a Complete each question with the best noun from Exercise 2a.

   1 How big a problem is _____ where you live?

   2 At what age can children be left without adult _____ ?

   3 When was a time you felt you could have died of _____ ?

   4 What do you do to protect your online _____ ?

   5 What problems might sudden _____ bring?

   6 Which plans or laws have faced a lot of _____ ?

  b Work in pairs. Ask and answer four of the questions in Exercise 3a.

2C Buildings, places, structures

1 Match the words in the box with photos A–H.

bungalow	dam	dock	hut
mansion	memorial	pier	reservoir

2 Complete the sentences with the nouns in the box in Exercise 1.

   1 While we were out in the forest, we came across an abandoned wooden _____ . It was a bit scary.

   2 For their wedding reception, they rented a great big _____ out in the countryside.

   3 After they retired, they moved into a little _____ by the sea. They like not having to go up and down stairs anymore.

   4 We walked out to the end of the _____ , where we bought an ice cream and looked round the souvenir shop.

   5 It hasn't rained much this year, and water levels in the big _____ outside town are very low.

   6 There was a war _____ in almost every town we drove through.

   7 They're worried that the _____ might burst and cause serious flooding.

   8 We stayed by a big lake and even had our own little _____ with a boat.

3 Work in groups. Which of the eight things in the box in Exercise 1 have you seen or visited? Say when and where.

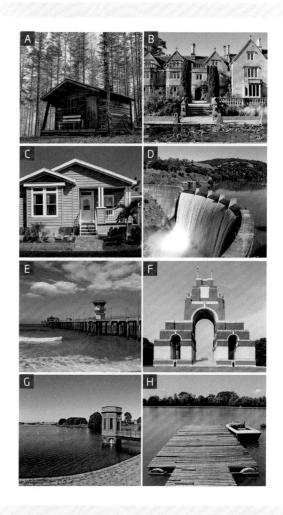

3B Crime

1 Complete the stories with the words in the boxes.

armed	held up	hiding	made off with	run

1 Did you see that story about those guys who _____ a bank in the centre of town? Apparently, they were quite heavily _____ and they _____ over two million in cash. They haven't been caught yet. They're basically all on the _____ now and the police think they've probably gone into _____ . I hope they get them soon!

custody	fire	raid	seized	wounded

2 I heard that there was a _____ on the gang's HQ first thing this morning and the police _____ over half a million pounds' worth of stolen goods. Apparently, when they turned up, the gang opened _____ on them and _____ three officers. They've arrested five people and are keeping them in _____ for further questioning.

assaulting	conviction	example	freed	offensive

3 He'd only been _____ from prison a few weeks before, but then he got himself arrested again for _____ a police officer and possession of an _____ weapon. He's got a previous _____ for a similar offence, so I think this time they'll really try to make an _____ of him. I expect he'll get at least five years.

bail	front	posed	trial	undercover

4 Apparently, the police had been running an _____ operation for months. One officer had _____ as a foreign businessman to gain the gang's trust and he found out that some of the clubs they owned were basically a _____ for illegal activities. They've arrested four men and they're due to stand _____ next month. In the meantime, the judge has set _____ at a million dollars each.

2 Complete the collocations with words from Exercise 1.
1 be _____ the run
2 _____ into hiding
3 _____ fire
4 _____ someone in custody overnight
5 have a _____ conviction
6 _____ an example of someone
7 _____ trial next month
8 _____ bail at £500,000

3 Think of TV shows, films or news stories that you can describe using six words or phrases from Exercise 1. Tell your partner about them.

3C Phrasal nouns and phrasal verbs

1 Match phrasal nouns 1–7 in bold with meanings a–g.
1 Make sure you stretch properly after your **workout**.
2 They had a **break-in** at the gym over the weekend.
3 They've given the **go-ahead** for the new stadium.
4 It was a brilliant game and there was a huge **turnout**.
5 There was a bit of a **mix-up** and they lost my tickets.
6 They gave the play a very good **write-up** in the local paper.
7 I'm exhausted. I'm just going to have a little **lie-down**.

a review
b illegal entry
c rest or sleep
d period of physical exercise
e permission for someone to start doing something
f a problem or mistake because someone was confused
g number of people at an event

2 a Complete the questions using phrasal verbs based on the nouns in bold in Exercise 1.
1 Have you been to any sports game or festival where very large numbers of people _____ ?
2 Have you ever lost your keys and had to _____ to your car or home? Why?
3 Do you ever _____ at the gym? if yes, how often? What do you do?
4 When was the last time you managed to _____ and have a little rest?
5 Do you ever _____ your notes after class or after lectures or talks?
6 Can you remember a time when someone _____ your order in a restaurant?
7 Can you think of a project that _____ despite a lot of local opposition?

b Work in pairs. Ask and answer the questions in Exercise 2a.

4A Prepositional phrases

1 Work in pairs. Complete the table by adding three of the words/phrases in the box to each column.

> any moment average a bad way the ball
> choice definition least other words
> rights second thoughts theory
> the top of your voice

on	in	at	by

2 a Choose the correct alternatives.

1 University education should only be available *at/by* your own expense.

2 Products that help you stop smoking should be available *in/on* prescription.

3 You shouldn't make judgments about people *on/at* the spot.

4 You can't judge the art of the past *by/in* today's standards.

5 People and organisations that miss their goals perform better *by/in* the long run.

6 Bread and water should always be *on/at* the house in restaurants.

7 It's better to get to a party early than arrive when it's *in/at* full swing.

8 It's normal to be *in/on* the red when you first start a business.

9 It's generally best to follow the rules and do everything *by/on* the book.

10 You shouldn't simply take what adverts say *on/at* face value.

11 *In/On* a personal level, this has been a great year for me so far.

12 It's lovely to be up *at/by* the crack of dawn, while everyone else is still sleeping.

b Work in groups. Discuss how far you agree with the statements in Exercise 2a.

4C Phrasal verbs

1 Complete each pair of sentences with the correct form of one phrasal verb in the box. In one sentence in each pair, you will also have to add an extra preposition.

> catch up crack down fall out fight back
> go on rub off stand in stand out

1 a If you want to be the best, you've got to play against the best and hope some of their talent _____ .

 b My mum was very musical so, I guess some of that must've _____ me.

2 a He's nearly two metres tall with orange hair, so it's fair to say he _____ the crowd.

 b Most kids don't want to _____ . They just want to be like all their friends.

3 a I just get so tired of her always _____ her problems all the time.

 b I'm not surprised you found him boring. He can _____ a bit when he wants to!

4 a Magda is off today and she's asked me to _____ .

 b My boss is away on a business trip, so her assistant is _____ her while she's away.

5 a I _____ my brother last year after lending him £1000 that he never paid back.

 b Can we not talk about politics? I don't want us to _____ .

6 a The police are _____ people who drive too fast on this road at the moment.

 b Too many people have been coming in late. From now on, we're going to be _____ .

7 a I missed three days of work last week, and I'm struggling to _____ at the moment.

 b I need to stay in tonight. I have to _____ some work.

8 a The local community have come together to _____ crime in the area.

 b He tried to grab my bag, but he clearly wasn't expecting me to _____ !

2 a Complete the questions using the correct form of phrasal verbs in Exercise 1.

1 Do you think it's better to look like everyone else or to _____ a crowd?

2 What do you think the police should start _____ where you live?

3 Do you know anyone who has _____ a close friend or anyone in your family? What about?

4 Which of your parents' likes and interests have _____ you?

5 Do you know anyone who's always _____ themselves or their job?

6 If someone tries to take your bag, is it better to let them or to _____ ? Why?

b Work in pairs. Ask and answer the questions in Exercise 2a.

5A Adverbs

1 a Choose the correct alternatives.

1 A: Did you check your essay for errors?
   B: I did, but not very *thoroughly/explicitly*. I didn't have time.

2 A: Did they agree to give you the money back?
   B: Very *reluctantly/readily*, and only after I threatened them with legal action.

3 A: I *freely/consciously* admitted I was wrong.
   B: Yes, but you aren't taking it very *seriously/sensibly*.

4 A: She spoke to each student *collectively/individually* about it.
   B: And did she find out who did it?

5 A: Do you remember Nicolas Bottas from school?
   B: *Vaguely/Sharply*. Was he the tall blond guy?

6 A: Where did Hugh go? He left rather *abruptly/freely*, didn't he?
   B: I've no idea.

b What verb is each adverb used with in the sentences in Exercise 1a? Can you think of one more verb that each adverb can go with?

2 Complete 1–8 with your own ideas. Then share your sentences with a partner.

1 I once deliberately …
2 I vaguely remember …
3 I (don't) always thoroughly check …
4 … has/have improved dramatically over the last few years.
5 I freely admit I …
6 I used to seriously think about becoming …
7 … is something I usually do very reluctantly.
8 … was a decision I made abruptly because …

5C Collective nouns

1 a Match collective nouns 1–6 with pairs of nouns a–f.

1	a herd of	a	ships/vehicles
2	a fleet of	b	keys/bananas
3	a mob of	c	wild elephants/people
4	a bunch of	d	attacks/failures
5	a stack of	e	angry people/youths
6	a string of	f	bricks/letters

b Match collective nouns 7–12 with pairs of nouns g–l.

7	a body of	g	cards/lies
8	a wave of	h	sheep/ducks
9	a flock of	i	work/evidence
10	a pack of	j	complaints/applications
11	a flood of	k	strikes/panic
12	a panel of	l	experts/judges

2 Complete the sentences with a completed collective noun from Exercise 1.

1 There's a growing _____ that suggests physical exercise can help tackle depression.
2 Vegan activists have carried out a _____ on butcher's shops over recent weeks.
3 The company has had to cancel hundreds of flights as it has been hit by a _____ by pilots and flight attendants.
4 We only advertised the position yesterday, but we've already had a _____ .
5 Has anyone seen a big _____ ? I dropped them somewhere and need them to get into my flat.
6 I thought he was telling the truth at the time, but now I see that the whole thing was a _____ .
7 A _____ of all ages took to the streets to protest against the new laws.
8 My upstairs neighbours are so noisy all the time! It's like living below _____ .
9 I have a special box in my bedroom where I keep a _____ that my grandma wrote to me.
10 The winner of the competition will be decided by a _____ from across the industry.
11 The road was blocked by a farmer and his _____ moving from one field to another.
12 A large _____ drove past earlier. I'm guessing it was probably the president and his staff.

3 Work in pairs. Take turns saying four true things about your life. Use words from Exercise 1.

I've always loved the band Queen. They left behind such an amazing body of work.

I probably need to tidy up my room. There are stacks of books all over the place.

6A Talking about the economy

1 Read the text. Match words and phrases 1–12 in bold with meanings a–l below.

> The early 2000s were a period of great economic **¹expansion** here. Business was **²booming**, people were earning plenty of money and there was a general feeling of hope for the future. There was also a strong belief in the value of the **³free market**. All that changed after the **⁴crash** of 2008. First one big bank nearly went bankrupt, then another. The crisis seemed to **⁵deepen** by the day and in the end, of course, it was **⁶the taxpayer** that picked up the bill. Local councils had their budgets cut, and workers in the public **⁷sector** had their wages **⁸frozen**. There was a lot of **⁹privatisation** as councils were forced to sell off land and housing – and even after years of this, we still have a huge trade **¹⁰deficit** and the big banks still haven't been **¹¹broken up**. The whole thing just isn't **¹²sustainable**. It's crazy.

a all the people who pay tax
b the sale of businesses or industries previously owned by the public sector
c system by which the buying and selling of goods is not state-controlled
d stopped from increasing
e capable of continuing for a long time without collapsing or damaging people, the environment, business, etc.
f part of the economy
g growth of size, number or amount
h separated into smaller parts
i sudden fall in prices/value
j the difference between the money you have and the money you spend or owe
k doing very well and making good money
l get worse

2 a Complete each question with one of the words in bold in Exercise 1.

1 What are the opportunities and threats a company faces when business is _____?
2 In your country, is it better to work in the public or the private _____? Why?
3 Can you think of one good reason and one bad reason why wages might be _____?
4 Can you think of one example of the _____ of a state company that's worked, and one that hasn't?
5 What factors might lead to a financial _____?

b Work in pairs. Ask and answer three of the questions in Exercise 2a.

6C Compound adjectives

1 a Match 1–6 with a–f to make compound adjectives.

1	fast-	a	friendly
2	environmentally	b	paced
3	old-	c	fact
4	hard-	d	populated
5	matter-of-	e	working
6	densely	f	fashioned

b Match 7–12 with g–l to make compound adjectives.

7	easy-	g	range
8	user-	h	behaved
9	open-	i	friendly
10	well-	j	earth
11	down-to-	k	going
12	free-	l	minded

2 Complete the sentences with the compound adjectives in Exercise 1.

1 Even after he became famous, he managed to stay _____, very normal and friendly.
2 The whole thing's a nightmare. It's one of the least _____ websites I've ever seen.
3 I might be _____, but I think the man should always ask the woman out.
4 I used to hate this kind of music, but I've got more _____ as I've got older.
5 She gets on with everybody. She's so relaxed, so _____.
6 We should all refuse single-use plastic packaging and choose more _____ products instead.
7 I don't mind kids coming in here so long as they're _____ and don't disturb anyone.
8 It's a _____ thriller full of twists and turns. I found it really exciting to watch.
9 Hong Kong is one of the most _____ cities on earth, where many people live in small flats in high-rise blocks.
10 She's the perfect employee: really _____, very reliable and never late.
11 They tried to break the news to me in a strangely _____ sort of way – as though it's something completely normal.
12 I don't buy eggs from factory-farm chickens. I only buy _____ ones.

3 Work in pairs. Which of the compound adjectives in Exercise 2 do you think are positive and which are negative? Give examples.

7B Secrets and lies

1 Complete the short stories with the collocations in the box.

> denied the allegations   leaked to the press
> plotting to remove   revelation has caused
> rumours circulating

> There was a story in the paper yesterday that several MPs in the Workers Unity Party have been [1]_____ the party leader. There had been some [2]_____ that they wanted to change the leader, but they had previously [3]_____ . However, yesterday, emails relating to the plot were [4]_____ . Not surprisingly, this latest [5]_____ further damage to the party who have slumped in the opinion polls.

> breathed a word   keeping something from me
> let slip that   made out that   sworn to secrecy

> My husband had been acting rather strangely. Twice I caught him secretly making phone calls and then ending them very quickly. When I asked him, he always [6]_____ it was to do with problems at work, but I knew he was [7]_____ as he's normally so open. Anyway, I was telling a friend of mine about it and I was quite upset and she [8]_____ he was actually arranging a surprise party for me. She told me she'd been [9]_____ . The party was last night and it was wonderful. I think I did well at pretending to be surprised. Anyway, I haven't [10]_____ about it to him.

2 Match sentence beginnings 1–6 with the best pairs of sentence endings a–f.

1 They have denied
2 He is plotting
3 She let slip
4 He made out that
5 She swore
6 Someone leaked

a to overthrow the government. / to become the new leader of the country.
b her friend to secrecy. / she wouldn't breathe a word to anyone.
c there was nothing to the rumours. / he was happy with the pay rise.
d that she actually knew already. / that she was going to resign.
e secret documents to the press. / the decision before it was announced.
f the rumour. / the accusation.

3 Work in pairs. Tell your partner about two of the following:

- a revelation in the news recently
- a rumour that is circulating
- a plot you have heard about
- a time you were sworn to secrecy
- a time you let something slip

7C Word building: affixes and word families

1 Match affixes 1–10 with meanings a–j.

1	dis-	a	after
2	-ful	b	again
3	-less	c	before
4	mis-	d	many/several
5	multi-	e	no/not
6	over-	f	too much
7	post-	g	too little
8	pre-	h	with
9	re-	i	without
10	under-	j	wrongly

2 Complete each sentence with the correct form of the words in the box and one of the affixes in Exercise 1.

> do   elect   estimate   hear   hope   match
> power   respect   school   storey

1 Prime Minister Mandini was _____ last year. He's now in his third term in office.
2 The President accused her opponents of _____ when they refused to accept the result.
3 I thought the People's Front might do OK, but I really _____ how well they'd do. They won an absolute majority.
4 The government says it's _____ it can get a deal to end the strike.
5 A lot of people feel _____ to bring about change because they feel they have no voice in politics.
6 I'm sorry I _____ you. I thought you said you needed to sit down.
7 I stayed at home till my daughter was five because there aren't many options for _____ childcare around here.
8 There's a _____ car park opposite our house but they have been trying to convert it into a community centre.
9 I went running yesterday and I think I _____ it, because I feel really stiff today.
10 The players complained about some of the referee's decisions in the _____ interview.

3 Write sentences using other words for each of the affixes in Exercise 1. Then share your ideas with a partner.

8A Jobs and companies

1 Complete the table below with the titles in the box. Add four to each column.

admin assistant   deputy finance director
GP   high-street retailer   HR service provider
management consultancy   programmer
multinational

Type of job	Type of company
freelance designer	defence contractor
CEO	property developer

2 Complete the sentences with the correct form of the jobs and companies in Exercise 1.

1 I'm a _____ . I specialise in branding and advertising and work with a few different clients.

2 While there are more women on the boards of top companies these days, there are still very few women who get the top job as _____ .

3 As a _____ here, you can expect to see 50-60 patients a day.

4 I work for a _____ that makes arms and provides military supplies for different countries.

5 A lot of _____ are facing stiff competition from online companies that can sell at lower prices because they pay a lot less rent.

6 The company made cutbacks, which means I no longer have an _____ to manage my diary, book flights and other day-to-day stuff.

7 The company uses an _____ to deal with pay, contracts and recruitment. They're based abroad.

8 The government contracted a _____ to look at the way the health system is run and recommend ways to improve efficiency.

9 The government has made computing a compulsory subject at school because it believes we'll need many more _____ in the future.

10 Most companies are controlled by _____ now whose head offices are based outside the country.

11 An abandoned factory building near here has been bought by a local _____ and they're going to turn it into a shopping centre and flats.

12 The company fired their _____ for hiding $50 million losses.

3 Work in pairs. Choose six of the situations in Exercise 2 and discuss:
• if you think the situations are good or bad. Why?
• what might improve the bad situations.

8C Expressions with *like*

1 Complete the expressions with the words in the boxes.

crazy   a dream   jelly   a light
watching paint dry

1 The whole event went like _____ .

2 I was out like _____ last night.

3 We were jumping up and down like _____ .

4 Honestly, it was so boring it was like _____ .

5 I tried to stay calm, but my legs felt like _____ .

flies   headless chickens   a lead balloon
nothing I've ever experienced   a tank

6 I thought it was very funny, but it went down like _____ .

7 He was about six foot six and built like _____ .

8 People were in a complete panic and running around like _____ .

9 People were dropping like _____ .

10 It was terrible – like _____

2 a Work in pairs. Use your own ideas and discuss which sentences in Exercise 1 might be linked with a–e.

a You must've been so happy when they scored.

b We had to watch this presentation about the history of concrete.

c There was some strange bug going round.

d This guy came up to us in the street and asked us to give him our wallets.

e I had to give this presentation at work.

f We were running a conference over the weekend.

b With your partner, choose three situations from Exercise 2a and create a short six-line conversation for each.

A: *You must have been so happy when they scored!*

B: *Yes – we were jumping up and down like crazy!*

A: *I'm not surprised - you were losing at half-time.*

B: *I know, I didn't think we had a chance.*

A: *I don't think anyone did.*

B: *But to win in the last minute of the match - unbelievable! It was a night I will never forget!*

9A Expressions with *it*

1 Match the expressions in bold in 1–11 with meanings a–k.

1 I can remember that once I bought my first car, I really felt I'd **made it**.

2 **Let's face it**, neither of us is getting any younger.

3 After months of having problems, they finally decided to **call it a day**.

4 I'm not saying it's going to be easy. **Far from it**.

5 I always love reading her comments. **Come to think of it**, though, she's not posted for a while.

6 Don't spend too long thinking about it. Just **go for it**. Why not?

7 I tried to stay as calm as I could, but in the end, I just totally **lost it**.

8 I really **put my foot in it**. I asked if she was his daughter, but it turned out it was his wife!

9 You think we should ask Max to organise it? **Come off it**! He's hopeless at things like that.

10 I was going to complain about it to the boss, but then I **thought better of it**.

11 Come on. **Spit it out**. I can't help if I don't know the full story, can I?

a I think what you've just said is stupid.

b stop doing something as you feel you've already done enough of it

c become very successful

d became extremely angry

e said something that accidentally upset or embarrassed someone

f If anything, the opposite is true.

g decided not to say or do something because it's a bad idea

h I'm going to say something unpleasant but true.

i used to add a comment when you've suddenly realised something

j try your best to achieve or win something

k hurry up and say what you're going to say

2 Complete the questions by adding the correct form of the verbs in Exercise 1.

1 Have you ever seen anyone just totally _____ it and start screaming and shouting at people?

2 Do you know any couples who've decided to _____ it a day recently?

3 Can you remember a time when you accidentally _____ your foot in it? What did you say or do?

4 Has there ever been a time in your life when you really felt like you'd finally _____ it?

5 Can you remember the last time someone said something that made you think '_____ off it!'?

6 Have you ever been about to make a big life change and then _____ better of it?

3 Work in pairs. Ask and answer three of the questions in Exercise 2.

9C Nouns and verbs with the same form

1 a Work in pairs. Look at the verbs in the box and discuss:

1 which are the only two verbs that <u>can't</u> also be used as nouns in the same form.

2 which three verbs are stressed differently when said as nouns. What's the difference?

adjust	alert	auction	blast	contrast	dip
dispose	exhibit	hike	insult	rebel	slump

b Complete the sentences with words in the box in Exercise 1a.

1 Most advertising is an _____ to our intelligence.

2 Going for a _____ in the mountains is a great way of relaxing.

3 Most teenagers _____ against their parents at some point. It's normal.

4 There's been a _____ in house prices this year. They're much cheaper than they were.

5 Museums shouldn't be allowed to _____ things that were stolen from other countries.

6 It's always best to _____ the police if you see someone acting in a suspicious way.

7 For most people, there's a definite _____ between what we say and what we do.

8 The best way to eat most biscuits is to _____ them in a warm drink.

2 Work in groups. Say how true you think each of the statements in Exercise 1b is.

10B Adjectives

1 Add the adjectives in the box to the correct category in the table below.

| autobiographical | chilly | committed | curly | fictional | humid | naïve | tanned |

Books	Weather	Appearance	Personality and traits
descriptive	frosty	chic	sharp
mainstream	harsh	filthy	dim

2 Complete the sentences with adjectives in Exercise 1.

1 I hate my hair. I wish mine was lovely and _____ like yours.

2 She's a really _____ kid. I mean, she is very quick to notice things.

3 It was the rainy season there and so it was really hot and _____ . I was sweating like mad.

4 He uses such wonderfully _____ language. You can really picture the place in your head.

5 Where did you go for your holidays? Somewhere hot? You're looking very _____ .

6 Sherlock Holmes must be one of the most famous _____ characters ever.

7 You might want to take a jacket with you. It's a bit _____ out there today.

8 Look at you! You're _____ ! I don't want you walking through the house like that!

9 Her first novel was largely _____ and drew on her experience of growing up in Tokyo.

10 I hate to say it, but I think it was a bit _____ of you to think you'd ever get that money back.

11 It's right up in the north and the winters are really _____ . It's dark for six months of the year.

12 He's a nice guy, but he can be a bit _____ sometimes, you know – a bit slow.

3 Which of the words can you use to talk about your own experiences? Compare your ideas with a partner.

10C Expressions with *get*

1 Match the expressions in bold in 1–10 with meanings a–j.

1 Why's it so funny? I don't **get it**.

2 I tried to change her mind, but **got nowhere**.

3 You're staying in to clean? Seriously? **Get a life**!

4 When he talked, no one could **get a word in edgeways**.

5 Don't **get on the wrong side of** her. She's got a temper!

6 **Don't get me wrong**. I like him, but he can be annoying.

7 I had a good long cry to **get it out of my system**.

8 I hate it when people do that. It really **gets on my nerves**.

9 After what she'd done to me, I wanted to **get even**!

10 He kept trying to talk to me so I had to tell him to **get lost**.

a Don't be so boring.

b manage to say something

c go away and leave me alone

d cause someone as much trouble as they've caused you

e annoys or irritates me

f Please understand me correctly.

g understand the joke

h make someone feel angry towards you

i get rid of a negative emotion by expressing it

j wasn't successful

2 a Complete the sentence endings and beginnings with words from the phrases in bold in Exercise 1.

1 I wouldn't want to get on the wrong _____ of ...

2 One thing that really gets on my _____ is ...

3 When I need to get something out of my _____ I ...

4 ... talks so much that no one else can usually get a word in _____

5 ... needs to get a _____ and spend less time ...

b Complete the sentences with your own ideas. Share your ideas with a partner.

I wouldn't want to get on the wrong side of Pat – he gets angry easily!

Communication bank

Lesson 1D

13a   Student A

Conversation 1
You're the landlord/landlady of a flat that Student B has been renting. You've gone round to visit because Student B is leaving and wants the €1000 deposit back. You don't want to give it back – at least not all of it – because you're not happy with the state they have left the place in. Think about what the problems are.

Conversation 2
You work with Student B, who has been with the company much longer than you. You joined a few months ago, Student B has been there almost a decade. Student B doesn't like the way you work, even though you've been getting good results. You feel Student B can be a bit bullying. You've been missing work to avoid a conflict with B, but have now decided you need to confront him/her.

Lesson 2C

10

Lesson 3B

12   Student A

1
A thirteen-year-old boy took his parents to court after accusing them of causing him a life of pain and suffering … as a result of the colour of his hair! A redhead, like both his mother and father, the boy argued that he should be awarded damages to compensate him for the teasing and unhappiness he'd experienced at high school, where he was known as Carrot Top!

2
A Philosophy student in Rotterdam took Erasmus University in Rotterdam to court after they ordered him to leave … because he smelled so badly no one could concentrate while he was in the room. While admitting to having rather smelly feet, he claimed that this decision damaged his chances of future employment and demanded to be allowed to continue with his degree.

4B Develop your writing

2b

1 1222
2 16th century
3 rich people's schools
4 90%
5 sweatshirt
6 £200

Lesson 5B

3

5B Develop your writing

3b

Journey to the bottom of a volcano

Sleeping on a ridge above a volcano is not for the [1]faint-hearted. You have to wear a gas mask to protect yourself from the toxic fumes and at night you only snooze, constantly aware that if you roll too far in your sleep you will fall off the narrow ridge and into the [2]fiery core below. Having spent three nights there, we were ready to make our descent.

Using ropes to rappel down in stages we made good progress but after half an hour, [3]a heavy downpour forced us to turn back. The volcanic gas turned the rain water to acid and the acid threatened to eat through our ropes and send us [4]tumbling down into the lava below. We spent a fourth sleepless night at the top of the crater, waiting for morning.

When morning came, the rain had cleared so we decided to try again. Supplies were [5]running low and we knew that if this attempt failed we would have to [6]abandon the mission and return home. Fortunately, the rain held off and we made good progress. As we got closer to the core we put on shiny aluminium suits to protect ourselves from the [7]scorching heat. We felt like astronauts but ones who were travelling in the wrong direction. The ground shook and trembled and the volcano felt like a bomb that might explode at any moment. The descent from the rim of the crater to the bottom took seven hours.

Reaching the bottom we looked out across a lake of lava as big as a football field. The earth beneath our feet trembled and the noise was [8]deafening. It was without doubt the most [9]awe-inspiring experience of my life. We unpacked the delicate equipment that we had brought with us and began the series of experiments which were the purpose of our journey. Then, experiments done, we packed up, took selfies and began the long journey back and began the long journey back – a [10]gruelling climb which took almost twice as long as the journey down.

Lesson 1D

13a   Student B

Conversation 1
You have been renting a flat for the last year and Student A is your landlord/landlady. You're leaving the flat now and want your €1000 deposit back. You've spent some time making sure the place is in a good state and are now asking for your money back. Some of the problems your landlord/landlady mentions may be real, but you either think they are not serious enough, had existed already or were not your fault.

Conversation 2
You have been working for the same company for the last ten years, and Student A started a few months ago. You're a steady worker and like to stay on top of things, but Student A leaves things till the last minute. You often have to work together and you're sick of having to wait and wait for A to be ready. You also find a couple of other things irritating about him/her (decide what things). You've made your feelings clear before and aren't scared of doing so again!

Lesson 3B

12   Student B

1
A thirty-year-old man in New York, who is refusing to leave home, is being taken to court by his desperate parents. The couple have been urging their son, who pays no rent and doesn't help with any household chores, to leave for many months now. They have even offered to pay over a thousand dollars to encourage him to move, but he has accused them of cruel treatment and has begged the judge to throw the case out.

2
A woman is taking her local TV station to court for giving a weather forecast that turned out to be completely wrong. The station had predicted hot, sunny weather for one particular Saturday afternoon, but in the end it poured with rain. The woman claimed she had dressed lightly, only for the heavy rain to cause her to catch the flu, miss a week of work and have to spend money on medication.

Lesson 10A

12   Student A

Work with Student B. Look at the questions that were investigated for previous Ig Noble Awards. Then discuss questions a-d below (you have the same questions as Student B).

1 Do chimpanzees copy humans as often as humans imitate chimpanzees?
2 What's the best way to carry a coffee cup?
3 How do people learn to use new products with many features?
4 How does contact with a live crocodile affect your desire to take risks?

a What area of science do you think each question is connected to?
b Why do you think researchers investigated these questions?
c How do you think they investigated them?
d What do you think the results were?

b Now read the information card on the right. Choose one of the Ig Nobel Award questions to talk about.

What's the best way to carry a coffee cup?
The Korean researchers won an Ig Nobel Award in fluid dynamics.
- The experiment compared the movement caused within the cup when carrying it in different ways.
- The cup was put in a machine that simulated the movement caused by walking.
- The least movement and, therefore, the lowest risk of spilling your coffee came from either walking backwards or holding the mug by the top, rather than by the handle.
- The experiment also compared the effects of using different-shaped containers and found that less liquid was spilled from wine glasses than from straight-sided mugs.

Do chimpanzees imitate humans as often as humans imitate chimpanzees?
This research won an Ig Nobel Award for anthropology.
- Over a three-week period, researchers at a zoo in Sweden watched the interactions between five chimps and visitors.
- The researchers were interested in when visitors copied a chimp action and vice versa – and in how accurate the imitation was.
- They found that chimpanzees and humans imitated each other more or less equally and that the chimps' imitations were almost as accurate as the humans' efforts.

Lesson 10C

10a Student A

Choose two jokes that you would like to tell or choose one and a joke of your own.

1. I'm single by choice … not MY choice, but still a choice!
2. How does a politician sleep at night?
   Well, first he lies on one side, then he lies to the other.
3. Do you find it hard to sleep after using your phone?
   Apparently, there's a nap for that.
4. Knock, knock. (Who's there?)
   Boo. (Boo who?)
   No need to cry, it's only a joke.

5. A guy is walking down a road and starts to hear this moaning voice '13 …13 … 13 …13 …' He looks round but can't see anyone, so he walks along a bit more and then he hears this terrible moaning again. '13 …13 …13 …'. He then notices it's coming from a nearby garden and there's a hole in the fence where the noise seems to be coming from '13 … 13 …13'. He goes up to the hole and peers through and he suddenly gets poked in the eye. Then he hears the voice again: '14 … 14 … 14 …'

6A Develop your reading

7

Ms Rashford, in keeping with her status, had a corner office with glass wall views over a central courtyard. This office, I told myself as I sat down, will one day be mine. *Ability is nothing without ambition!* I reminded myself.

'Come in,' Ms Rashford said as I knocked gently on her open door. She was staring at her computer and didn't even look up to acknowledge me.

'Good morning! I'm Justin Alsop, Junior Assistant,' I said as I offered her my hand to shake. She looked up at me but didn't take my hand. 'On probation …' I added, feeling a little uncomfortable.

'I know who you are,' replied Ms Rashford after a pause. 'So far today I've been copied in to forty-eight of your emails. Yesterday sixty-six. Last week two hundred.'

'I like to stay busy,' I replied smiling, but somehow I couldn't help feeling like a schoolboy about to be punished.

'Do you know what we do here, Mr Alsop?' said Ms Rashford after another lengthy pause.

'Absolutely,' I replied. 'We're a financial management services company. We help our clients invest their money wisely.' I'd learned the company mission statement off by heart on my first day in the job.

'Exactly,' said Ms Rashford, still not looking up from her keyboard. 'What we don't do is waste time. We don't reply to colleagues simply to say that we are going to reply to them later.'

'Well, it's a courtesy really …' I said, a bit defensively.

'And how many emails have you actually replied to?' she asked, pointedly. I don't mean the 'I-will-reply-later reply. I mean actually replied to the request in the email.

'Well, so far today none but I've been very busy with …'

'And yesterday?' she interrupted.

'Well, yesterday also none, but the emails I need to respond to are printed out in a pile on my desk and …'

'Printed out?' she almost shouted, taking off her glasses to stare at me. 'Why did you print them out?'

'Well I find it helps me to answer them' I replied, rather weakly.

'Well clearly not,' she responded, 'seeing that you haven't actually answered any yet.'

It was at this stage that I began to get the nasty feeling that I wasn't going to get the promotion I'd hoped for.

'You're on probation, aren't you?' said Ms Rashford finally.

'Yes' I replied.

'Regretfully, Mr Alsop, we are terminating your employment here at Hakeford with immediate effect.'

And with that I was jobless, again.

Despite the initial shock, by the time I'd cleared my desk and said a tearful goodbye to my colleagues, who managed not to cry, I began to feel a strange sense of positivity coming over me. After all, as someone once said, *Every failure takes you one step closer to success.*

Lesson 6C

12   Student A

Choose two events that you went to at the festival. Write notes about what happened, what you thought of each event and if you'd recommend it.

Soul Stars Choir
One of the country's leading soul and gospel choirs presents a show highlighting the different styles and songs that have marked the development of soul music - an uplifting journey that takes in Gospel, Country, Blues and even Latin and African rhythms.

Festival Free for all
Do you have a talent you want to share? Why not come and take to the stage at our weekly show featuring eight cabaret acts and comedians from the fringe. Just sign up when you arrive and help make our evening even more entertaining. Every Tuesday.

Innervisions of Terror
Innervisions of Terror is an intense experience that takes you into a dark space – literally and metaphorically. Sit in complete darkness while live and recorded sounds allow your imagination to run wild in a performance that is different every time.

The Light Fantastic – with Circo Maravilla
One of the world's top circus and cabaret companies bring their celebration of light, movement and music to our big tent. Expect daring circus tricks, spectacular scenery and costumes and a big rock soundtrack from a live band.

Midnight in Leeds
A moving low-budget drama about a failing businessman trying to keep his life together. A surprise hit at the Birmingham film festival last year, Andy Walker's film about a small man's struggles touches on the biggest issues of our times from globalisation to love in a digital world. Showing daily throughout the first two weeks of the festival.

Lesson 7C

11

1 Everyone who can vote should be legally required to do so.

2 You should pass an IQ test first before you get the right to vote,

3 All major policies should be decided by a referendum.

4 There should be an upper limit on voting. If under-18s can't vote, over-75s should be stopped too.

5 All voting should be done online. It's the safest way of making sure there's a fair vote.

6 The best electoral system is one which generally results in coalition government.

Lesson 10C

10   Student B

Choose two jokes that you would like to tell or choose one and a joke of your own.

1 You know that guy who had an accident and lost his whole left side? Well, apparently, he's all right now.

2 What's so great about whiteboards?
Well, if you think about it they're pretty re-mark-able.

3 I think my friend's a terrible driver, but the other day we came back to the car after we'd been shopping and someone had left a note on the windscreen saying *Parking fine*. So maybe he's not that bad after all.

4 Knock, knock. (Who's there?)
Annie. (Annie who?)
Annie thing you can do I can do better.

5 When the US space agency NASA started sending people into space they suddenly realised that biro pens didn't work in zero gravity. After several years and $12 billion dollars of investment they developed a pen that wrote in zero gravity, was virtually indestructible, and was self-regenerating, meaning it had no need for ink. The Russians used a pencil.

Lesson 7D

10a

Main reason for moving

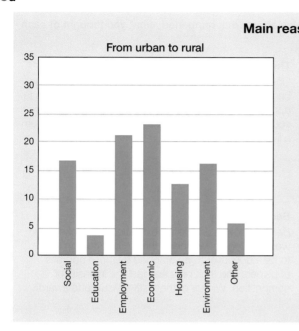

From urban to rural

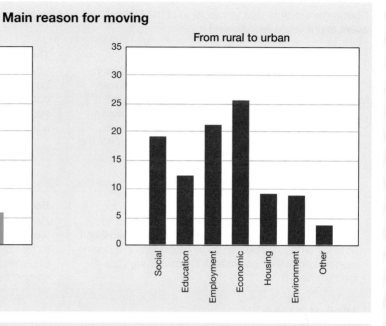

From rural to urban

Main reason for moving

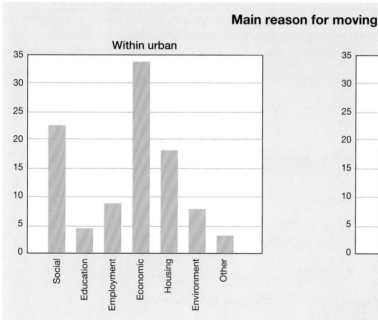

Within urban

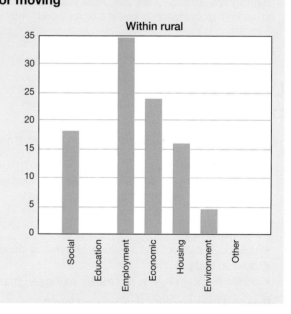

Within rural

Lesson 6C

12   Student B

Choose two events that you went to at the festival. Write notes about what happened, what you thought of each event and if you'd recommend it.

New Lives with Migrant Nation

New Lives is an experimental piece exploring the migrant experience. Using the app Cahoot, the audience vote on the turns the story takes for our lead characters, who have left their homes to start a new life in the city. At times, the actors improvise scenes with audience members taking roles from characters' lives. How will the work evolve? What will be the ending?

The Light Fantastic – with Circo Maravilla

One of the world's top circus and cabaret companies bring their celebration of light, movement and music to our big tent. Expect daring circus tricks, spectacular scenery and costumes and a big rock soundtrack from a live band.

Devil Rhymes

Terri Larson reads from her latest collection about life, love and literature. Her poems are intensely personal and at times simply hilarious. If you've never been to a poetry reading before then be warned: the devil always has the best rhymes.

Best in Show

Best in Show is a fantastic exhibition that looks at the world of dog shows round the world. You don't have to be a dog lover to be grabbed by these portraits of owners and their pets and feel the intensity of competition. Winner of the festival visual arts award.

Midnight in Leeds

A moving low-budget drama about a failing businessman trying to keep his life together. A surprise hit at the Birmingham film festival last year, Andy Walker's film about a small man's struggles touches on the biggest issues of our times from globalisation to love in a digital world. Showing daily throughout the first two weeks of the festival.

Lesson 8A

11   Student A

You're a **sustainability manager** for a huge furniture store chain [Decide the name].

Job description
- advise the company on how best to use its resources
- help to reduce the amount of pollution produced
- reduce impact on the environment

Responsibilities
- develop, implement and monitor environmental strategies
- draw up budgets
- communicate your plans and market your green strategies to colleagues and customers

Personal background / How you got into it
- studied Environmental Management at university
- actively involved in environmental campaigning in your free time
- the job pays well and you feel like you're making a positive difference to the world

Think about how you will answer questions 1–6.
1 What do you do?
2 What is it that that involves, then?
3 Do you enjoy it?
4 How did you get into that?
5 What's the money like?
6 What are the hours like?

Lesson 8A

11 Student B

You're the **Chief Listening Officer** – the CLO – for a major art museum [Decide the name].

Job description
- head the public relations and marketing department
- oversee all digital and face-to-face communication

Responsibilities
- provide reports and insights on the effectiveness of the museum's communication style
- track what's said about the museum
- provide fast response to any complaints, issues, or misinformation

Personal background / How you got into it
- have a degree in Business Management and a Master's in Marketing Communication
- very active user of a wide range of social media and keep up-to-date with the latest trends
- promoted from the social media manager, who mostly manages marketing campaigns
- it's an extremely well-paid position.

Think about how you will answer questions 1–6.
1 What do you do?
2 What is it that that involves, then?
3 Do you enjoy it?
4 How did you get into that?
5 What's the money like?
6 What are the hours like?

Lesson 10A

12 Student B

Work with Student A. Look at the questions that were investigated for previous Ig Noble Awards. Then discuss questions a-d below (you have the same questions as Student A).

1 Do chimpanzees copy humans as often as humans imitate chimpanzees?
2 What's the best way to carry a coffee cup?
3 How do people learn to use new products with many features?
4 How does contact with a live crocodile affect your desire to take risks?

a What area of science do you think each question is connected to?
b Why do you think researchers investigated these questions?
c How do you think they investigated them?
d What do you think the results were?

b Now read the information card on the right. Choose one of the Ig Nobel Award questions to talk about.

How do people learn to use new products with many features?

This research won an Ig Nobel Award for literature.
- Researchers asked 160 people about their use of electronic devices.
- They also studied two smaller groups of people who kept a diary on how they used mobile devices (group one) and medical devices (group two).
- The conclusion was that, firstly, most people do not read manuals.
- Secondly, most people do not use all the features of the products they own.
- Having too many features and being forced to consult manuals also appears to cause negative emotional experiences.

How does contact with a live crocodile affect your desire to take risks?

This research won an Ig Nobel Award for economics.
- The study asked visitors to a crocodile park to either use a gaming machine before they entered the park or after they had handled a live crocodile.
- The study found that the people who had handled the crocodiles and were in a generally positive emotional state took more risks than those who had not.

5C Develop your reading

1b

1 c

2 b (although according to research the average child only plays with 12 of them)

3 c

4 b

5 a

7C Develop your reading

7

Despite this setback, Mike wasn't deterred. He started dating again and decided to allow his investors to vote on his choice of partner. One of his dates bought shares in Mike in order to influence the vote and Mike decided that she was the one for him. Shareholders approved the choice and Mike offered his date an initial three month 'relationship contract'. Not, perhaps, the most romantic gesture but, despite this, she accepted!

Lesson 8B

12

SLEEP QUIZ
- How could you stop yourself nodding off in a very boring meeting or class?
- Is having an afternoon nap good for you?
- What's the best way to get over jet lag?
- Is it healthier to be a night owl or an early riser?
- Can you catch up on sleep with a lie-in after several sleepless nights?

Think of two more questions about sleep or sleep problems.

8B Develop your writing

1b

1 born mid 1940s to mid 1960s: baby Boomers

2 born mid 1960s to early 1980s: Generation X

3 born early 1980s to late 1990s: millennials

4 born 2000 to present day: Generation Z

Lesson 8C

12

Invent a dish you could make with some of the ingredients. Decide how much you need of each ingredient and what you would do with them.

Ingredients		
whole chicken	red/green pepper	coconut milk
prawns	green beans	pastry
onion	potato	water
celery	garlic	oil
carrot	chili	salt and pepper
tinned tomatoes	parsley	
	spice (e.g. coriander/cumin)	

Irregular verbs

Verb	Past simple	Past participle
be	was	been
become	became	become
begin	began	begun
bite	bit	bitten
blow	blew	blown
break	broke	broken
bring	brought	brought
build	built	built
burn	burned/burnt	burned/burnt
buy	bought	bought
catch	caught	caught
choose	chose	chosen
come	came	come
cost	cost	cost
cut	cut	cut
do	did	done
draw	drew	drawn
drink	drank	drunk
drive	drove	driven
eat	ate	eaten
fall	fell	fallen
feel	felt	felt
find	found	found
fly	flew	flown
forget	forgot	forgotten
get	got	got
give	gave	given
go	went	gone
grow	grew	grown
have	had	had
hear	heard	heard
hide	hid	hidden
hit	hit	hit
hold	held	held
hurt	hurt	hurt
keep	kept	kept
know	knew	known
learn	learned/learnt	learned/learnt
leave	left	left

Verb	Past simple	Past participle
lend	lent	lent
let	let	let
lie	lay	lain
lose	lost	lost
make	made	made
mean	meant	meant
meet	met	met
pay	paid	paid
put	put	put
read	read	read
ride	rode	ridden
ring	rang	rung
run	ran	run
say	said	said
see	saw	seen
sell	sold	sold
send	sent	sent
shine	shone	shone
show	showed	shown
shut	shut	shut
sing	sang	sung
sit	sat	sat
sleep	slept	slept
smell	smelled/smelt	smelled/smelt
speak	spoke	spoken
spend	spent	spent
spill	spilled/spilt	spilled/spilt
stand	stood	stood
swim	swam	swum
take	took	taken
teach	taught	taught
tell	told	told
think	thought	thought
throw	threw	thrown
understand	understood	understood
wake	woke	woken
wear	wore	worn
win	won	won
write	wrote	written